From Value in Production to Value in Exchange:
Marxist Political Economy Revisited

# Studies in Critical Social Sciences



VOLUME 373

The titles published in this series are listed at *brill.com/scss*

# From Value in Production to Value in Exchange: Marxist Political Economy Revisited

*Critical Reconstructions of Political Economy*

VOLUME 11

*By*

Ben Fine

BRILL

ISSN 1573-4234
ISBN 978-90-04-76625-9
ISBN 978-90-04-76626-6 (PDF)
DOI https://doi.org/10.1163/9789004766266

Library of Congress Control Number: 2026942270



Brill and Koninklijke Brill BV are part of De Gruyter Brill.
www.degruyterbrill.com

Questions about General Product Safety Regulation: productsafety@degruyterbrill.com

# Contents

# Preface and Acknowledgements

Marxist Political Economy was not my first love within my study of economics. That honour goes to social choice theory, encountered in my first week as a student of mathematical economics. It has been a love that has continued to tax and engage me, if only from time to time (most recently, see Fine and Mendes Loureiro, 2021). Marxist political economy, though, has been my constant companion for more than fifty years and has been most important to me in scholarship that goes far beyond the world of academia. Along the way, I have made many friends and encountered many hostilities. Sometimes it is the one, sometimes the other, if sometimes alternating and sometimes both at the same time. I have collaborated for short and sharp periods, as well as for long and enduring ones. All have contributed to making my Marxist political economy what it is, and I thank each one of those with whom I have been involved without reservation and to the extent of their influence upon, and joint endeavours with, me. For I have learned and benefitted from them even in unresolved disagreement.

This is the first of two volumes on Marxist political economy. It mainly covers theoretical issues. Whilst some chapters were first drafted relatively recently, most are of much longer vintage and reflect the formation of my core understanding of the approach I take and its substantive content. There continues, however, to be ample room for development, improvement and wider scope of application, especially in light of continuing debate and contemporary shifts in the nature of capitalism. These will be reflected in the second volume which will include relatively more recent contributions.

CHAPTER 1

# Value Theory and Marxist Political Economy: A Personal Journey

## 1 Introduction

This is the first of two Volumes on Marxist Political Economy (and the tenth and eleventh in the series as a whole on the *Critical Reconstructions of Political Economy*).[1] It is primarily focused on theory, especially Marx's value theory and its implications for economic reproduction, and corresponding categories of analysis such as price, profit, interest and rent. Whilst most of the Chapters derive from publications much later, the core understandings presented were primarily developed during the 1970s and first appeared in Fine (1975a)[2] at an elementary level and in Fine and Harris (1979) in more advanced form with some coverage of major debates and differences. Indeed, whilst often asked subsequently to contribute on value theory, I have been inclined to refuse on the grounds of having nothing new to say. In retrospect, I can see that I generally made exceptions in two circumstances (but see Fine, 1980b and 1983a, or Chapter 3 to this Volume, and Fine, 1983b). One has been special occasions – marking anniversaries around Marx or particular journals. In this case, contributions took the form of insisting upon the continuing validity and relevance of value theory despite or, more exactly, because of developments in contemporary capitalism that others took to signal its demise. Otherwise, contributions have been motivated by response to criticism on my contributions on Marx's value theory (often co-authored) or by criticising alternative approaches that reject value theory, especially by getting it wrong.

Value theory has always been heavily contested and subject to varieties of (mis)interpretations across many dimensions. To the fore have been two overlapping questions: what did Marx really mean; and is he correct in his analysis? The first question will remain controversial for a number of reasons. First, Marx's thought on these, as with other issues, evolved over time. Second, in any case, he is not always consistent. Third, there are issues around how to translate his works. Fourth, at times, especially in drafts, Marx will adopt and work with the concepts of those he is seeking to assess critically. Fifth, Marx's own

1 Thanks to Alfredo Saad-Filho for comments on an early draft.
2 Subsequently in its seventh edition as Fine and Saad-Filho (2026[1975]).

 | HTTPS://DOI.ORG/10.1163/9789004766266-002

terminology changes over time as well as his conceptualisations. Sixth, Marx's own thoughts need to be contextualised both in terms of the circumstances of his world and the scholarship on which he draws, refashions and/or rejects. Seventh, (re)interpretations (although, more often, I told you so, on value theory and more generally) follow from the making available of ever more of Marx's voluminous unfinished and working manuscripts.

I have never been able, let alone sought, to be on top of all of these issues and, to the extent that I am, it is extremely uneven. I only read Marx in English. I have some but limited knowledge of his intellectual influences and so avoid by necessity if not virtue the syndrome – you can only understand Marx if you understand Hegel, and Hegel if you understand … and so on. I am conscious of issues of methodology, most of which are not covered in what follows (alongside the significance of concepts such as mode of production and forces and relations of production). In other words, I am no Marxologist, and my own understanding and its presentation to others are influenced by my own trajectory and those I have sought to address and why – I am mathematician and economist by initial training, and contribution to political economy and critique of mainstream (and heterodox, as appropriate) economics is my subject matter. This leads to what might appear to be incomplete and even naïve accounts from the perspectives of those trained in the finer points of dialectics and Marxology more generally, but needs must and not necessarily a bad thing for those readers for whom the finer points of Marx's methods, and its sources, are alien.

In short, across what Marx said and whether he is right or wrong, I have much to say although much more as reference points rather than the main objective which is to make the case for what is value theory, why it is valid and how it is to be developed and applied. I note that, surreptitiously and not intentionally, the overview that follows shifts in presentation from the evolution of my own thinking (on Marx) to this is what Marx meant, with a presumption that the two are aligned. That is for the Marxologists to decide (although their wider knowledges are no guarantee of validity). I am secure in the comfort that my own interpretations and presentations draw upon a wide reading of Marx and the drawing of levels of coherence out of his key concepts across the works consulted – something that is notably absent for most contributions for which value as such, its accumulation, the reproduction schema, the transformation problem, falling profitability, finance, and rent, are not treated as an integral whole as opposed to being fragments to be joined together.

As will be apparent, the differences between the value theories of Ricardo and Marx are crucial to my approach so that I take what is termed the value form seriously not only methodologically but also (or what is the same thing) as the key to understanding the underlying determinants of more complex outcomes in which the forms have effects and are not merely obfuscating appearances. Traditionally, within Marxist political economy, analysis of the value form is heavily associated with critical discussion of the neo-Ricardian approach to the transformation problem. But it is not accidental that my work goes much further within the economic realm but also extends to social reproduction. Thus, there are passing references throughout this Volume to issues such as what are the determinants of consumption and the value of labour power, and it is significant that these contributions were written whilst I was working on these topics both empirically and theoretically as contributions on value theory were being drafted. Also important in addressing value and its forms is specifying both where their boundaries fall (and evolve) and how to relate them to those aspects of social reproduction that are non-value whether, for example, wage labour that is not employed by productive capital, or labour that is not wage-labour at all (or even activities that are not labour at all, not least conflict).

## 2 Engaging Value

By the early 1970s, I was well into the intensive study of Marx's *Capital*, Volume 1, with Volumes 2 and 3, and the three Volumes of *Theories of Surplus Value* to follow. I am more than ready to confess that I was hooked. As someone previously trained in both mathematics and the mainstream economics of the time, I was simply fascinated by the combination of resonances with what I already knew and, yet, the complete and absolute breaks with it in terms of how the subject matter was treated alongside how compelling factors were covered that were notably absent from the mainstream as if the issues involved simply did not exist.

I also took unbelievably extensive hand-written notes – rather than deploying today's facility of copy and paste from electronic versions – writing out quotation after quotation by hand, underlining the focused or scattered treatments of key concepts and the propositions attached to them. After photocopying each of these pages of notes a number of times, where necessary I cut out bits and pieces covering the same topics and pasted them onto new sheets. In this way, I collected together Marx's contributions in these volumes on key aspects of his political economy. I had a filing cabinet drawer full of folders covering topic after topic.

I suspect no one would do this today. It would be much easier not only to copy and paste but also to search upon key concepts from electronic versions of the materials. Who knows whether needing to rely upon more 'manual' methods made a difference to how well I absorbed the material and how

I interpreted it. It did form the basis for my work on Marx's political economy for years to come although I must have felt I had squeezed as much as I could out of the notes that I had taken as they were all discarded upon some office move or other.

There were two major uses to which I put these materials. The first derived from teaching for an optional course for the MSc in Economics at Birkbeck on Theories of Distribution. For this I covered both Classical Political Economy (especially, Smith, Ricardo, Malthus and J. S. Mill)[3] and Marx, seeking to locate distribution both in the history of thought and wider framings of their treatments, most notably with the *production* of surplus value as the basis for distribution in Marx. Of necessity, to get to distribution through Marx – to incorporate not only wages and profits but also interest and rent – implied getting to the end of Volume 3 of *Capital* and beyond. Ultimately, as mentioned, preparing these materials for teaching led me to write a short overview of Marx's political economy (Fine, 1975a), a book that has got to its sixth edition, doubling in length, with seventh edition in preparation, having been translated into numbers of languages and picked up a co-author along the way (Fine and Saad-Filho, 2026[1975]).[4]

The second outcome from my endeavours was to engage in the debates around Marx's political economy that were raging at the time. The context was one of sixties student radicalism, the collapse of the post-war boom into seventies stagflation, and contestation over how both to interpret the end of the 'golden age' and to use Marxist political economy in doing so. In this, I was heavily involved in the Conference of Socialist Economists (CSE), and its Bulletin which later became the journal *Capital and Class*. By the mid-seventies, apart from collective running of the CSE, I was closely involved in such work with Laurence Harris, who had joined Birkbeck, alongside political activity with him through membership of the Communist Party of Great Britain.

Indicative of engagement through CSE is that I published three pieces in Issue 12 of its Bulletin (Fine, 1975b and c; and Fine and Harris, 1975a), the latter on the British economy, one on the circulation of capital, with an earlier one on productive and unproductive labour (Fine, 1973), each of which necessarily drew heavily from Volume 2 of Capital.[5] The third piece was a review

3 To some degree, my engagement with distribution through neoclassical economics and Classical Political Economy informed my next two books (Fine, 1980c and 1982, respectively) following a more advanced and developed reading of Marx (Fine and Harris, 1979, see below).

4 On rough calculation upon perusal of publisher returns, it must have sold many more copies than all of my other books put together.

5 The Bulletin was printed using typed stencils and a Gestetner with Andrew Glyn playing a leading role until taken over at Birkbeck. He complained to me that I wrote too much.

of the book on Marxist economics from the sympathetic mainstream mathematical economist, Michio Morishima. In addition, there was a fourth later contribution co-authored with Laurence Harris, the second but last, in what was intended to be a series of reviews of the current position of the British economy (Fine and Harris, 1976a).[6]

## 3 Get the OCC Right and All Else Follows

It is important that this and continuing theoretical work, grounded in value theory, was accompanied by the empirical work on the British economy because they dovetailed with one another. For the empirical, emphasis was placed on the restructuring of the British economy, with emphasis upon the concentration and centralisation of capital in the context of the formation and growth of multinational corporations, nationalised industries (and the role of the state more generally) and the role played by different interests in such restructuring (with these being relatively weak and ineffective in the UK due to the role of finance, with insufficient influence otherwise through the state from either labour or industrial capital). These considerations, covered in detail in Fine and Harris (1985),[7] drew in particular upon accumulation of capital as bringing about productivity increase through an increasing organic composition of capital (OCC) as developed in detail in Volume 1 of *Capital* as the source of relative surplus value.

As is as well-known as it is well-used, the OCC is extremely prominent in debates around Marxist political economy, especially as a key element in the so-called transformation problem, the law of the tendency of the rate of profit to fall (LTRPF) and, to a much lesser extent, Marx's theory of rent. But, as is apparent from my contributions at this time, within the vast majority of the literature, the OCC has been and continues to be widely and heavily misrepresented, equally across those sympathetic to as well as those critically dismissive of Marx. This can be put relatively simply by distinguishing between three different definitions of the composition of capital, the technical (TCC), the value (VCC) and the OCC.

6 These empirical analyses were accompanied by a discussion of how to go about such endeavours but it was not published in the Bulletin (Fine and Harris, 1975b).

7 Much delayed to publication due to a writer's block in my co-author, and with some co-authorship on my part with Kathy O'Donnell and Martha Prevezer on the British coal industry.

The starting point for these, and the connections between them, is the (rising) TCC. For Marx, productivity increase specifically under capitalism is heavily governed by, although not confined to, the increasing working up of raw materials by labour into final products (not least through the use of machinery within a factory system). This is measured in physical terms by the TCC. But the TCC is reflected in value terms in two different ways, although both generally designated across the literature as C/V since the distinction between them tends to be overlooked. One, the OCC proper according to Marx, is to assess the C and the V at prevailing values – those in place prior to increasing productivity – bearing in mind that there will be a variety of raw material and fixed capital inputs (as well as varieties of labour) involved. In this way, the OCC is a direct reflection of the (rising) TCC within production, only expressed in value terms.

However, the consequence of the rising TCC (and OCC) is to modify (reduce) values, and this will lead to different measures of the TCC in value terms, after the modified values have worked their way through economic reproduction as a whole. Indeed, if all values are reduced in proportion, relative values of C and V will remain just the same as before (apart from, as highlighted by Marx, the heavier use in proportion of fixed capital, and its depreciation as the condition for the rising TCC). The recalculation of (rising) sectoral OCCs by reduced values leads to the formation of the corresponding VCCs, as it were after modified values have been realised in exchange to reflect the extent to which sectoral productivities (and values) have been differentially affected.

From a narrow perspective, this is no more than an index number problem – how do we reduce to a single dimension the shifting ratios of raw materials to labours within the production process. We can use, for example, either ex ante or ex post values, or some other sort of pricing. Thus, changes in the TCC and OCC for metal manufacturing will be the same irrespective of the value of the metal used if they use the same methods of production. But their VCCs will differ according to (changes in) the values of the metals, similarly for carpentry that uses mahogany rather than pine in making the same furniture. So, the TCC/OCC couplet is seeking to measure what is going on in production; the VCC incorporates this alongside changes in the values of the raw materials used not least from the changes in the TCCs/OCCs themselves.

So much for making (clear) the distinctions between TCC, OCC and VCC. But what is the point in doing so? First, there is no point in the context of equilibrium since the motivation for the distinctions derives from analysing *changing* conditions of production (OCC) and, in particular, their impact upon exchange (VCC). In equilibrium, the two collapse into one another as values at the time of production will be identical to values during exchange. Second, and more constructively, the distinctions point to the modifications of values through rising OCC within production but that such modifications need to be realised through purchase and sale of commodities embodying surplus value (VCC). Third, this means that most treatments of the so-called transformation problem have got it entirely wrong. It is generally understood as a set of equilibrium prices (of production) for equalised rates of profit across sectors given different (technical) compositions of capital within those sectors.

But, as already implicitly suggested, this is not Marx's problem. Rather, he is concerned with how differing rates of productivity increase across sectors (rising OCCs) give rise to the formation of prices of production in exchange. This is not about equilibrium at all but about changing productivities across sectors. Perversely, standard treatments of the transformation frame it in terms of the consequences of differing OCCs whereas they actually focus entirely upon the VCCs as if they were the OCCs which they are not. This derives from exclusive attention to the impact of differing (equilibrium) ratios of values (and prices) in production whatever their source as opposed to those that derive from rising TCCs/OCCs specifically, i.e. changing conditions not those of equilibrium.

I have spent a little bit of time on the TCC/OCC/VCC syndrome even though it is fully covered elsewhere in the book and, in my overview here, its treatment is brought forward within the materials covered in the three Volumes of *Capital*, with the transformation appearing within Volume 3, without my having as yet had much to say about Volumes 1 and 2. This is justified here on the grounds of catching the reader early the better to be able to dispel misconceptions that may already have been experienced, so common are they across the literature. Hopefully, what has been prematurely presented at this stage is comprehensible to readers, and the basis on which to follow more detailed treatments later with a more open mind. In other words, the idea is to shake the reader out of complacency by my arguing in the relatively simple terms of the distinctions across the compositions of capital that Marx is not looking at equilibrium even though most commentators, including the sympathetic, tend to do so and have got some of his basic concepts and problems wrong – talking about the OCC when they mean the VCC and ignoring the OCC altogether having lost its distinction with the VCC. As will be argued, this is vital for Marx's political economy as a whole and for its integral consistency across the transformation problem, the falling rate of profit and Marx's theory of rent.

## 4 Commodity Fetishism as Commodity Form

So, now, if we backtrack to the issues raised in the three Volumes of *Capital* before the transformation is broached, it is possible to see that, with it, Marx is dealing with what is termed the value form. How is the production of (relative) surplus value realised in exchange in the context of the (differentiated) accumulation of capital across sectors. More generally, the value form is about how value is expressed as exchange value. As such, it encompasses a huge range of structures, processes, agencies and relations. The most prominent analysis of the value form is to be found in Marx's treatment of commodity fetishism – that commodity relations as relations between producers (of value) appear as something that they really are even if concealing something entirely different that is more important. Value relations between labours are expressed as equivalencies as use values (relative prices).

Commodity fetishism is such a powerful insight that it has tended to have a number of potentially limiting effects. First, there can be the presumption despite Marx's emphasis to the contrary, that commodity fetishism is an illusion[8] – on the contrary, commodity relations really are relations between things but they conceal the underlying class relations of how (surplus) value is produced by labour in production.

Second, commodity fetishism is in no way confined to this aspect alone. As it were, exchange value as such conceals any number of relations that underpin its existence, the most compelling these days, for example, being the extent to which commodity relations are also (extremely damaging) environmental relations. But search a commodity for sale as closely as you wish and you will find little, if any, evidence of the role it has played in, or how it has been dependent upon, environmental factors in its journey to the market (lest it be claims to being environmentally friendly as the way to enhance chances of sale). All the relations that go into the provision of commodities, the who, how, where and when, are concealed in the value form. Search the commodity itself and, at most, you are liable only to find traces of its passage to sale as well as the same applying to the underlying determinants of that passage.

Third, the complexities and multiplicity of determinants in the passage of value to value form is also one of what might be termed real effects. Not everything is predetermined in the creation of value just as a wedding conditions but does not determine a marriage (let alone a divorce). Most obviously, production of (surplus) value in the form of commodities does not guarantee its sale (nor its profitability). Crucially, this has given rise to a wide-ranging and abiding tension within value theory itself. In principle, and in general terms, this is very simple. Do the real effects of the value form negate the definition

8 Of course, there can be illusions that are false – significant for Marx is that workers are paid for all the work that they perform (their labour) as opposed to their capacity to labour (their labour power) with surplus value resulting from the difference between the value of what they are paid and the contested amount of labour they perform in return.

of value itself so that the definition of value has to be modified in order to be able to accommodate the complexities of the value form. In the vernacular, there are so many determinants of price that the distance between it and value (as labour time) are so great that value has to be modified in definition if not abandoned altogether.

The fierce debates on value theory that raged across Marxist political economy in the 1970s, and their implications, can be seen in retrospect often to have been engaged in these terms if not always realised as such. Rather, they were more focused on particular issues, especially the transformation problem and the LTRPF, with the distinction between productive and unproductive labour of some significance. I was myself heavily influenced by the contributions of Rubin (1975 and 1978) on the value form but have never been seduced towards abandoning value theory as a result of its being invalid in some sense because of the complexities of the value form.[9] The reason is simple – value theory is about how the labour exerted in production is represented in exchange for which the complexities connecting the two is certainly a challenge to be unravelled but not a rationale for conflating value with its form.

More specifically, in case of the transformation problem, the major conflict was between those who wished to retain Marx's value theory and those (dubbed neo-Ricardian or Sraffian)[10] who sought to abandon it, first and foremost, as an inadequate and/or unnecessary theory of price (and the rate of profit). What is characteristic in general of both approaches, as already explained above, is to locate the transformation problem in some sort of equilibrium setting and to focus essentially upon the role of differences in the VCC whilst using the term OCC to represent it.

At one extreme in the debate,[11] Marx's "solution" can be made correct with some sort of trick or two, and more or less revision to certain conditions on the relationships between both aggregate value and aggregate price and aggregate surplus value and aggregate profit. From my perspective, the aggregations are not a problem given that price and profit are the forms taken by value and surplus value, respectively, so that in aggregate total price and profit must be

9 The approaches of Pilling (1972 and 1980), as acknowledged in Fine (2012d), and Elson (ed.) (1979) have also been particularly influential in my thinking on these issues.

10 I have reserved the term neo-Ricardian for those who reject Marx (and value) for his treatment of the transformation problem (and LTRPF) but retain value theory as a sociology of exploitation. Sraffians are deemed to reject the lot, with value theory as both wrong and irrelevant.

11 Typically, these serve as fixes to the artificially created problem of linking equilibrium values to equilibrium prices and have little or no connection to the material processes of economic reproduction.

the form taken by the total value and surplus value, respectively, although the transformation indicates that this is not correct at the level of individual commodities. Just to reiterate, Marx's transformation is not about equilibrium prices for given VCCs but how, for equalisation of rates of profit, there must be redistribution of surplus value to those sectors that have relatively increased productivities through rising OCC. Further, this has to be achieved through the formation of VCCs.

At the other Sraffian extreme in the debate, value theory is rejected altogether on the grounds that it cannot form the basis for a correct theory of equilibrium prices and (rate of) profit, or is an unnecessary detour if doing so. Underlying exogenously-given, technical conditions (generally input-output tables) together with some sort of distributional fix (the wage rate, for example) are sufficient to calculate prices and profits but values as such are not, although they can themselves be calculated from the technical conditions (but so what for Sraffians, for they are not needed?). By substituting the notion of determination as causation with the ability to determine mathematically, i.e. to calculate or solve, Sraffians erroneously dismiss value as being of any analytical significance at all.[12] With this foul blow, all of Marx's value theory is swept aside for failing as an equilibrium price theory for linear (constant returns to scale) technology.

As observed especially by Pilling (1972 and 1980), the Sraffian approach to value theory, like Ricardo's, is instrumental. Let us define value as labour embodied in products and see how well it serves as an equilibrium theory of price. But Marx's value (form) theory is different and differently motivated – how does value, created by labour out of production, find expression through exchange and with what consequences, for exploitation, accumulation and beyond. This shifts the discussion towards methodology and, in place of instrumentalism, the requirement that the concepts that we use be validated by showing how they correspond in thought to the material realities that they are deemed to represent (not equilibrium for starters). In a sense, the tensions – between remaining loyal to value theory and rejecting it as the complexities of its form come to the fore – do themselves have to be reproduced in thought as an expression of material realities. Otherwise, value theory is abandoned altogether as the easy option, with value and its forms mangled together.

The means by which to retain value theory rests, first and foremost, upon abstraction – identifying the simplest concepts that can be reproduced as their

---

12 So, more simply, $2x = 4$ (or complicated sets of linear equations around values, prices and profits) tells us nothing about the causes, of $x = 2$, just as a weather forecast calculating that it is going to rain does not cause it to rain.

forms at more complex levels, like value and price, leading to the reproduction of the complex and concrete forms of capitalism in thought. Further, this involves identifying the structures, relations, processes and agencies through which the simple become complex. In these respects, Volume 1 of *Capital* is primarily concerned with how value and surplus value are produced, not least: the identification of labour power as a commodity as indicative of capitalist relations; the corresponding roles of capital and labour as classes; the processes involved in the production of absolute and relative surplus value through accumulation and rising OCC; and with what are some of the structural consequences for social as opposed to economic reproduction.

## 5 Straddling the Three Volumes of 'Capital'

Significantly, this method is pursued in detail in Volume 2 of *Capital*, although this Volume is heavily neglected (and much misrepresented) in much Marxist Political Economy. First, it details the structures underpinning the value form – the distinction between the spheres of production and exchange. Second, this allows the structured processes of circulation to be specified across its constituent parts: different departments of the economy (beginning with means of production and consumption); constant as opposed to variable capital; and fixed as opposed to circulating capital. Third, it distinguishes between productive and unproductive labour. Finally, it specifies the balances across structures for economic reproduction (simple, expanded and extended reproduction – the latter two involving accumulation, one with unchanging conditions and the other with increasing OCC, respectively). These balances have generally been interpreted as conditions for equilibrium. But I have argued this is wrong (Fine, 2012a). For the balances involved, and there are three of them, are independent of whether the economy is in equilibrium, whatever that might mean within a Marxist framing given there are always systemically generated disturbances (as opposed to reliance upon random shocks or imperfections as within orthodox economics).[13]

13 Ironically, with Morishima (1973) for example, Volume 2 of *Capital* is heaped with praise for anticipating both the equilibrium and growth theories, and conditions for them, of orthodox economics itself. I shared time with Morishima at the LSE in the early 1970s where I was doing my PhD. He was genuinely interested in, and impressed by, Marx through the prism of mathematical economics, no doubt reflecting his Japanese origins where Marxism had been strong within his generation.

The three balances are those in the flow of values and of use values in one direction, and the flow of money in the opposite direction (at prices as the form taken by the values). Disruptions can occur as a result of shifts in any of these balances and, should they be or become generalised from whatever source, whether within or across production, circulation or distribution, there will be a crisis of economic reproduction. Otherwise, the levels at which the balances are achieved cannot be predetermined by the schema of reproduction themselves. As they are primarily presented in value terms with, for example, the condition for simple reproduction being $C_2 = V_1 + S_1$, the scale of production in use values is contingent upon levels of productivity.

As a result, the reproduction schema have primarily been used as the means of characterising crises, of being out of balance, contingent upon what is taken to drive the accumulation of capital. There can be disproportionality between sectors, underconsumption across them, overproduction, distributional conflict or inadequate monetary flows. As presented in Fine (1975b), different theories or ideologies of what drives economic reproduction (or not in case of crises) follow from exaggerated attention to particular aspects, especially those located in the sphere of circulation or exchange. For Marx, as the driving force of economic reproduction, it is the production and accumulation of surplus value that is imperative even if contingent on how balances are realised in circulation, which can themselves be the proximate cause of crises and certainly the more complex form in which they appear.

In this respect, Volume 2 plays a vital role in forging the link between Volumes 1 and 3, in ways that have been overlooked and misrepresented (most notably as an equilibrium analysis), especially once further aspects of method are brought into play. For, whilst Volume 2 provides insight into the structures, relations, processes and agencies of economic reproduction in moving from simpler to more complex concepts, such abstraction, and its conscious and verified correspondence in theory to movements in the economy itself,[14] have a number of aspects that have as yet not been brought to the fore.

First and foremost, in this respect, these are best recognised through the distinction brought out above for Volume 2 between balance and equilibrium. Across all theory, and disciplines, it is understood that equilibrium may not

---

14 I put conscious here, and it is important, because as is explicit in Marx's theory of commodity fetishism, and characteristic of Marxist approaches to ideology and theory more generally, these tend to be illusory, not necessarily 'wrong', reflections of reality. This is not to suggest that abstraction by others cannot be fictitiously inventive as well, but why with the content that it has will have material roots as well as create the space for speculative inventiveness – see above also.

exist, may not be unique and may not be stable. But the presumption is that it remains as it is unless disturbed. Balance is otherwise since it is the momentary resolution of forces that are inevitably sources of change or disturbance themselves, reflecting systemic tensions or what Marx calls laws deriving from tendencies. And, as already indicated, the single most important tendency under capitalism is the accumulation of capital and the forms that it takes, with rising OCC to the fore.

In this light, Volume 3 is not simply, nor predominantly a theory of distribution (the original motive for my reading in preparing a course on the topic across Marx and others). Thus, the transformation problem is not about equilibrium prices but about the tensions that are created across production, distribution and exchange when there are differential rates of increase in the OCC across sectors, and continual disruptions in the formation of prices of production in exchange (the VCC).

This is the context in which to situate (the fierce and continuing debate over) the LTRPF. The two main sides in the debate – what have been dubbed the Sraffians/neo-Ricardians and the fundamentalists – tend to share a number of features in common. First is to treat the LTRPF as if it is an empirical law. Does the rate of profit fall or not, within the theory and so within reality? Second, in deference to Marx's own treatment, admittedly in three short Chapters, reference is made to the OCC. Third, however interpreted, these treatments of the LTRPF can proceed as if the whole of Volume 2 does not exist as well as exposition of the transformation problem by Marx himself that immediately precedes the treatment of the LTRPF in Volume 3 of *Capital*. It is as if the laws of production (rising OCC and accumulation derived from Volume 1) translate, or not, directly into a theory or postulate of falling profitability.

As is apparent from work throughout the 1970s with Laurence Harris (brought together in Fine and Harris, 1979, following 1976b and 1977, in debate with Hodgson, 1977) and in continuing contributions (Fine, 1991) my position is very different. For the fundamentalists, with (S/V)/(1 + C/V) making up the rate of profit, if C/V (interpreted as the OCC) rises the rate of profit must fall. Maybe there are some countertendencies but these cannot prevail. The major reason given, apart from the (wrong) idea that Marx says so, is that the rising OCC involves the relative expulsion of living labour from the value of commodities (with machinery displacing its role) so that the source of surplus value as the basis of profitability is undermined by the accumulation of capital itself.

Neatly attractive though this account may be, it is simply wrong even in theory, let alone empirically. For the rising C/V is part and parcel of the production of relative surplus value, increasing both S/V and the rate of profit. It might appear that the rising OCC must inevitably outweigh the rising S/V but this cannot be shown. As a mathematical economist, I had no problem hitting a brick wall in trying to show this. Later in life, I found an analogy which I liked, as cars began to indicate how many miles were left on a drive before fuel ran out. It is common experience that as you drive, you may find that you can still go further than when you set out, even though you have already used some petrol, for example because you drive from the city centre onto a motorway. In theory, there may be a rate of increase in miles per gallon that means you never run out of petrol no matter how far you go. The further you go, yet even further you are still able to go on your even faster increase in miles per gallon. Implausible in practice but it cannot be dismissed in principle. And, for the LTRPF why should not the increase in S and decrease in V, i.e. increase in S/V, be so much that it dominates the rise in C/V?

This is exactly the thrust of the Sraffian response, drawing upon the Okishian theorem. Basically, if capitalists individually choose higher rates of profit (from new techniques such as those deriving from a rising OCC), then the new equilibrium configuration of prices must involve rising profitability. In simpler terms, for the rate of profit to fall from one equilibrium to the next, there must be an increase in wages greater than the effect of productivity increase. So, falling profitability must derive distributionally from rising wages as opposed to some handwaving around rising OCC.

How did we differ with and reconcile these accounts. First is to reject the notion that Marx is putting forward an empirical law (in the tradition of Classical Political Economy, for which profitably falls for Adam Smith due to limits in the extent of the market, and through declining productivity of agriculture for Ricardo). Rather, his law is tendential, a systemic force deriving from accumulation and the rising OCC. By the same token, it co-exists with counteracting tendencies (CTs which he specifies).[15] Most important in these is the increase in S/V (arising out of relative surplus value) and the potential reduction in of C/V arising out of productivity increase across production of means of production. Crucially, these CTs are not of the sort that may or may not happen. They are part and parcel of, irreducibly attached to, the rising OCC.[16] You cannot have the LTRPF without having these CTs, two sides of the same coin.

As a result, it is not, however, a simple matter of adding the LTRPF and CTs together arithmetically and coming up with falling or rising profitability. Rather, it is how these two systemic tendencies interact with one another to give rise to more complex outcomes, one of which might be crises. Where the Law as Such and CTs differ is not in their causal role – each derives from

15 Mainly drawn from previous writers in the classical tradition and not reworked.

16 In contrast, say, to benefits from trade.

accumulation – but from their different levels of complexity. To use the vernacular, they are at different levels of abstraction but are not causally unequal. The Law as Such, as Marx dubs it, derives directly from production, whereas the CTs are synonymous with the formation of value and the VCC, as they reflect the formation of new values after the results of production (rising OCC) have worked themselves out from production through distribution and exchange. Indeed, Marx's treatment of the interaction of the LTRPF and CTs focuses not upon empirical movements in the rate of profit but on whether the *mass* of surplus value produced can continue to be satisfactorily accumulated in light of the structures, relations, processes and agencies engaged in such economic reproduction.

In short, the LTRPF and CTs remain at a relatively high level of abstraction and, as previously suggested, do not lead to immediate empirical predictions in the rate of profit. Indeed, it is remarkable that both sides of the debate between fundamentalists and Sraffians more or less presume that once the rate of profit falls, for whatever reason, this triggers a crisis. This does not follow at all – it might induce a reduced capacity to invest and incentive to invest but, equally, it is better to get some profit rather than less, to preserve the worth of your sunk fixed capital investments, or, alternatively, to invest more to accrue productivity in the competition to survive. Significantly, there were those arguing that the post-war boom ended, for example in the UK, because of falling profitability from each of the LTRPF and profit squeeze through wage increases. Yet, even today, fifty years later, there are arguments over the empirics of whether and when the profit rate fell. So, individual capitalists reducing investment and precipitating a crisis cannot have done so through knowledge of general conditions. And, last and by no means least, the rate of profit always depends upon the value of fixed capital and, as a crisis looms, firms go bust and can be bought up at a low cost through merger or acquisition, leading to a step increase in the rate of profit for those who survive.[17]

In a sense, this is to make sporadic raids into how the LTRPF and the CTs interact with one another to give rise to more complex outcomes rather than to leap from a falling rate of profit at an abstract level to immediate complex phenomena. In Volume 3 of *Capital*, Marx does go about this more systematically, both logically and historically, indicative of further aspects of his method.[18]

17 The depreciation, or devaluation/destruction of value, of capital in a crisis is intimately related to its restructuring through the agencies of industry itself, finance and the state – the focus of our empirical work on the British economy as mentioned previously.

18 The logical and historical within Marx are best illustrated and most prominent through his approach to modes of production and stages within modes of production (Fine and Harris, 1979). See also Fine (1992).

The logic is to investigate further the categories associated with the restructuring of capital through which the tensions between the LTRPF and the CTs assume more complex forms. This involves close attention to the financial system and leads to an extremely sophisticated theoretical account by Marx of the various different types of capital in exchange and their relationship both to interest, the accumulation and restructuring of capital and the circulation of value more generally. This, however, can only take us so far until historically, or conjuncturally, the relations between industry and finance (and the state) are specified. In Volume 3, these logical and historical aspects are mixed together in unfinished form but the theory is clear enough, with Marx uniquely specifying a distinction between interest-bearing capital and industrial capital (and the division of aggregate surplus value between them), and also between interest-bearing capital and other forms of capital in exchange (most notably merchant's capital, itself subdivided into various categories, which shares with industrial capital, the tendency for the rate of profit to be equalised).[19]

It is apparent, then, right or wrong, that during the 1970s, I had developed a detailed account of Marx's value theory.[20] With the exception of capital in exchange, the integral nature of my understanding, and of its representation of Marx's own political economy, came together in many respects in my contributions on Marx's theory of landed property, and rent as the economic form that it assumes in appropriating (surplus) value (Fine, 1979 and 1980a and b, debating Ball, 1980 and Catephores, 1980).[21] At length is addressed the formation of value within sectors and across sectors in general prior to taking into account the role of landed property in influencing (usually, but not necessarily, obstructing) the accumulation of capital. Differential rent arises out of competition within the sector and absolute rent from competition between sectors (and whether capital flows onto new or, more intensively, onto old – already in use – land). Crucially, the well-known result attributed to Marx, and more

19 These issues, and their implications, are fully covered in following Chapters. Note that the tendency for equalised rates of profit underpins the transformation of values into prices of production but, as always with Marx, tendencies have countertendencies attached, for which interactions between them give rise to more complex outcomes. In case of equalisation of profit rates, this goes hand in hand with accumulation within sectors to be more competitive than rivals through productivity increase and higher rates of individual profitability.

20 Note that I was asked to edit a volume of contributions on value theory that had appeared in the journal *Economy and Society* (Fine, ed. 1986). Those of my own that appeared there, as well as a substantial overview and introduction, are not reproduced in this Volume.

21 Note that my contributions on rent were more inspired in the first instance by detailed research on the British coal industry (and coal royalties) and the role of landed property in mineral extraction more generally (Fine, 1990b and 1994, for example).

often than not dismissed as arbitrary, associates absolute rent with a lower than 'normal' OCC with its potentially being made up out of the correspondingly positive difference between value and price of production.

Clearly, such a result depends upon how the OCC is interpreted and, as this has generally been wrong across the literatures for both the transformation problem and the LTRPF, it is hardly surprising that the same should apply to the theory of rent, and that there should be no connection with the other two problems, just as there was none forged by most of the literature between them. The transformation, the LTRPF and the theory of rent appear to others to be discrete. By contrast, my own treatment forges a unity across the three issues, with absolute rent deriving from the choice between intensive and extensive accumulation of capital, resulting in absolute rent increasing price by at most the difference in surplus value that would be produced by intensive as opposed to extensive accumulation on new or old land, respectively. In contrast to many dismissals of Marx's theory of absolute rent as being arbitrarily contingent upon a lower OCC within agriculture – why not any other sector subject to some sort of monopoly 'rent' – I show, following Marx, that absolute rent is contingent upon the lower OCC within agriculture as a result of its lower pace of intensive accumulation because of the intervention of landed property.

## 6 Short Overview of Chapters

Explicitly or otherwise, the themes covered above are addressed in more detail throughout this Volume. Chapters 2, 4 and 5 insist upon the continuing salience of value theory, properly understood, observing that there is a tension between remaining committed to value theory and addressing the increasing complexities of capitalism as it evolves that appear to invalidate value or require it to be modified. In other words, do the increasingly varied, complex and weighty value forms invalidate value itself or pose the challenge to relate value and value form afresh and/or even further. For me, it is premature to reject value as opposed to meeting the challenge.

Chapter 3, uniquely across this collection of Volumes, puts together two separate publications, albeit each of them short. One offers a rare critique of Sraffa's interpretation of Ricardo – of relevance because it is shown how Sraffa cornifies, that is, departs from Ricardo's commitment to labour as the source of value just as Sraffians seek to displace Marx's value theory through physical technical relations. The other topic in Chapter 3 is the so-called 'historical' transformation problem – was there ever a time when commodities exchanged at their values? Rather than giving an answer as yes or no, the point is made that value is transformed (other than for a Ricardian embodied labour approach) so that its very nature in terms of production relations, and the forms they take in exchange, need to be specified prior to addressing whether value equals price or not. The value of contemporary capitalism is very different from that of petty commodity production of an erstwhile era – and so are its corresponding relations to price. So, it is the nature of value as well as the forms that it takes that need to be uncovered in relation to one another.

Each of the contributions in Chapter 3, like many of the other Chapters, offers more or less direct criticism of other contributions and contributors as the way of elaborating and defending value theory and its implications.[22] Chapters 6 and 7, in debate with Jim Kincaid, moves from addressing the neo-Ricardian/Sraffian critique of value theory around price and profit formation in exchange to the broader criticism that exchange itself is a determinant of values since, if it ain't sold, it ain't socially necessary labour. This is the basis of underconsumptionist theories (and the inability to realise surplus that has been produced, see next Volume in this series). The most telling criticism of this is simply to point out that, whilst (social) use value is a prerequisite of a commodity, this does not mean that value cannot be destroyed once it has been produced simply because it has not been sold. Crises, after all, are the destruction of value, not merely the failure to create it.

Chapter 8, in critique of Groll and Orzech, focuses on the compositions of capital, TCC, OCC and VCC, in greater depth than above. Groll and Orzech are to be congratulated for almost uniquely highlighting the distinction between the OCC and VCC, and make some further progress in pinpointing them as belonging to production and exchange, respectively. But, from my perspective, what they do is wrong in and of itself and in interpretation of Marx, and in finding unity across treatments of the transformation, falling profitability, and rent. For them, the distinction between OCC and VCC derives from cyclical movements which would place the cyclically determined VCC, correctly, at a more concrete, even directly empirical, level of abstraction than the OCC. But it would also not see it as at the same causal level, deriving from accumulation itself and at a more abstract level than cyclical movements which are the consequences of the interactions between the LTRPF and its CTs at a more concrete level and requiring more logical and historical analysis of how the two tendencies interact in specific conditions of accumulation of capital.

22 I am acutely conscious that the contributions that are subject to direct criticism are not reproduced here. But, hopefully, they are both fairly and sufficiently represented within the critiques to allow for an understanding of my responses other than, possibly, for relatively minor points.

Chapters 9 and 10 address the transformation problem, the so-called "new interpretation" and Fred Moseley's approach, respectively. Whilst the 'solutions' they propose are very different (and mutually critical, especially from Moseley), what they do share in common is effectively the treatment of the transformation as an equilibrium determination of prices from values – as opposed to the formation of prices from values in the context of differential productivity shifts across sectors, deriving from accumulation, rising TCC/OCC and VCC formation, as contradictory processes. In the case of the new interpretation in particular, this involves all sorts of analytical and arbitrary acrobatics in order to preserve aggregate equalities between surplus value and profit, and value and price, but the result is to crunch the complex relations between value and price into a single value-price dimension, thereby precluding (and excluding) analysis of the LTRPF and CTS.

Chapters 11 and 12 offer an exposition of Marx's theory of capital in exchange (also debating Carlo Panico). Marx's analysis in Volume 3 of *Capital* is extremely complex (and unfinished). The key points are that such capital does not produce value but it appropriates surplus value whether as profit or interest. Logically, there are two categories (and many sub-categories) of capital in exchange – one, merchant's capital, most readily associated with buying and selling, is subject to an equalising rate of profit with industrial capital. The other, though, interest-bearing capital, is not and appropriates surplus value in the form of interest at the expense of, and prior to, the distribution of surplus value across capitals that are subject to profit rate equalisation. The major difference with Panico is that he effectively reduces capital in exchange, through a Sraffian-type analysis, to the first category – as does most orthodox monetary analysis with the rates of profit and interest tending to equalise with one another (subject to some sort of monopoly of finance and speculative activity). Whilst these distinctions may have appeared to be of limited relevance at the time of writing, they have become imperative in making sense of debates over financialisation (see next Volume in this series and Fine, 2022, most recently).

Finally, building upon rather than contesting Kohei Saito's scrutiny of newly available manuscripts drafted by Marx, Chapter 13 revisits my approach to Marx's theory of landed property and rent. Saito emphasises just how much Marx was drawn to developments in the chemical manufacture and use of fertilizer across agriculture as the means of increasing productivity. This is precisely a reflection of a rising OCC, quite apart from the simultaneous degradation of nature that results from the exhaustion of its 'free' (commodified but not commodity) 'gifts',[23] with relevance for climate change and the environment.

---

23 See Chapter 5.

CHAPTER 2

# The Continuing Imperative of Value Theory

## Postscript as Personal Preamble

This Chapter ultimately appeared as Fine (2001b), drafted upon request for a special issue of *Capital and Class* to mark its 25th anniversary – although *C&C* itself had been preceded by and remained for a time at least as subtitle, the Bulletin of the Conference of Socialist Economists (CSE). Previously, a longer version had appeared in Greek, again upon request (Fine, 1997a). It was modified and submitted for *C&C* before being shortened. The longer version is the basis of what appears here.[1]

By this time, the CSE had move on from its initial character which was primarily focused on debating and promoting Marxist political economy. It was very much a collective organisation in (self-)publishing the Bulletin, if eventually using a professional printer rather than gestetner, running the membership, and organising workshops and working groups, with the annual conference as a showpiece.[2] Whether due to this or not, once *C&C* was turned over to a commercial publisher, the nature of CSE began to change, slowly but surely if without sharp breaks and conflicts. There was also a turnover of leading figures from the "old guard" which had established and run the CSE.[3] Rather

1 It included the following. *Select References and Bibliography*: For overviews of value theory and its implications from various point of view, see Aglietta (1979), Dobb (1940), Elson (ed.) (1979), Fine (ed.) (1986), Fine and Harris (1979), Foley (1986), Lebowitz (1992), Meek (1956), Rosdolsky (1977), Rubin (1975), Steedman (1977), Steedman (ed.) (1981), Sweezy (1968) and Weeks (1981). For discussions focusing on money, see de Brunhoff (1976) and Arnon (1984). For views on Marx's method, see Colletti (1976), Moseley (ed.) (1993), Oakley (1983, 1984 and 1985), Pilling (1980), Reuten and Williams (1989) and Shamsavari (1991). On specific aspects of value theory, see Duménil (1983/84), Lee (1993) and Lipietz (1982).

2 It is surely not accidental that the subsequent International Initiative for Promoting Political Economy (iippe.org) should also have focused on an annual conference, working groups and workshops.

3 Under the leadership of erstwhile CSE stalwart, Robin Murray, many CSE members joined the Industry and Employment Branch of the Greater London Council (GLC), abolished by Mrs Thatcher in 1985. I myself worked there half-time as Research Editor, affectionately dubbing it the GLCSE. It may well be that the shift in focus and activity from CSE to GLC had some impact on the evolving nature of the CSE itself, something that did not occur in the earlier period of the CSE's involvement in formulating and debating the Alternative Economic Strategy (AES) of the 1970s. Rather, the latter reinvigorated debate over reform versus revolution, engagement with and within the Labour Party or not, the causes of the end of the

HTTPS://DOI.ORG/10.1163/9789004766266-003

than focusing upon Marxist political economy as such, it involved a wider take upon its role within the social sciences. In addition, the organisation increasingly became a journal with an annual conference with the loss and vitality of individual membership's collective participation, not least in working groups and workshops. In parallel, my own involvement in, even devotion to, CSE and *C&C* eroded.

Nonetheless, it is significant, and was welcome, that I was asked to contribute to the anniversary issue, and I continued to publish in *C&C*, if not over the last fifteen years (Fine, 2006a and 2007a, on critical realism; and Fine et al. 2010, on value theory once more, for the hundredth special issue – I seem to be ceremonially hauled out for such occasions).

Otherwise, at the time of publishing this piece, I was in the middle of a two-year research professorship to study economics imperialism, and so had plenty of time for researching and publishing. Significantly, *C&C* had been where I had launched my work on economics imperialism, seeing the mainstream's information-theoretic (or market imperfections more generally) as a revolution within the discipline as well as the basis on which to appropriate the subject matter of other disciplines if not other disciplines themselves (Fine, 1997b). As a result of this, and much more besides, I took the opportunity to reference much of my ongoing work in the discussion of value theory, not just to showcase it and shoehorn it in (as I suspect was the case) but primarily to illustrate just how much value theory could inform topics as diverse as the history of economic thought, the system of provision approach to consumption, the transition from apartheid in South Africa, the horrendous social capital and so on, quite apart from the shift from Sraffianism to the new interpretation as a response to the transformation problem.

## 1 The Dialectics of Debate[4]

The circumstances that gave rise to *Capital and Class* (and the old Bulletin before it) are very different from those of today. Then, in the wake of student radicalism, the collapse of the post-war boom and the ideology of Keynesianism,

post-war boom and its particular impact upon the UK as the 1970s' sick man of Europe, and conflicts between and within socialist/Marxist organisations, not least with the rise of Eurocommunism.

4 The article (Fine, 1997a) on which this Chapter is based was revised whilst in receipt of a Research Fellowship from the UK Economic and Social Research Council (ESRC) under award number R000271046 to study The New Revolution in Economics and Its Impact upon

mainstream economics was in disarray prior to the rise of neoliberalism. It was under assault from within, not least with the Cambridge critique of capital theory, and from without with the growing interest in Marxist theory and radical political economy. Further, intellectual, academic and personal practices were far more integrated. Currently, mainstream economics as a discipline is ever more esoteric, intolerant of heterodoxy and riddled with the crudest methodological and theoretical inadequacies. Yet it possesses such a stranglehold that the discipline is lost to political economy as a terrain on which to argue for alternatives. Radical political economists within economics are ageing, compromising and increasingly eccentric. For value theory, new 'solutions' to the transformation problem are more marked by these influences and the search for originality than by a dual attachment both to the topic's intellectual traditions and the realities of capitalism that are the object of study.

But this is just a specific conjunctural instance of a more general feature of debate over the labour theory of value (ltv). For it has always been open to rejection by some even as it has been accepted by others, with both sides appealing to the same factors. This paradox in the realm of theory is not accidental. For as society becomes more developed and complex, does this undermine the validity and necessity for value theory, or does the latter remain essential as the abstract basis on which to reconstruct and comprehend complex outcomes? Two separate methodological issues are involved here. First is whether the features of the capitalist economy that are common across all of its history are amenable to explanation by reference to value theory – do we need the ltv to explain wages and profits, or the course of economic growth and crises? The second issue is whether particular periods of capitalism, especially the more developed, reinforce or undermine the validity of value theory – as in monopolisation, for example, or the growth of unproductive labour in the service sectors. The ltv has always been on the defensive across these analytical divides. It has been charged with underlying analytical weaknesses and for inflexibility in responding to historically new features of capitalism. In short, is value theory, for example, appropriate at all as the basis for a theory of price and, if so, does it remain appropriate for monopoly pricing?

In this Chapter, whilst highlighting this dialectic, I intend to put emphasis on the positive case that has been established for the ltv rather than, as is characteristic of most of the favourable literature, seeking to defend the theory against the mountain of criticism to which it has been subject. Almost

Social Sciences. Thanks to Costas Lapavitsas and Alfredo Saad-Filho for extensive comments and suggestions on an earlier draft. I hold them entirely responsible for any errors or deficiencies.

inevitably, the positive case for value theory has been overshadowed by the weight of criticism levelled against it. The basic reasons for and methods underlying the ltv have become inadvertently set aside or, as is to be suspected for much of the literature, not even consulted or known as a parody of Marx's political economy is paraded for ritual attack and defence. I intend to demonstrate that there are fundamentals to the ltv that are internally coherent. Further, this coherence provides the basis for unravelling the increasing complexities and specificities of the capitalist mode of production as they have emerged over time – even though these complexities have induced rejection of value theory on the basis of incoherent and inaccurate understandings of it.

At a more mundane level, as a proponent of value theory, the positive account offered here will also be personal to a greater extent than intellectual modesty might otherwise reasonably allow. But I do want to illustrate the arguments offered here by showing how value theory has informed my own work and to reference it accordingly. It might, thereby, help to inform the future work of others. To this end, I have only referred to my own work in the text but I suggest important sources, other than Marx himself, in the bibliography (see first footnote to this Chapter).

## 2 Smith, Ricardo, Marx

Adam Smith provides an excellent starting point. He argued that the labour theory of value would hold but only in that rude society, or primitive communism as Marx called it, in which labourers simply hunted deer and beaver as required for personal consumption. Significantly, in view of the theme laid out above, as soon as the economy developed to allow for the presence of rents and, ultimately, profits, Smith argued against the labour theory of value and replaced it with a components theory of price, with the latter naturally made up of the contributions or claims from wages, profits and rents. For Smith, once labour was no longer the sole element in price, the labour theory of value needed to be jettisoned. The addition of the simplest element of economic complexity was sufficient both for this purpose and for Smith to embrace a components theory that was either tautologous (a price is made up of its constituent parts) or erroneous (since the three components are not independent of one another as they mutually exhaust net product, a complicated point that need not detain us here but see later).

Implicitly, and explicitly from the vantage point of Marx's value theory, Smith's contribution raises two crucial methodological issues. The first concerns the status of the argument in favour of the labour theory of value when

Smith deems that it does hold. However, in a rude society, there would be no (market) exchange (except for random disposal of accidental surplus which would not be tied to labour time of hunting). This implies that there are no prices, so there is no need for a value theory at all! Quite clearly, Smith has gone through an inadvertent mental exercise. Suppose the rude society were like a capitalist society – would the labour theory of value hold? It is a totally meaningless question, and this implies there must be considerable doubts about the notion of value that Smith has constructed.

There is, in this context, considerable difference with one aspect of Marx's own materialist method, one that is highly attractive in terms of the appeal to realism. For this depends upon justifying the use of particular concepts by demonstrating their correspondence, even if necessarily within the theory itself, with the realities of the society under consideration. From this perspective, concepts such as value, price and exchange are invalid if applied to the rude society. By whatever intellectual route that value is derived as a concept, it is merely a general, mental, ahistorical and asocial construct for Smith, which may or may not be useful for explaining exchange in the rude society (where the question is irrelevant) or more developed economies with returns also accruing other than to labour (where the labour theory is rejected necessarily on the basis of a concept of value which has not been designed specifically for them). In contrast to such instrumentalism in the understanding and use of the labour theory of value, Marx's own approach can be understood by first establishing whether value exists or not. If not, it has no analytical status by way of correspondence to, or reproduction in thought of, reality itself. When the answer, however, is in the affirmative, it leads to a number of subsequent questions – which labour counts towards value, by how much does it count and by what (social) mechanisms does it do so, and what are the relations between value and more complex economic and social outcomes (that might lead the many to reject the ltv)?

The second methodological point that arises out of Smith's rejection of the labour theory of value is whether value, however defined and understood, and price should be seen as identical to one another or not, at least as some sort of centre of gravity once the peripheral or particular issues, such as advertising in the modern world, are set aside. For Smith, it is a matter of whether value as labour time is identical to price or not. If not, value has to be amended until it does equal price, as in his components theory. Of course, such natural prices, as they are called, are perceived as the centre around which actual price fluctuations occur. This, in itself, is potentially an arbitrary division between those factors that determine the natural price and those that determine the deviations around it. In some sense, one set is supposedly more fundamental than the other. This opens the way for any number of factors to enter the fundamental set, as is the case for price theory based on generalised theories of supply and demand.

Again, Marx's approach is different and not arbitrary. Value as labour-time is understood as an abstract and simple category derived from production. It cannot be directly observed, or held in the hand as it were, but is the basis on which the more complex exchange categories, such as price, are constructed both in reality and, correspondingly, within theory. In other words, the theory has an analytical structure or structure of abstraction in which more complex categories like price reproduce rather than displace the simpler categories like value. This reflects the previous methodological point in that the existence of value has already been established. It cannot simply be thrown away because of the complex forms that it assumes and which are its effects. Only if price is seen as the form taken by value in exchange, just as the element carbon can assume the form either of coal or diamonds depending upon the way it is structured and worked upon (by natural forces long ago), so the value/price nexus forges the relationship between producers as it becomes a relationship between buyers and sellers of goods. Carbon does not cease to exist nor to be of analytical relevance simply because it can take the form of a number of different products.

In short, the value relationship is quantitative in terms of the labour time expended by individual workers but, qualitatively, it is much more besides. The existence of complicating factors, some of which are considered fundamental and some not – such as equalised profit and random or unsystematic factors, respectively – are by no means a reason for rejecting value theory but the very basis on and for which it is constructed. It is perhaps unfortunate that the dialectical view of this perspective in terms of essence and appearance or substance and form often expresses the second aspect of each couplet as *mere* phenomenal aspects (or forms and appearances). Whilst, in a sense, appropriate for a grand vision of fundamentals, it can lead to an unwarranted denigration of the importance of critical features of the capitalist economy. If prices are the *mere* form of value, is profit the *mere* form of surplus value, and the financial system the *mere* monetary form of capital? On the contrary, these are not lightweight symbols of the essence like the face of a monarch on coinage but material relations with effects even if they are derivative from the class relations between capital and labour. But I anticipate. The important point, though, is that value theory does not fall merely by virtue of the complexity through which it moves through the world of capital(ism).

Turn now to Ricardo. Even though he shared some of the methodological deficiencies with Smith, he was firmly committed to the ltv. He was determined to explain as many features as possible of the capitalist economy on the basis of value theory as he understood it – which is, as for Smith, the labour time required for production. Ricardo demonstrated that Smith's argument was, at least in part, wrong – that the formation of a separate claim on production other than from labour was not a reason in itself why price should diverge from value. Rather, if profits as an element of price were non-zero or increased, this would be at the expense of wages, and prices could continue to equal (labour) value. Unfortunately for Ricardo, although this argument is correct as far as the mere presence of profits is concerned, once there are differences in what is now termed the composition of capital, prices do deviate quantitatively from values, with higher prices relative to values for those products that have high capital-intensity, since they are liable to command disproportionately larger amounts of profit relative to labour time of production. Once again, as Ricardo realised giving rise to what is now termed the transformation problem in Marx's value theory, the ltv appears to falter as it confronts the simple distribution of profit between capitalists (with differing compositions of capital).

Setting these difficulties aside, Ricardo attempted to explain rent on the basis of his value theory. He succeeded, by asserting that value should be determined by the labour time of the worst piece of land in use, with rent making up the difference in productivity on better lands. But by attempting to deal with a more complex form, rent, this creates an inconsistency in Ricardo's value theory, one which he never resolves. For, there are now two value theories, one for agriculture on the margin of cultivation, the other for manufacturing which is presumably based on average production conditions. Why should value in industry not also be determined at the margin of the worst producer, other producers reaping profits in the form of what Marshall termed quasi-rents until, at least, they were eroded by the catch-up in technique or whatever by the erstwhile marginal producers.

For Marx's value theory, these issues have to be treated differently. But first consider some of the methodological issues raised previously. The opening chapters of Volume I *Capital* can be considered as establishing that value does exist but only in societies dominated by commodity production. The process of exchange necessarily establishes an equivalence between the different types of labour that are used in production, although that equivalence is rarely, if ever, direct. Rather, the relation between (the labour of) producers is expressed as a relationship between commodities, as use values, in terms of relative prices. Only for convenience is it assumed that commodities exchange at their value for, then, the distinction between value and price, as previously discussed, can be made prominent – even if those unaware of this motivation see the abstraction merely as a simplifying assumption, as unjustified and as inconsistent with Marx's treatment of price of production in Volume III of *Capital*. Further, it becomes apparent in Volume I that value is most extensive, indeed predominant, only under the capitalist mode of production for which, it is not only the proletariat that joins the market, being both able and compelled to sell its capacity to work. Means of production and means of consumption are in general also brought into the orbit of exchange. The value relationship then, as for other modes of production where commodities are less pervasive, is not synonymous with the market. For it represents a set of entirely different economic relations between producers and those that command them, as well as differences in other socioeconomic relations, such as (access to) consumption (with major access through the market from whatever sources of revenue).

In establishing the nature of the value relation, as a relation between producers and not simply as quanta of labour time, Marx pinpoints the peculiar character of the money commodity. Initially, this is constructed on the basis of a particular use value, gold. But Marx, even at this early stage in his analysis, establishes that gold as a general equivalent for other commodities, soon takes on a symbolic role – first of all with the debasement of the currency through wear and tear and even clipping and filing, and eventually through paper symbols themselves. What this demonstrates is that the distinction between value and price is such that the one can be represented by the other even with the increasing displacement of commodity money from the processes of exchange.

In short, Marx's theory of money is in part based upon the notion that commodity money is displaced by symbols of money and, hence, indirectly, symbols of value – although ratification of such symbols ultimately requires the intervention by the state. Paradoxically, it is precisely this displacement in its most modern form, in which the functions of commodity money, gold, are more or less confined to the reserves of central banks, that lead many to reject Marx's monetary theory where they have genuinely considered it. How can a theory of commodity money, based on value theory, be of relevance when commodity money is no longer in use. In riposte, it can be argued that Marx's monetary theory implies the displacement of commodity money. How this occurs needs to be explored in theoretical and empirical context, moving beyond the mere symbolic circulation of values as commodities to incorporate the symbolic, at times fictitious, circulation of surplus value. But, this is to anticipate, although it does root consideration of the currently evolving financial system within the bounds of the production system on which it depends for its profitability however much it might wish otherwise.

Although the abstraction that value equals price draws the qualitative distinction between the two and establishes value as a social relation between producers specific to a commodity producing society, the importance of this abstraction is arguably more important for another reason – the light that it sheds on class. For, throughout Volume I, once value is established as a legitimate category, Marx is primarily concerned with exchange only to a limited but crucial extent. His concern is primarily with the single most important exchange within capitalism – between capital and labour – treating the economy, as it were, as a single enterprise. On this basis, Marx initially addresses the single most important question – how is it possible that surplus value can be produced when every commodity exchanges exactly at its value. His answer is remarkably simple; the commodity labour power, the capacity to labour, is what is purchased by the capitalist but at a value itself that bears no necessary quantitative relation as such to the quantity of labour performed by that capacity. Surplus value arises out of the ability of the capitalist to extract more working time, and hence value, than is required to purchase labour power. Interestingly, having answered this question qualitatively, the vast majority of Volume I is concerned both theoretically and empirically with how do capitalists extract surplus value quantitatively. By proposing the concepts of absolute and relative surplus value, Marx draws attention to the extensive (longer, harder work) and intensive (productivity increase through mechanisation) methods of production by which capital exploits labour. Each requires the accumulation of capital to proceed.

Value theory, then, gives rise to and ties political economy to a number of notions: the classes of capital and labour are divided by a fundamental conflict over the production process – this is prior to distributional considerations as suggested by Ricardian-type analyses; accumulation of capital is imperative for the capitalist system; and there are definite methods by which the expansion of surplus value is pursued, with Marx suggesting, to be breathtakingly brief, that productivity is systemically pursued through the relative displacement of workers from the production process as given amounts of raw materials are worked up into final products through the use of machinery, etc.

## 3 Value and Capital

A number of distinguishing, positive features stand out from Marx's value theory, although they are often overlooked or even discarded by those subscribing to some form of Marxism. First, methodologically, Marx's value theory is based on a dialectic in which the concepts employed are shown to have a correspondence to the reality under study both socially and historically. Further, abstract concepts are based on simple concepts such as value – itself derived from the notion of the two aspects of the commodity as exchange and use value – which are reproduced and not displaced by the emergence of more complex concepts such as price. This method can be illustrated by the three Volumes of *Capital*. In Volume I, Marx is concerned with establishing the nature of value and, then, how – as a concept rooted in capitalist production – (surplus) value is produced. Qualitatively, the latter depends upon the exchange between capital and labour, stripping away, or abstracting from, all other forms of exchange; quantitatively, it leads to a thorough analysis of how the production process is directed towards both the intensive and extensive exploitation of labour and what are some of the results of this – in the accumulation of capital, the factory system, limits to the length of the working day, the emergence of a credit system, the formation of a reserve army of labour, etc.

In a sense, then, Volume I, can be considered as being primarily concerned with the use value of that unique commodity, labour power. The focus of Volume II is upon the exchange value of commodities more generally and how, with the intervention of money, the accumulation and reproduction of the capital-labour relation can be sustained. This is not, however, simply a shift from one sphere of activity, production, to another, exchange but, rather, a refinement of the concept of value itself. For far from being an analysis of equilibrium – at which word, all genuine Marxist scholars should reach for their critical red pen, ready to strike out – Volume II is concerned to show how economic reproduction is simultaneously a balance between value magnitudes (as in its famous equations) and a balance between use values across the sectors of means of production and means of consumption (with a further analysis, often overlooked, at the different ways in which these values circulate as revenues with money, or credit, as an intermediary).

In short, Volume II has nothing to do with equilibrium although it can be interpreted in this way by those seeking analogies with various strands of orthodox theory. Rather, it reconstructs the concept of value, as understood in Volume I (and not just a quantum of labour time but the whole capital-labour relation as laid out there) in the more complex form of balance and movement, at whatever quantitative level, between sectors of the economy. In addition, the refinement of the concept of value allows a variety of more complex forms to be defined more rigorously and fully – unproductive labour is that wage labour which is not engaged in the production of surplus value (because used for commerce or non-profit-making services), fixed capital is that part of constant capital which only releases its value into circulation over a number of periods of production, etc.

Volume III of *Capital* is concerned with the distribution of surplus value but not merely in the simple sense of who gets how much of the surplus value that has been produced. Note, however, that even this superficial interpretation presupposes, correctly in line with Marx's method, that the surplus value has to be produced before it is distributed. If, though, the distribution is simply interpreted as a cake-division exercise, as in the (neo-)Ricardian (or Sraffian) interpretations, then the concepts of surplus value and profit collapse and the former simply serves as a superfluous accounting exercise. In contrast, Marx deals with the distribution of surplus value as a refinement of the concept of value, in which the results of the previous two Volumes are brought together and used to develop more complex and concrete categories in terms of the economic processes by which production and exchange are integrated in the circulation of capital and commodities as a whole (with the distribution of surplus value as one amongst many consequences).

Thus, the so-called transformation problem addresses the formation of prices of production. Whilst this has incorrectly been seen as an equilibrium theory of prices (and the rate of profit), a careful reading, drawing the distinction properly between the value and organic compositions of capital, reveals that Marx's pre-occupation is entirely otherwise and remains much more sharply and abstractly focused. It is concerned with the question – how does the inevitable development of productivity at different paces across the different sectors of the economy allow for the tendency for capital to be equally rewarded according to the quantity of capital advanced. For, when the rate of change of productivity differs across sectors, profitability would change in favour of those performing better. Prices have to adjust, and capital move, for profitability to move towards equalisation. But the situation is more complex than this in that productivity and corresponding price changes and movements of capital will have knock-on effects for the input costs (values) of means of production and in the prices (values) of items of consumption.

This is an appropriate starting point for raising Marx's law of the tendency of the rate of profit to fall, LTRPF, (and counteracting tendencies), although the LTRPF and the transformation problem have traditionally been treated separately – but sharing in common the capacity to attract target practice for those seeking to reject Marx's value theory. This separation between the two 'problems' – what happens to prices and profits for given values and what happens to them when values are changing – has been almost universal even amongst those sympathetic to, and supportive of, Marx. The approach adopted here is different. The LTRPF is seen as more complex and different than an empirical prediction or mathematical proof of movements in the rate of profit. Rather, it deals at a relatively abstract level with the co-existence of the consequences of accumulation, as laid out in Volume I, and the need for these to be coordinated through the mechanisms of exchange as detailed in Volume II. Quite apart from a host of socioeconomic change attached to the accumulation of capital, such as monopolisation, urbanisation, the reproduction of a reserve army of labour, etc, the exchange system has to accommodate the shifting rates of productivity and profitability analytically laid out in the treatment of the transformation of values into prices of production. Marx draws the conclusion that this cannot always be done without the accumulation of capital being punctuated with crises from time to time.

Volume III does, however, go much further than this by confronting the previously developed categories with specific types of capital. Volume II highlighted the need for commodities to be sold; this can become a specialised activity within exchange undertaken by merchant capital, tending to earn equal profitability with industrial capital but without itself creating any (surplus) value. Volume II has also shown how money is continually entering and leaving the circuits of capital, thereby creating a pool of idle money. Volume I suggests that capital prospers to the extent that it can command money-capital through the credit system. Through these insights, Marx forms the notion of interest-bearing capital, the borrowing and lending of money for the purposes of producing and appropriating surplus value (upon and around which any number of other forms of credit and money-dealing can be incorporated or evolve).

Volume III also considers circumstances in which there are potential obstacles to the accumulation of capital in the form of landed property. In contrast to Ricardian and most other rent theory, Marx is concerned with how the presence of class relations on the land affects the access of capital to a vital means of production and thereby modifies the pace and nature of accumulation and through which rent emerges as a consequence. For this reason, Marx's theory is organised around the potential for a lower organic composition of capital (properly understood) and the necessity for, but the limits that this imposes on, (absolute) rent. Paradoxically, this yields the result that there is no such thing as no rent land (a totally common and commonsense experience), although Ricardian theory insists that the worst land must pay no rent but for monopoly rent (which would not distinguish the intervention of land from monopoly conditions in other sectors or factors of production).

The immediately preceding discussion is intended to show how the distinctive method of Marx's value theory is embedded in one particular interpretation of the flow of argument through the three Volumes of *Capital*. It is perhaps worth reiterating that on every occasion in which Marx introduces a more complex concept, this is often deployed positively by critics (even supporters of Marx) as a means to reject his analysis. Volume II, for example, has induced theories of underconsumption, as in the work of Baran and Sweezy and many others, for which the notion of (unrealised) potential surplus suffices and value theory as such is no longer necessary. The transformation of values into prices of production and surplus value into profit is reconstrued as a transformation, and generally, an equilibrium problem. Merchant capital, and even unproductive labour in the state sector devoted to non-commercial activity such as education, are conceived of as akin to any other sector of activity and equally a source of profitability, possibly indirectly. Interest-bearing capital is indistinguishable from credit in general, in whatever purpose to which it might be put, and is geared to the exchange process as a whole and is not specific to the accumulation of capital and creation of surplus value. And rent is simply the consequence of a more or less powerful monopoly over a particular factor of production. Paradoxically, in each of these cases, Marx is accused of being insufficiently sophisticated, whereas it is his critics who are generally responsible for collapsing socioeconomic structures, processes and agencies into an unduly simplistic mould – as if, for example, education could produce and appropriate profits in exactly the same way as an industrial sector, the capitalist economy could be in equilibrium, an inability to sell prove an insurmountable and chronic problem, etc.

I have attempted to deal with many of these issues of method in my writing although others, to whom I refer in these to the best of my knowledge, have done so in greater detail and with greater success and insight. Fine (1989) provides an elementary overview. Fine and Harris (1979) provides a survey of many contributions to Marxist political economy, although it is on the basis of the relative emphasis upon, and interaction between, the three *structures* – on which see below – of production, exchange and distribution and reflects a heavy Althusserian influence in vogue at the time of writing. Fine (ed.) (1986) provides readings on the value debate, including those of my own that have addressed both the transformation problem and rent theory, with the latter specifically employed in a historical and empirical account of the British coal industry in Fine (1990b). Fine (1982) develops the interpretation of the law of the tendency of the rate of profit to fall as an abstract law leading to more complex outcomes and shows how it is the antithesis of alternative accounts based on comparative statics and, hence, equilibrium. Fine (1985–86 and 1988) argues for the distinctiveness of Marx's theory of interest-bearing capital.

## 4 Class, Structure, Tendency, and History

This long account of the first distinctive feature of Marx's value theory (from abstraction to more concrete complexity as a reproduction in thought of material relations) will allow most of the others to be handled much more briefly.

Second, then, the value theory incorporates a particular understanding of class, one based on the fundamental conflict between capital and labour over production. The increasingly complex way in which (surplus) value is reproduced has its counterpart in an increasingly sophisticated understanding of class and of class relations. For there is the implication of differentiation of the capitalist class – by sector, productivity, by fractions across industrial, merchant and interest bearing capital – and also of the class of labour by the same factors as well as by skill, employed or not, etc. Once again, greater complexity induces a rejection or refinement of Marx's theory of class for a range of criteria leading to stratification. This is so even before the social reproduction of the capital-labour relation is considered where political, ideological and other socioeconomic relations become involved (as in gender, race, nationality, etc). Whilst it is essential to avoid economic reductionism (the capital-labour relation as such cannot inform us directly any more about these issues than it can about the exact outcomes for prices and profits), value as a class relationship is an essential foundation on which to examine other (non-economic) issues and especially politics, ideology and the state.

Third, Marx's value theory is attached to a particular understanding of socioeconomic structures. This is not simply a matter of the basic class relations from which the logical possibility of other classes can also be derived by their divergence from the simple but fundamental dichotomy between capital and labour. The self-employed, for example, constitute a category that is neither proletariat nor bourgeois but is defined relative to them. Such derivation of categories also applies to other socioeconomic structures. As is apparent, capital defines a fundamental distinction between production and exchange, and also between economic and social reproduction, the latter comprising those relations that are conditioned by, but which are not incorporated within, the direct orbit of capital.[5] Thus, the nature and determinants of the state and the role of the family system (and domestic labour, for example) can be identified but not filled out by an abstract analysis of capital alone. Such structural divisions can only be identified qualitatively.

It is important to recognise that these structural divisions can themselves only be identified qualitatively by abstract value analysis. We know that the freedom of labour implies that it is not reproduced solely by capital, although this by no means implies that economic and non-economic freedoms are

5 Subsequently, I have argued (much more clearly) that economic is contained within social reproduction not a structured dualism with it as has often become commonplace in the recent renewal of interest in social reproduction around the environment, pandemics and care/welfare, and intersectionality (Fine, 2024, for example).

either guaranteed or mutually exclusive (consider, for example, the right to demonstrate). Similarly, which particular activities occupy the realm of production, exchange or lie outside the direct control of capital altogether (as in provision by the state or the household on a non-commercial basis) is variable both historically and within and across countries.

Transport and storage, for example, could be incorporated under the control of either industrial or merchant capital. Privatisation and commercialisation (introduction of user charges) of public utilities illustrate a shifting boundary between productive and unproductive labour either between the public and private sector or even within the public sector itself. And the domestic provision of consumption goods is generally believed to have been undermined by the assault of capitalist mass production. But even here, the shift in structural boundaries has often been in the opposite direction as capitalist production has enhanced the scope for domestic provision, as in home entertainment and a host of consumer durables from building tools through to microwaves. I have attempted to deal with many of these issues both in theoretical and empirical detail in Fine (1992, 1997 and 1998b), Fine and Leopold (1993), Fine et al. (1996), and Fine (1998b). Both in identifying structures and in constructing appropriate theory and construing empirical evidence, value theory has proved invaluable.

Value theory has, however, often been rejected on the basis of structuralist arguments whether the latter are recognised as such. This is especially so in case of what has been termed categoricism, for which a particular inequality or difference is identified empirically and then 'explained' by being referred to as a structure. This can take the form of class analysis, as in the notion of capital and labour in conflict over distribution, or along different lines, as in theories of patriarchy and racism in which these are used as structures to explain disadvantage. Inevitably, categoricism is antagonistic to Marxism, not only because it, possibly erroneously, identifies structures which are perceived both analytically and empirically to contradict emphasis on class but also because, methodologically, structures are erroneously interpreted as the most fundamental of categories – to a large extent, an approach that was itself encouraged for a time by Althusserianism. This begs the question of where these structures originate and how they are reproduced for, otherwise, how can they ever change or be transformed.

In short, Marxism in general and value theory in particular do not deny the existence and significance of socioeconomic and other structures but this is not to embrace a methodology of structuralism, whether categoricism or not. More specifically, structures need to be analytically justified on the basis of class relations and the socioeconomic processes to which they are attached for which the theory of value is an exemplary illustration as suggested by the ground already covered above, as in the distinctions between production and exchange, and between economic and social reproduction. But structures can also be understood as the consequence of more complex, historically contingent outcomes, as I have tried to demonstrate with the economic history of the South African economy (Fine and Rustomjee, 1996), and the way in which consumption and food systems are constructed and evolve (Fine and Leopold, 1993; Fine et al. 1996; and Fine, 1998b).

Fourth, an important part of these analyses is to specify the socioeconomic processes by which structures are reproduced and transformed. Like class relations these are abstract and are the basis on which the more complex structures are reproduced (or not). Often, the underlying processes are mutually contradictory as in the imperatives towards vertical integration and disintegration, for deskilling and reskilling, and, of crucial significance in value theory, how productivity increase via the accumulation of capital is experienced both as a boost to profitability in the form of lower production costs and as a threat to profitability in the form of more intensive competition for markets. For equilibrium analyses, these processes interact harmoniously and, subject to no upward adjustment in wages and rational choice by capitalists of least cost production techniques, must enhance profitability. In contrast to Marx's theory of the tendency of the rate of profit to fall, there is no attempt to understand how the forces generated by the accumulation of capital and productivity increase place enormous strains on the economic structures and processes of the value system, and the social formation within which it is embedded. In this respect, Marx's value analysis is uniquely successful in the links that it forges between the theory of value and productivity *change*. Orthodox economics does not even address the issue and has always used equilibrium analysis with given technology, although value as price can change from one equilibrium to the next in a comparative statics for one set of given technologies as opposed to another. Ricardo did very little better, with value being determined in a similar way in industry but in a dynamic but relatively trivial way for the distinct theory of value used for agriculture. The value contributed by labour time on better lands increased simply by virtue of the use of other, possibly equivalent, labour on lands of worst quality.

Smith contributed a much more penetrating if chaotic understanding and can even be credited with having first addressed the issue of how to define value as productivity is changing. This was a consequence of his motivation to explain the wealth of nations in which he ultimately gave priority to the growing division of labour as a source of productivity increase. Within the context of his components theory of value, he argued that wages would be higher with the *growing*, and not the level of the, division of labour. It follows that price depends upon the pace of productivity increase. Although not in the context of the labour theory of value, this implies that Smith indirectly establishes an equivalence in the formation of price between technologies of the past and technologies of the present (through the wages, profits and rents that are the components of the raw materials, previously produced, but which are added as indirect costs to the direct cost components that make up current production). In doing so, he made the elementary error of overlooking that he cannot use the same wages, etc for the indirect costs as for the direct costs since he has already argued that the latter are amended by the growing division of labour.

In Fine (1982), I discuss these aspects of Smith's value theory in greater detail. What is remarkable is that he unconsciously poses the issue of how do previously produced materials enter into value when conditions of production are themselves changing? To my knowledge, only Marx has answered this question in a non-trivial sense, avoiding both comparative statics (i.e. a sequence of equilibria for each of which technology is given) and a simple neutrality in the improvement in productivity for which all prices decline in proportion. But Marx shifts the analytical terrain on which the issue is addressed. On the one hand, not surprisingly, the labour theory of value displaces the components theory. This, in itself, implies an acknowledgement that different labours, in different sectors, of different skills, exercised at different times with different levels of productivity are all brought into equivalence with one another through the system of commodity exchange (although these differences are often referred to as a rationale for rejecting the labour theory of value). On the other hand, the outcome is not tied to an equilibrium theory of natural prices but to the laws of development of capitalism as they are expressed through its relations, tendencies and structures.

Fifth is the historical aspect to Marx's value theory. As already observed, its applicability is limited to those societies in which there is the presence of commodity exchange which only attains its peak with capitalism. This is not only to justify the use of value as labour-time on materialist grounds but also an acknowledgement that value is a social relation between producers whose interaction with one another is through the system of exchange in complex and potentially historically variable ways. These elementary historical and social insights should suffice to recognise that the labour theory of value is not adequate if based solely on the idea of value as a quantum of embodied labour. For then, of course, in a sense, we do not need to know anything about social relations at all in understanding value, as in its application to Smith's rude society, just as we do not need to know about other objects or substances if we want to know how much iron is embodied in a particular object. Of course, the notion of the labour theory as labour embodied has been seen by critics from mainstream economics as arbitrary and has led to parodies in terms of iron or energy theories of value.

## 5 From the Historical to the Contemporary

Once, however, value is seen as a relation that is historically and socially specific, then it is possible to recognise that value does itself change with the underlying socioeconomic relations by which it is constituted. Interestingly, the historical specificity of value has been the focus of a debate – the so-called historical transformation problem. Here, the issue has been whether there was an early period of capitalism or even simple commodity production, as suggested by Engels, during which commodities exchanged at their values which was then followed by the situation of developed capitalism for which exchange at value no longer obtains. According to the argument offered here, as laid out in Fine (ed.) (1986), this is an inappropriate way to view the historical transformation. For, rather than a given value exchanging at price in one historical instance and then at price of production at another instance, the nature of value itself is different according to whether it is attached, for example, to simple commodity as opposed to advanced capitalist production – a rather obvious point if value is seen as a relation of production through which labour time is represented in exchange. Both the nature of production relations themselves as well as the way in which they are integrated through exchange are entirely different.

Whilst such insights are what gives value theory its analytical strength, the issues concerned are otherwise seen by critics as indicative of weakness. How can an economic theory based on labour-embodied be appropriate both for simple commodity exchange and for advanced capitalism? And, of course, the answer is that it cannot as Smith discovered two hundred years previously in erroneously confining his particular understanding of the labour theory of value to the rude society. Today social scientists and commentators tend to be much too sophisticated to review Smith's arguments and are bedazzled by the increasingly complex economic and social developments that appear to reinforce the irrelevance of value theory.

In general, this has led to two broad responses. One is to rely upon empirical and descriptive analyses which are relatively void of theoretical considerations. Where theory is involved, it tends to be simplistic, presuming a correspondence between correlation and causation, however many variables are statistically embroiled together. This implies an absence of relations, structures and tendencies – an analytical structure of concepts and causation – except in the sense of categoricism outlined above.

The other response is to be conceptually inventive but without consciously rooting such innovation within existing theoretical frameworks, and certainly not within that provided by value theory. The most obvious and relevant example of this is provided by the theory of post-Fordism, critically assessed in Fine (1998a), although it is now being supplemented by the idea of globalisation. For each of these, value theory has ultimately been totally discarded although, as post-Fordism was initially given a Marxist gloss by Aglietta, it has taken a little time for it to gain its "freedom" from value which is now indisputable. Consequently, standard concepts within Marxism, which were rooted theoretically in value theory and historically in the current phase of capitalism have more or less disappeared without trace – notions such as imperialism and monopoly capitalism (with monopoly being seen as the form in which competition takes place rather than as its antithesis).

Such flights of fancy pale into insignificance when set against many of the offerings associated with post-modernism. Here, the critique of Marx's value theory, especially as it has evolved in the work of Baudrillard, concerns his neglect of the use value aspect of the commodity. It is wrongly argued that this is taken to constitute the physical properties of the commodity by Marx, and it is also suggested that in the social construction of use value, the meaning and significance of the commodity to the consumer is almost limitless. In contrast, it is imperative to recognise that the culture of consumption is a material culture, one that is deeply embedded in the relations and mechanisms through which those commodities are produced and eventually find their way into consumption. Value theory takes as one of its starting points that the commodity must constitute a social use value (otherwise it cannot be sold) and it must also be produced; far from precluding an incorporation of the role of the nature and meaning of the commodity, this is one of its most important determinants without which the role of other factors, including culture and subjectivity, become arbitrary. To put it bluntly for a moment, are we really to believe that the meaning of Coca-Cola, and the way that this meaning is purveyed through massive advertising campaigns, is independent of the way in which Coca-Cola is itself produced, distributed and sold? In short, as has been argued in Fine and Leopold (1993), an appropriate understanding of modern consumption depends upon developing and not rejecting value theory in the context of the social construction of the use value of the commodity in which this is not artificially detached, as in much post-modernist discourse, from the value relations by which we have commodities at all.

## 6 The Tasks We Face

The constructive rationale, then, for the ltv that has been outlined is well established through Marx's own work but, equally, through the value theory debates conducted in and around *Capital and Class*. My own views are laid out in Fine (ed.) (1986). In other publications, I have sought to develop and apply value theory in greater complexity, addressing issues such as privatisation, the British coal industry, the British economy, women's employment, labour market structures and dynamics, the political economy and culture of consumption in general and of food in particular, the South African economy, and social capital (the last of these containing references to other work, Fine, 2001a). Throughout analysis has been rooted in fundamental principles derived from the ltv, originality deriving from retaining elements of political economy that enable the reconstruction of value in more complex forms. Yet, at the outset, I suggested that the increasing complexity of capitalism simultaneously both strengthens the case for the labour theory of value, to uncover underlying determinants, and strengthens the resolution of opponents in view of the apparent inconsistency of value with those complex outcomes. This means that the intellectual balance for and against is dependent upon the vigour, resolution and skill with which value theory is elaborated by its supporters, quite apart from the economic, political and ideological climate within which debates are engaged. In the academic world, mainstream economics has rarely been stronger and has never been prepared to confront the ltv on any terms other than as labour embodied in an equilibrium framework, for which rejection of value is the only possible outcome. Many supporters of value theory have been seduced by the associated arguments involved. This is despite ingenious analytical devices that draw piecemeal upon aspects of capitalist reality to seek to preserve the ltv through one or other transformation.

The most prominent in this vein is the new solution to the transformation problem. It suggests that the latter's problems can be resolved by treating the value of labour power as the wage revenue (with value equivalent) received ex post rather than as a quantity of ex ante labour time (attached to a 'subsistence' wage bundle). Without the space to provide details (Fine et al. 2004), the new solution suffers from collapsing the complex determinants of the value form (price) into a single step, thereby precluding appropriate consideration of intermediate factors and processes. Accordingly, its theories of money, the value of labour power, and the structures and dynamics of the capitalist economy (especially value formation in the presence of technical change) are both underdeveloped and insecurely founded within the value theory that is purportedly being defended. In effect, the new solution is merely a sociology of exploitation, using the ltv to establish that exploitation obtains whenever wages do not exhaust total revenue. This exercise is both limited in importance and scarcely needs value theory in any case – profits as evidence of exploitation is clear to all who care to see.

In light of the new solution and the more general commentary above, the prospects for value theory from a radical tradition within economics have rarely looked bleaker. But, as I first argued in *Capital and Class* (Fine, 1997), economics is currently colonising the other social sciences as never before. This is as a result of its own internal developments, deriving from information-theoretic economics, in which the market and non-market, the individual and the social, are all seen as reducible to optimising in response to market (informational) imperfections. On the other hand, social sciences other than economics have always been much more open to serious treatment and acceptance of value theory, at least to the extent that they need to cross the artificial boundaries dividing the academic disciplines and confront economic issues in the form of political economy rather than on the basis of the esoteric and blatantly unreasonable assumptions that are so characteristic of orthodox economics. In addition, Marxism itself is also treated seriously as an alternative and as a source of insight for non-Marxist analyses in complete contrast to economics. At the same time, there has been an uneven retreat both from neoliberalism and the excesses of postmodernism across the social sciences. As a result, there is a wish for a greater material, even economic, content to analysis – a return to the real not least in the warmth with which the nebulous notion of globalisation has been received. The prospect is for the social sciences other than economics to prove an intellectual battleground in examining the economic. Given the traditional, and warranted, antipathy of social sciences towards economics, the potential for reviving commitment to the ltv is strong. But it has to be won and cannot be taken for granted.

In short, there is ebb and flow in the factors that promote and undermine the place of the ltv in the current intellectual climate. By virtue of the arguments that I have made here, I hope to have convinced some at least not only of the analytical value of value but of the necessity with which its classical Marxist content must be defended, promoted and developed. Debates within *Capital and Class* remain an essential starting point.

CHAPTER 3

# Juggling the Transformation Problem

## Postscript as Personal Preamble

This Chapter puts together two short pieces. Each covers a topic that has rarely been addressed. The first is the so-called historical transformation problem – was there ever an occasion in history when commodities sold at their values? To my mind, this is a bit like asking the question, was there ever a time in history when the economy was in general equilibrium. But the posing of the question enables the point to be reinforced that value is based within production relations and takes a value form through exchange. Both the production relations and the forms they assume are subject to historical variation.

The second piece is on a logical rather than a historical mission, seeking to emphasise the extent to which Sraffa tends to 'cornify' the economy, treat it in terms of technical relations rather than social relations of production – even if, in his own hands, as opposed to his followers, his *Production of Commodities by Means of Commodities* (not labour) (Sraffa, 1960) is never used to dismiss Marx's value theory. As a result, cornification of the economy has been well-recognised by Marxist value theorists in their dispute with Sraffians but, piggybacking upon Faccarello's (1982) contribution, I show that Sraffa does himself sideline labour as the source of value in his treatment of Ricardo (who remains loyal to the notion of labour as the source of value despite the problems that it creates for him as a result of adopting an embodied labour as opposed to a value form approach). So, as it were, Sraffa is at least implicitly complicit with Sraffianism through his treatment of Ricardo if not of Marx.

## 1 On the Historical Transformation Problem[1]

In this short rejoinder to a short reply from George Catephores (1980) by himself to a fourth appendix from my article on Marx's theory of agricultural rent Fine (1979) which engages with Morishima and Catephores (1975), I cannot hope to settle questions concerning the historical transformation problem. Instead, I will attempt to focus on the differences which exist between Catephores and myself. Catephores brings to the fore my criticism

1 Originally appearing as Fine (1980a).

HTTPS://DOI.ORG/10.1163/9789004766266-004

of Morishima and Catephores (M&C) on two counts and three errors. Let us begin with the errors. First, I argue that M&C identify Marxian and Ricardian value theory, and Catephores denies this by suggesting two things. First, that the presuppositions for the existence of value are necessarily present in M&C's theory but, secondly, there is a technical definition of value as labour embodied that is neutral between Ricardo and Marx. This is, in fact, precisely the neo-Ricardian position on value; that, in some way, the social relations necessary for the existence of value can be evaporated to leave a technical definition as labour embodied in commodities.[2] Catephores' view that not a word of criticism exists against the embodied labour idea is simply astonishing in the light of the extensive debate that has raged for and against this position.[3]

The second error is that M&C impose this notion of value on other epochs. I do not see how he can deny this. A logical and a historical notion of value as labour embodied is put forward as a virtue by M&C to investigate whether this value has been identical to price during any period of history. The third error is a corollary of the second as a result of this investigation. M&C impose the economic structure of advanced capitalism on less developed stages by treating the relations between production, distribution and exchange as if they were the same even if they allow the conditions within these spheres of economic activity to vary (more or less competition, free flow of labour and commodities, etc). This is analogous, for example, to treating slavery as a special case of capitalism in which we simply have no labour mobility. In contrast, we must emphasise that what constitutes production, distribution and exchange has first to be determined prior to a calculation of what constitutes value. Indeed, as Marx makes clear in the *Grundrisse* (see its *Introduction*) and elsewhere, there is a role for an analysis of production (and labour) in general (as suggested by the notion of labour embodied) but only in the context of its incorporation with an analysis drawn from a specific stage of development of production. Before this is done, it is not even possible to identify what is the labour to be added up in the embodiment because production itself has not been located. What is production for a slave society, of slaves themselves for example, may be reproduction for capitalism. Even in advanced capitalism, what constitutes value production is open to question (and struggle) as is evidenced by the existence of nationalised industries or public services, for example, for

2 Catephores makes clear that his objective is the neo-Ricardian one, to place "at the centre of interest … the compatibility of exploitation of labour with the existence of a free, perfectly competitive market", p. 334. This, as the Sraffians have shown, can be done with no reference to value at all so that the concept becomes redundant. See Fine (1980c) for the distinction between neo-Ricardians and Sraffians.

3 See Fine and Harris (1979) for a survey, but also Elson (ed.) (1979) and Himmelweit and Mohun (1978) for other recent contributions.

which a logical analysis based on embodied labour can provide no answers particularly in the absence of historical underpinnings. In short, M&C's use of a logical (technical) construct of value contains an error of method, for an ideal construct is imposed not only on earlier epochs but also upon advanced capitalism itself. As observed earlier, the logical, ahistorical concept of value has not been drawn from the society to be analysed, even if certain presuppositions are presumed for its existence, so that the idea of value is analysed rather than its real existence.

So much for the three errors. On the two counts, the first concerns the question of whether value is purely a logical construct and requires no historical underpinnings and we have already attempted to indicate a negative answer. The second count concerns the challenge to me to identify an epoch during which commodities exchanged at values. As I hope I have made clear, this challenge presents a need to analyse nothing short of the economic relations of the societies concerned. It is not open to the M&C confrontation of an ahistorical notion of value with the facts of history, a task that confusedly leads Catephores to state in the same paragraph that, "we did not intend to analyse the historical past … rather, we compared the mercantilist part of capitalism with its free trade era", p. 335. However, whilst evading the task of pinpointing dates, my original article did make clear the conditions necessary for the divergence of values and prices under the capitalist mode of production, and that is that the competition between capitals of different sectors should not be subordinated to the competition within sectors and this requires the establishment of the monopoly stage (and in particular the credit system as a means of capital mobility). Indeed, production of commodities which exchange at their values can still be identified in the contemporary world particularly in the underdeveloped economies where precapitalist or underdeveloped capitalist relations persist, although the value itself may be determined by advanced capitalist methods.

Finally, I close with two further comments. My criticism of M&C should not be seen as a defence of either Engels or Meek who were originally the object of criticism for M&C. In particular, there are considerable doubts about Engels' interpretation of the logical-historical method and his application of it to the historical transformation problem.[4] He seems much closer to M&C than to Marx and constructs ideal modes of production to justify the historical

4 Engels (1971) argues that the logical order of concepts corresponds to their historical order. This is both incorrect and at odds with Marx who states and shows the opposite in many places. See the "Introduction" to the *Grundrisse* where he seems to assert that the logical and the historical order of development of particular categories either tend to occur in the same or opposite sequence.

existence of value which allows M&C quite rightly to deny their existence.[5] Second, Catephores criticises me for emphasising the form of value, but he does so with perhaps an over-formal understanding of this as price. The form of value concerns not only its creation by labour but also its formation through to exchange. This has price as its final result but the mediation between price and value is not subject to an invariant set of economic relations and it is these which have to be analysed before value can be specified and determined let alone compared with price.

## 2 On the Economics of Ricardo and Sraffa[6]

Sraffa's (1960) contribution to economics has been examined and debated in great depth in two separate but related areas. The first concerns the critique of neoclassical theory as is indicated by the subtitle of his book, *Prelude to a Critique of Economic Theory*, and the substance of its preface. The second involves the debate surrounding the legitimacy and interpretation of Marx's value theory. This application never seems to have been intended by Sraffa. Nevertheless, those following him have seized upon his analysis to refute and reject Marx's value theory.[7] The controversy has been focused upon the so-called transformation problem although it has significance for most of Marx's major propositions, particularly the law of the tendency of the rate of profit to fall.[8]

The intention here is not to examine these debates.[9] It is to bring to the fore an area that has been neglected in the controversy surrounding Sraffian economics, the interpretation of Ricardo.[10] Sraffa was himself the main editor of Ricardo's works and wrote an interpretative introduction to them that has been highly influential (Sraffa, 1951). Sraffa's followers have always taken the

5 Banaji (1979) argues that Engels requires careful interpretation. Weeks (1980) goes further accusing Engels of neo-Ricardianism, further arguing that for value to exist it requires the relations of advanced capitalism.

6 Originally appearing as Fine (1983a).

7 Most notably in the case of Steedman (1977).

8 The Sraffian critique of this is associated with Okishio (1961).

9 For the author's views on the Sraffian critique of neoclassical economics, see Fine (1980c, Ch. 5). For value theory, see Fine (1980c, Ch. 6) and Fine and Harris (1979, Ch. 2). For the law of the tendency of the rate of profit to fall see Fine (1982, Ch. 8) and Fine and Harris (1979, Ch. 4). See also Steedman (ed.). (1981), Elson (ed.) (1979) and Weeks (1981).

10 Sraffa (1926) also made a major contribution in his discussion of economies of scale. This has been neglected altogether although it would be important to assess how this informs and is informed by his economic thinking as a whole.

implications of his work much further than he has himself, and possibly much further than he would wish. Even though there is only less than two pages in Sraffa (1960) on the relevance of this work for Ricardo, it has been used to interpret Ricardo by the Sraffians. It is this interpretation which has remained relatively unchallenged.[11]

For this reason, Faccarello's (1982) contribution is to be especially welcomed. He disputes in detail Sraffa's own interpretation of Ricardo and hence, by implication, anyone who would take it further. The extent of the cavalier attitude of the otherwise cautious Sraffa is revealed in his dependence upon evidence of this type (Sraffa, 1951, p. xxxi):

> Although this argument is never stated by Ricardo in any of his extant letters and papers, he must have formulated it in his lost 'papers on the profits of Capital' of March 1814 or in conversation.

As Faccarello reveals, the argument to which Sraffa refers is one more likely to have been formulated by Malthus as the only possible way that he could understand Ricardo's theory of price in which demand played no part. For Malthus, dependent upon the interaction of supply and demand, this must imply a one commodity world and lead to a corn-profit model. It is this interpretation of himself by Malthus to which Ricardo is responding. This both explains why it is not Ricardo's argument and why it might appear to be so.

Such is the elegance of Faccarello's critique. However, he confines himself to this issue of Ricardo's economics, as indeed does Sraffa in his *Introduction*,[12] prior to Ricardo's more mature thought for which a labour theory of value has been both adopted and been found to be problematical. As a result, the question of the Sraffian interpretation of Ricardo's mature economics is left unaddressed by Faccarello. Nor does Faccarello address the question directly of why Sraffa should have been bent towards the particular (mis)interpretation that he adopts.

The second of these questions is rather easier to answer than the first. One major characteristic of the Sraffian system is that it deals in economic categories as things, as a technical relationship between inputs and outputs. It is, of course, one of the criticisms of the Sraffian system that this reification is

11 A major exception is Hollander (1979) who simply reads Ricardo through a neoclassical retrospective.

12 Sraffa (1960, p. 93) also appears to refer only to premature value theory in Ricardo.

extended to the category of labour itself.[13] Accordingly, the interpretation of Ricardo (and necessarily Marx) is liable to suffer from the same process of reification. As a result, the 'cornification' of Ricardo, treating his economics as a corn-corn or a corn-profit model, is a natural interpretation for Sraffa and the Sraffian system (i.e. pushing labour as source of value into the background).

In his mature thought, Ricardo became committed to a value theory based on labour time and remained so despite the problems that this created for the theory of price and profit within his system.[14] The problems concern the divergence of price from such simply conceived value once account is taken of factors such as the differing durability and compositions of capitals. Sraffa suggests that the labour theory of value permits Ricardo to abandon the supposedly previously held corn-corn model and to rely upon value theory in its place. In his *Principles*, however, with the adoption of a general theory of value, it became possible for Ricardo to demonstrate the determination of the rate of profit in society as a whole instead of through the microcosm of one special branch of production (Sraffa, 1951, p. xxxii):

> as a result, the rate of profits was no longer determined by the ratio of the corn produced to the corn used up in production, but, instead, by the ratio of the total labour of the country to the labour required to produce the necessaries for that labour.

Here Sraffa appears to leave the matter at this within his *Introduction*, but for Sraffians the problems of Ricardo's price theory are to be corrected by their own system. As in the critique or correction of Marx's transformation of values into prices, this involves the abandonment of value theory based on labour time. The result is that Ricardo's mature thought is also subject to 'cornification' at the expense of his own emphasis upon labour. Propositions concerning distribution, for example, based in Ricardo on the division of value between

13 Consider the title of Sraffa's book: *Production of Commodities by Means of Commodities*! Where's the labour as producer other than a commodified thing like any other?

14 In the draft of a manuscript whose completion was interrupted by his death, Ricardo (1951b, p. 397) wrote, "that the greater or less quantity of labour worked up in commodities can only be the only cause of their alteration in value is completely made out as soon as we are agreed that all commodities are the produce of labour and would have no value but for the labour expended upon them."

capital and labour are replaced by propositions concerning the division of the net produce of the standard commodity between the two classes.[15]

The standard commodity reduces the many commodity model of the economy to one as if it were a corn-corn model. Consequently, distribution can be analysed in terms of this thing (or more exactly this composite bundle of things) without any special reference to labour or value based upon it. Ricardo's supposed problem of finding a unidimensional axis on which to measure distribution has been solved just as his problematic based on labour time has been abandoned.

The cornification of Ricardo by Sraffians is also apparent from their tendency to identify their standard commodity with the invariable standard.[16] Ricardo observed that relative prices would change as a result of wage changes and he wished to minimise this variation by the choice of a money commodity as an invariable standard that was produced by an average composition of past and present labour. Ricardo was acutely aware that such an invariable standard could only serve as an approximation. By contrast the standard commodity is an exact theoretical solution to an entirely different problem, of finding a commodity which is produced hypothetically by a sequence of uniformly declining

15 The use of the standard commodity to interpret both the early and mature work of Ricardo led me (Fine, 1982, Ch. 3) in the pursuit of the critique of the Sraffian interpretation of Ricardo confusingly (and erroneously) to run together the two periods of Ricardo's thought as if he always held a value theory based on labour time rather than earlier holding to the more general principle of difficulty of production (but with the common exclusion of demand). See Faccarello (1982).

16 Sraffa (1960) is himself guilty of this but, as usual, to an unknown degree. He merely observes that, "the conception of a standard measure of value as a medium between two extremes also belongs to Ricardo", p. 94. The fact, however, that ham lies between the two extremes of bread in a sandwich does not identify it in any other way with other categories of medium and extremity. Sraffa makes an association and no more although he does go on to observe a paradox. Continuing the above quote: "... and it is surprising that the standard commodity which has been evolved from it here should be found to be equivalent to something very close to the standard suggested by Adam Smith, namely 'labour commanded', to which Ricardo himself was decidedly opposed." The paradox is easily resolved, and unsurprising, since Sraffa's standard has little to do with Ricardo's (or Adam Smith's). Here Sraffa also reveals a tendency to read "the connection of this (i.e. his) work with the theories of the old classical economists" by cornifying them. In the two and a half pages of Appendix D, *References to the Literature*, he manages to do it to a remarkable number of authors. He proceeds by extracting what can be interpreted to be Sraffian within them.

labour inputs expended in the periods extending into the indefinite past.[17] The two standards cannot be legitimately identified with one another.

In conclusion, it is hoped that Faccarello's critique of the significance of Sraffa's contribution to the assessment of Ricardo's economics has been widened further.

---

17 Broome (1978) cast doubts on the invariability of the standard commodity. See also Fine (1982, Ch. 3) where the difference between the Ricardian and Sraffian standard is examined in more detail. At more of a methodological level, it is to be observed that the standard commodity of Sraffa serves as an ideal construction for expositional purposes and its validity as a category of political economy has to be established separately. Do the classes struggle over the distribution of the standard commodity? By contrast, Ricardo addresses himself to the immediate workings of the economy. What is the money commodity that would minimise price variations as a result of wage changes? The nature of Ricardo's answer (and of his question) is determined by his treating all economic categories at the same empirical level whilst remaining committed to a (more abstract) value theory based on labour-time. Sraffians do much the same other than to abandon the value theory. In this light, it is unfortunate that Sraffians are often termed neo-Ricardians because of their belief in an inverse relationship between wages and profits. This is a term best reserved for those who support this proposition but continue to defend value theory based on labour-time. See, for example, the critique of Steedman (1977) by Armstrong, Glyn and Harrison (1978).

CHAPTER 4

# Value is as Value Does: Twixt Knowledge and the World Economy

## Postscript as Personal Preamble

This is the second of three Chapters on the merits, defence and promotion of Marx's value theory. Core material is to be found across all three Chapters to a greater or lesser extent, focusing on how value and its forms are irretrievably attached to one another in moving from the abstract to the concrete, and in deciphering the contradictory tendencies attached to the accumulation of capital and its economic and social reproduction. This Chapter (correctly) anticipates that the increasing complexity of, and the differences in the forms, taken by capital accumulation will lead to a tendency to degrade the treatment of value theory either by its rejection altogether or by its willy-nilly adoption or revision in light of the complexities and diversities of contemporary developments.

More specifically, two case studies are included that illustrate these comments. One is on the world economy/market which, it is argued, is taken by Marx as his starting point with national economies as more concrete, and by the multiple factors determining their reproduction. This is to challenge the highly popular and prominent alternative of treating the world economy on the basis of what has been termed methodological nationalism; that is, as a set of nations trading or whatever with one another, and with a metropolis exploiting a periphery through whatever mechanisms of unequal exchange.[1] Irrespective of the distribution of economic activities across nations, Marx's theory of accumulation provides for uneven and combined development both within and between them – from domestic industry through to the factory system – and how such 'development' is distributed across activities and associated conditions cannot be explained by the exploitation of one nation by another for, then, all production would shift to the exploited country.

The second case study addresses the so-called knowledge economy and, in particular, how particular firms or activities can generate such large returns.

1 This is not to say that Marx's own views remained unchanging on such issues (Anderson, 2025). Note also that what I have termed the developmental state paradigm, touched upon in passing within the Chapter, is also based on methodological nationalism.

HTTPS://DOI.ORG/10.1163/9789004766266-005

The answer is to be found by delving into Marx's own treatment of knowledge in production and the consequences of both collective and skilled labour (which have the potential to produce at lower individual value and so appropriate surplus rather than monopoly profits).

The Chapter closes with an Appendix, discovered on searching for the electronic file for the article. I turned up the draft for an email,[2] seeking a correction to the introduction to the Special Issue of *Capital and Class*, in which our contribution was misrepresented. I have not searched to see if a correction was made and have no record of a response.

## 1 Introduction[3]

There has been an enduring paradox in debate around Marx's value theory (Fine, 2001b).[4] This is that both proponents and opponents appeal to the same phenomena as the basis for their positions. Value (even if transformed into price of production) does not equal market price, so reject the labour theory of value says one. This is precisely why we need value theory says the other. And this is before we move onto skills, rent, interest, world economy, non-wage labour, knowledge, monopoly, crises, and so on.

As proponents of value theory, for us, this paradox is resolved by the simplicity of the stance adopted on what it is: a theory that seeks to trace out how labour-time exercised within capitalist production is attached to market forms, with corresponding consequences. As this is not a matter of right or wrong,

2 I used to draft emails at home, put them on a floppy disk and send them from a connected desktop once at SOAS, rather than dial up onto the internet as was then required at home (no cloud in those days). In any case, I wanted to avoid being on the internet at home if at all possible to avoid always being at work, especially at home, something I still retain by not having the internet on my mobile phone (which I seek to confine to emergency use). This makes me appear what I am, technologically backwards. But at least it means I have records of some old emails that would otherwise have disappeared into the ether once sent, unlike today's conditions of mass storage.

3 Based upon Fine et al. (2010) in response to a request for a submission for the one hundredth issue of *Capital and Class*. Thanks to Alfredo Saad-Filho for comments on parts of an earlier draft.

4 See also debate between Kincaid (2007, 2008 and 2009) and Fine and Saad-Filho (2008 and 2009). Note how the latter identifies two major sources of complementary *supportive* misinterpretation, but often dismissal, of Marx: the intrinsic critique associated with Rubin (in which the exchange form of value absolves of the responsibility to trace the routes from production to circulation); and the extrinsic Ricardian critique (in which more concrete forms, starting with price but potentially unlimited in scope, are presumed to be incompatible with value).

but of material reality, the challenge is one of reproducing the structures, processes, relations and agencies in thought. In this respect, properly interpreted as such, Marx endowed us with a rich body of theory, addressing value in the complex context of the accumulation of capital, its laws of production, and their reproduction through distribution and exchange. Taken seriously and constructively, his contribution suffices to dismiss interpretations that either view value theory as a, generally inadequate, theory of (equilibrium) price or, even if more favourably inclined, impose ideal fixes to value theory rather than tracing out the complexity of value relations – as is often an error in most 'correct' treatments of the so-called transformation problem (Fine et al. 2004). The point is not to use value theory to get some ideal price theory correct but to select and reproduce material processes in thought. Thus, it is hardly surprising that controversies over abstract issues such as the transformation problem should prove so bitter, pervasive and long-lasting, for they reflect very big differences in interpretations of Marx as well as his method. By the same token, if anyone has been lucky enough to get the solution right (and plenty believe they have), there is no guarantee that such virtue will extend appropriately into other areas of application.

Of necessity, rather than weakness, Marx's own value theory is both selective and, hence, incomplete but for two different reasons. First, there are a multitude of determinants in the passage from production processes through to exchange, use and reproduction. Marx's own pre-occupation, as a reflection of capital within its most advanced stage, is with the formation of exchange relations as productivity is enhanced through accumulation of capital (both transformation of value into prices of production and law of the tendency of the rate of profit to fall) and the distribution of surplus value in the form of industrial and commercial profit, interest and rent (Fine and Saad-Filho, 2026[1975], for elementary expositions). Whilst quantitative relations are involved, the primary concern is with the appropriate logical derivation of categories and their location in the structure of abstraction and, not quite the same thing in practice and certainly not methodologically, the nature and structure of causation. Second, though, logically derived analyses – such as the difference between productive and unproductive labour, the nature of interest-bearing capital, and the impact of landed property – can only be taken so far before more historically specific developments have to be taken into account and incorporated to make any legitimate progress. This is important in both posing the most relevant issues as well as in addressing them appropriately.

These observations are borne out by our judicious selection of two topics by which we seek both to defend and to extend value theory. For each, necessarily briefly, we address, even tease out, Marx's own contribution, whether this is recognised by subsequent literature and, if so, whether it has been falsely interpreted and/or rejected and, ultimately, offer an alternative within value theory.

The first of these applications is to locate the world market within Marx's value theory. Significantly, a later volume of *Capital* may at times have been intended to be dedicated to the topic (wages and the state also) so, no doubt, it potentially falls within the scope of value theory as understood by Marx. And, even if under different nomenclature, most notably as globalisation today, the need to address the world market is both imperative and indicative of a different nature (and history) than would or could have been addressed by Marx himself during his own lifetime. Further, the world market as such has rarely been satisfactorily or fully addressed by subsequent Marxists. Is it simply the global economy considered in abstract as an instance of capitalist accumulation (with co-existence of capitals and non-capitals in articulation with one another)? Or is it national systems of accumulation with their own dynamics, even if articulated with one another to form the world market. Each of these two extremes seems to miss something from the other: how do we address distinct national economies (or are they a fiction?) if working at the abstract level of the world economy; and how does the world economy impact upon national economies rather than vice-versa? We confront these issues by demonstrating how the world market is present both at the outset of Marx's theory of capitalism (both logically and historically) and reproduced (similarly) at more complex and concrete levels in tandem with value theory itself.

Thus, as laid out in section 2, our position is, as was Marx's intention, to proceed from the world market as constituted both logically and historically out of the ensemble of exchange relations based on, but not reducible to, the production and realisation of capital accumulation at a global level. In other words, the challenge is both to derive the forms logically taken by capital accumulation and to constitute them as they are historically materialised and evolve in practice.

A very different issue, and challenge, for Marxist value theory is addressed in Section 3, one that predominantly reflects contemporary developments however interpreted (and exaggerated) and which could hardly have been anticipated by Marx himself. This concerns the so-called 'knowledge economy', variously termed and interpreted within Marxist and non-Marxist scholarship and strategising. As previously indicated, we offer a partial overview of different approaches, concentrating on those that reject value theory in light of the emergence of the knowledge economy. We suggest that they display a limited understanding of value theory, of knowledge itself, and of the contribution that is already present for the understanding of knowledge within Marxist theory. The knowledge economy is extremely diverse in terms of functions and substance, ranging over the enhancing of productivity, the generation of new products and processes, and the governance of economic, social and ideological reproduction. None of these is new, although the balance and content across them is subject to transformation and, equally, amenable as such to value theory, once delineating the role within it of the distinctions between conception and execution and individual and collective labour through cooperation.

In our concluding remarks, we shift gear to discuss the role that value theory might play in the future. As remarked at the outset, in life as in theory, the dialectical tension between rejecting and accepting value can only strengthen as capitalism incorporates new forms and complexities as it evolves.

## 2 Value in the World Market

Marxist political economy has traditionally been strong in its 'global' aspects. This has been so for two reasons. First, logically, it takes abstract categories such as those associated with value as it starting point. And the same applies to class, capital, and labour, each of which can be projected to the global level. Second, historically, more or less immediately after Marx's death, the most important developments within Marxist political economy concerned what have become the classical theories of imperialism. These necessarily placed capitalism as a world system on the agenda with, especially through the influence of Lenin, considerable emphasis placed on monopoly, finance, cartelisation of world markets and inter-imperialist rivalries to the point of global warfare.

Despite, even because of, this affinity to the global, there have been tensions in Marxist theory on how to address capitalism as a world system, not least since the abstract categories, which allow it to be taken as an object of study, can equally be projected to a national level or even other levels above or below. There is a chicken and egg problem of what comes first, the global or its constituent elements, especially where the specification of national capitals or economies are concerned.

Marx himself is not free of such conundrums. For him, "The world market itself forms the *basis* for this [capitalist] mode of production" (Marx, 1894, p. 451), emphasis added. And, yet, the "[*e*]*stablishment* of the world market" is also regarded as one of the "[t]hree cardinal facts about capitalist production", p. 375 emphasis added. One way of addressing this issue of how the global can be both pre-condition for, and consequence of, capitalism is by focusing on its origins in the emergence of capitalism itself for which Marx has much to contribute. But, first, observe that a methodological principle is involved in that it is not simply a matter of logically deriving the relationship between the global and capitalism in abstract thought but of rooting it in material processes for which history is the starting point. As Marx puts it, "the modern mode of production ... developed only where the conditions for it had been created in the Middle Ages" (Marx, 1894, p. 450). Indeed, for Marx (1973, p. 675):

> [C]apital did not begin the world from the beginning, but rather encountered production and products already present, before it subjugated them beneath its process. Once in motion, proceeding from itself as basis, it constantly posits itself ahead of itself in its various forms as consumable product, raw material and instrument of labour, in order constantly to reproduce itself in these forms. They appear initially as the conditions presupposed by it, and then as its result. In its reproduction it produces its own conditions.

The world market was definitely picked up by Marx as one such condition or category. In particular, in the shifting relationship between the capitalist and non-capitalist worlds, as the former is emerging, gaining predominance and transforming the latter, the world market is both a precondition for such historical processes and is itself transformed by those processes, not least as more is produced and traded capitalistically.

Significantly, this can all be related to the prior dependence of the world market on the presence of trade or merchant's capital which is one of the "antediluvian forms of capital" (Marx, 1894, p. 728). And, whilst merchant's capital is enabled "to appropriate for itself a preponderant part of the surplus product: partly by acting as middleman between communities whose production is still basically oriented to use-value", it "subjects production more and more to exchange-value by making luxuries and subsistence more dependent on sale than on the immediate use of the products", p. 448, translation modified. Further, the dynamics involved are also made explicit, pp. 450–51:[5]

> [W]hereas in the sixteenth century, and partly still in the seventeenth, the sudden expansion of trade and the creation of a new world market had an overwhelming influence on the defeat of the old mode of production and the rise of the capitalist mode, this happened in reverse on the basis of the capitalist mode of production, once it had been created.

5 See also Marx (1867, p. 918).

> The world market itself forms the basis for this mode of production. On the other hand, the immanent need that this has to produce on an ever greater scale drives it to the constant expansion of the world market, so that now it is not trade that revolutionizes industry, but rather industry that constantly revolutionizes trade.

It is not just that capitalist commerce expands (with the production of surplus value and its realisation through commodity-capital) but non-capitalist production and commerce become integrated with, and determined within, its orbit.

This view of the world market – in part, the 'global' of the time – is important in that it differentiates Marx as a thinker from his contemporaries. As Gareth Stedman Jones (2007) correctly argues, Marx is in part a child of his time in that, like D. Diderot (1713–84), G. W. F. Hegel (1770–1831), J. B. Say (1767–1832), James Mill (1773–1836) and many others, he looked upon the emergence of the 'world' as a pinnacle in the development of the material conditions of human life, notably made possible by revolutions in transport and communication from the sixteenth century onward. They could ponder the world-historical implications of these changes, even justifying the perpetration of violence by West Europeans as harbingers of 'civilisation'.

But for Marx, the fate of such civilisation lay less in speculative and cosmopolitan thinking and more by way of the laws of capitalism, with the world market as its *result* in all of its diversity of capitalist *and* non-capitalist forms. His extensive study of non-European and pre-capitalist societies needs to be assessed in this light. Significantly, Stedman Jones acknowledges that this entailed Marx recognising that capitalism would not sweep uniformly across the globe but, incorrectly, draws the conclusion that for Marx, this should have entailed his "abandonment of *Capital*" as a consequence, for he perceives it to have been written in "the universal and unilinear terms" largely shared by Enlightenment thinkers and Marx (Stedman Jones, 2007, p. 198). But this conclusion is hasty, lacks evidence and enforces Marx into this Enlightenment way of thinking. By contrast, in view of the broader intellectual project to which Marx was committed, study of non-capitalist societies represents a sharpening of his long-standing 'global' standpoint by incorporating more determinations into the world market as opposed to homogenising them into a single outcome. Instead of predicting the inevitability of the conquest and destruction of extra-European societies by Europe, Marx pays more attention to the transformation those societies experience once they are drawn into the world market where capitalist relations of production prevail (Marx, 1867, p. 345). In Marx's refined framework of analysis in *Capital* and later, these societies, or national economies in general, are viewed as particular moments in the reproduction of a differentiated capitalism (and not just capitals) on a global scale, a point Stedman Jones appears to fail to appreciate. Further, the existence and persistence of such differentiated societies in the world market requires an abstract theory of capital to be developed, in its different forms in production and exchange, in its different stages of development, and how these mutually co-exist. In other words, not least as laid out in *Capital*, value theory provides the constituent elements of a theory of the world economy but the elements can only be put together through incorporating an historical content.

In particular, this is so in addressing the *international* or *global*, as opposed to the *national*. For this is not purely a theoretical matter but reflects the way the capitalist world was formed and has evolved. As covered in the last Part of the first Volume of *Capital*, "the colonies, the national debt, the modern mode of taxation, and the protectionist system" in the world market are offered as "the chief moments of primitive accumulation" (Marx, 1867, p. 915). They demonstrate that the *global* dynamics of capitalist development were already in place as early as its formative stage. For the colonies, this is not only in the sense of resourcing primitive accumulation on the side of capital but also in playing a much more active role in production itself. As Pomeranz and Topik (2005, p. 226) emphatically argue, "the first industrial factories were the sugar mills of the [colonial] Americas", in the seventeenth century, not Manchester cotton mills! According to this view, even if capitalist relations had emerged in Western Europe, only in their colonies were some elements first put into practice. The colonial factories involved huge sums of money on top of "some of the most sophisticated technology of the era, and a large workforce", p. 227. Further, Sidney Mintz (1985, p. 51) highlights three *human* as well as *technical* elements that suggest modern industrial (factory) production first appeared in the seventeenth century Caribbean sugar plantations based upon slavery, not free labour: discipline; efficiency-maximising organisation of the labour force; and time-consciousness. All are essential features of *capitalist* labour organisation.

If it is an exaggeration to say "the factories of the Caribbean were holding a mirror in which Europe could see its industrial future"[6] (Pomeranz and Topik, 2005, p. 228), certainly it was only after such periods of 'experimentation' with a factory system on the basis of slavery that its full-scale application was realised in 'mother' countries.[7] With commodities, finance and organisation of

6 See Trentmann (2009) for the early impact of colonies on capitalist *consumption*.

7 Debate on the active role of the colonial economies in the rise of capitalism was ignited by the publication of Eric Williams' *Capitalism and Slavery* in 1944. See Solow (1987) for a critical overview.

production itself derived from the colonies, the presence of the global prior to the national is evident at the birth of capitalism itself. As such, globalisation is not a new phenomenon, as if the dream of the Enlightenment has only been realised today, albeit in the form of a nightmare. For national economies were from the outset formed in a global context, and each could only obtain its position vis-à-vis others in the world market (Hont, 2005).

The preceding discussion explains why Marx should take the world market as starting point but, at the same time, abstract from its constituent elements. As he puts it himself (Marx, 1867, p. 727fn):

> We here take no account of export trade ... In order to examine the object of our investigation in its integrity, free from all disturbing subsidiary circumstances, we must treat the whole world as one nation, and assume that capitalist production is established everywhere and has taken possession of every branch of industry.

Initially, then, value analysis and the world market as a single nation are one and the same.

In this light, though, the 'world market' is something of a misnomer. To be sure, the most elementary and systematic form in which capitalism is constituted as a global economy (as opposed to violence and plunder) is through commodity relations (value formation across sectors). But these are combined out of very different modes of (commodity, in part, as opposed to capitalist) production and equally diverse methods of production of different and shifting levels of productivity (value formation within sectors), from the factory system through to sweatshops. In short, the world market is the articulation of commodity production through competitive accumulation across a spectrum of producers, and is addressed as such by Marxist value theory (Saad-Filho, 2002, for a full account for factory production).

By the same token, commodity relations are forged through the mediation of money so that world money itself is an elementary category that must prevail irrespective of the forms and content that it assumes as it evolves in relation to the historical complexity of the world market (and world finance). Once again, though, the nature of world money is both logical (significantly able to be present within the opening Chapters of Volume I of *Capital*) and, for the latter, not exclusively confined initially to a source of plunder as with primitive accumulation. Indeed, *Capital*, especially but not exclusively Volume III, offers an extraordinarily rich account of the development of money within exchange, with interest bearing capital at its pinnacle, as that form of money capital that underpins competitive accumulation through the broader 'credit system' as a whole (which also incorporates commercial and personal finance).

Further, across the accumulation of capital in its money, productive and commodity forms, (each with its own constituent elements), the state also intervenes as well as developing economic forms of its own in taxation, monetary instruments and policies, and other policies that both facilitate (or even obstruct) and condition the pace and composition of capital directly (as in nationalised industries, for example) and economic and social reproduction (health, education and welfare, repression and reform, etc). Again, logical and historical analyses complement one another, as a system of nation-states, and international relations more generally, draws upon, reproduces and transforms, but is not reducible to the world market even as this is itself reproduced historically, and in thought, in more complex and developed forms.

As argued in this vein in Fine and Harris (1979), value theory can be attached to a periodisation of the world economy, through the sequenced internationalisation of commodity, money and productive capital, with earlier dominant forms complementing the new as the latter emerge, and with the corresponding location of the state as an agent of economic and social reproduction. However, the current phase of capitalism, since the collapse of the post-war boom, has been characterised by the resurgence of finance, with financialisation (and its broader expression as neoliberalism) tempering the pace of accumulation and progress in the economic and social conditions to which it is attached (Fine, 2007b and 2009a, for example). This involves not only the proliferation of financial markets themselves but also the heavier penetration of finance into the restructuring of industrial capital (as with 'stakeholder value') *and* economic and social provision (most notably for pensions and housing finance for example), with the corresponding form and severity of the current crisis as a result.

Irrespective of the veracity of this unduly brief perspective on the current configuration of values on the world market, the method is to proceed from such value analysis in its full development as laid out in *Capital* to the historical complexity attached to outcomes at disaggregated levels such as the role of China, the US, or the dollar. Here, on a longer view, the contrast with other approaches can be observed. Even though they may highlight crucial aspects of past or contemporary capitalism, the issue is one of locating these contributions appropriately within an analytical framework for which abstract value theory is essential as the theory of the capitalist mode of production. For theories of the developmental state, for example, the order of analysis is reversed and development (inevitably capitalist) is perceived to be the potential or actual result of adoption of appropriate policies without reference to the world economy except as conditioning, not prior determining, factor. There is no acknowledgement of combined and uneven development with an implicit presumption that all states could be developmental without success of some being, in principle, contingent upon failures of others. By contrast, for world systems theory, the world economy tends to be rigidly structured, precluding the possibility of successful capitalist development, unambiguous evidence to the contrary in light of East Asian NICs and, most recently, China, each of which has both reflected *and* transformed the world market.

Often, if often inadvertently and with major exceptions such as Lenin's *Imperialism*, the Marxist tradition has proceeded from the national to the international rather than vice-versa. It has, in recent literature, enabled if not necessarily pre-determined major errors in interpretation of contemporary capitalism. Brenner, for example, is right to have sifted the empirical evidence both to point to the slowdown of accumulation over the period of financialisation and to show that this does not derive from working class demands or rewards. But, with his overhang hypothesis of investment constrained by incumbents (and excessive competition between blocs of national capitals, with the USA, Japan, and Germany to the fore), he fails to acknowledge both the multiplicity of ways in which restructuring can take place through the levers of competition and the extent to which restructuring has occurred albeit in the context of slowdown.[8] Harvey's notion of accumulation by dispossession can also be seen to be an important aspect of contemporary capitalism but, again, its prominence is a consequence of the rise of financialisation and the inertia it has imposed on accumulation through re-investment of surplus value.[9] And Glyn's (2007) continuing approach of emphasising international competition and real wages as too high (at the expense of profitability) or too low (at the expense of realisation) is useful in pointing to the impact of China on the world market (and vice-versa). But, apart from underestimating the role of financialisation (in potentially sustaining demand when wages and other expenditures are weak), this fails to acknowledge that (international) competition cannot lower the rate of profit for capital as a whole, as lower prices for producers who sell output means lower prices to those who buy it (or lower value of labour power for consumption goods). In these instances, cause is

8 Significantly, dos Santos (2009) and Lapavitsas (2009) do emphasise financialisation, adding financial exploitation/expropriation of wages as a leading element in the crisis. This appears to represent a divergence from Marx's value theory and displays an anomaly in that the slowdown is not explained and appears to become inexplicable as, with Brenner, not only are workers unduly exploited in light of stagnant real wages but, in addition, they are also exploited by finance as well within exchange. Together with neoliberal command of the state, it is inconceivable how circumstances could otherwise be more favourable to capital accumulation! Fine (2009b) for a critique.

9 See Fine et al. (1999 and 2005) on Brenner, and Fine (2006b) on Harvey.

conflated with consequence, as is dramatically revealed by the acute shifts in position that have been taken on the Chinese economy, as major competitor bringing down capitalism prior to the crisis but as potential source of recovery in its wake. The insertion of the Chinese into the world economy is considerably more complex than as source of cheap labour, and of demand and supply (and as sump for US dollars to match its trade deficit). Accumulation on a world scale is both more than, and different from, this.

## 3 Too Much Knowledge Is Dangerous

Knowledge, especially science and technology, plays an important role in Marx's theory of capitalism. Production of relative surplus value requires ceaseless innovation, mostly through adoption of new production methods based on new technologies. Incorporation of science and technology into machinery is a precondition of the specifically capitalist mode of production, where mass production and commodity exchange are generalised. Generation and use of knowledge are socially constructed and determined. Indeed, for Marx (1867, p. 493), "Technologies lay bare the process of the production of the social relations of [human] life". But Marx does not provide a detailed study of knowledge despite the rich historical and concrete accounts of machinery, concentrated in Volume 1 of *Capital* and scattered elsewhere throughout his work.

Specifically, if abstractly, Marx reveals the interrelations between knowledge and labour, not least as one of conception and execution. As "purposeful activity", p. 284, labour both presupposes and generates knowledge. Knowledge production or conception is the activity of constructing in the head ideally what is to be realised, and determines the "purposeful will" of labour. Humanity is distinguished from other species in that conception precedes execution even when labour is simple. Knowledge signals an "exclusively human characteristic". At this level, the distinction between conception and execution has the following characteristics. First, this distinction is ontological. Despite feedback mechanisms such as learning-by-doing, conception always precedes execution but, in turn, can only be realised through execution. They are two distinct but interrelated moments of production. Second, the distinction as such, drawn at the most abstract level of analysis, is ahistorical, excluding any determinations specific to capitalism. A key question is how this distinction is developed and reproduced specifically under capitalism. Third, if more specifically, the key issue is the role of knowledge in value production. Workers employed by capitalists to produce chairs do produce (surplus) value and have some knowledge of what they are doing. But does labour that designs the chair produce (part of) the value of the chair or not? Such knowledge labour is not the same as commodity-producing labour in that design is reusable irrespective of the number of chairs produced, see later.

Initially, consider capitalist forms of co-operation in the labour process. For Marx (1867, p. 454), co-operation is "the fundamental form of the capitalist mode of production". And, in addition, cooperation is associated with both the formation of the collective power of labour and the tendency to separate the production from the use of knowledge in the exercise of collective labour, corresponding to the separation of conceptualising and executing production. First, when different individual workers collaborate, they work together to achieve common goals. Under co-operation, individual workers not only perform individual labours but the productivity of collective labour exceeds the sum of individual contributions both quantitatively (how much) and qualitatively (what can be achieved).

Second, in its simplest form, co-operation, can take place by gathering workers together but, in most cases, co-operation involves coordinating and organising the production process. Further, as labour becomes collective, so the knowledge and goals of labour also become collective. This gives rise to a group of workers that are more or less dedicated to the realisation of these goals and the coordination and adjustment of the production processes. Marx mentions the emergence of overseers in this context, but knowledge work as such is not identified. Rather, and equally within the Marxist tradition, emphasis is placed upon the coercion to create surplus value collectively, for which knowledge and supervision of labour-time as well as activity itself are essential. Third, though, skill consists of knowledge at the collective level as well as drawing on the skills of individual workers. Collective skill or knowledge cannot be reduced to a set of individual skills as it includes knowledge that exists irrespective of individual workers, not least as embodied in fixed capital. Finally, the separation between conception and execution "is completed in large-scale industry, which makes science a potentiality for production which is distinct from labour and presses it into the service of capital" (Marx, 1867, p. 482). In contrast to "manufacture", which is based on handicraft and "excludes a really scientific division of the production process", p. 458, the proportion of collective (and other) skills tends to be marginalised from productive workers in machinery-based production. Science is incorporated into the labour process "as an independent power" (Marx, 1894, p. 880).

In sum, in capitalism where production is based on co-operation, conception and execution are, necessarily imperfectly and incompletely, detached from one another and infused with value relations. And the same incomplete detachment applies to conception itself to the extent that it is removed from production and appropriated within the realm of science and technology as distinct from production. One notable consequence is that as knowledge production is monopolised by and centralised into a group of workers distinct from execution and even from production itself, workers involved in the labour process are degraded and the labour process correspondingly transformed.

Such polarisation of conception and execution, and its impact on waged work, have been the main theme of labour process theory. Braverman's (1974) notion of deskilling suggests there is a tendency in capitalism to deprive workers of skills, fragmenting and sub-dividing work into a set of functions. "Semi-artistic" workers in simple co-operation are transformed into partially skilled workers in manufacture (Marx, 1867, p. 504), and into versatile unskilled workers in machinery-based production, "to the level of an appendage of a machine", p. 799. The deskilling thesis, however, has been criticised from a number of perspectives: in some cases, it goes hand-in-hand with the emergence of new jobs requiring different kinds of skills than those of craft workers; the notion of skill in Braverman is partial and takes craftworkers as ideal; the broader social determination and construction of skills are neglected; Braverman ignores the importance of consent and autonomy, as opposed to contestation, as part of capitalist and worker strategies; and the corresponding role of subjectivity of workers and class struggle in the formation of the labour process is overlooked (Wardell, 1999; and Meiksins, 1994). Marxist labour process theorists have argued that deskilling is a tendential law, inherent in the capitalist mode of production as an underlying force (Hassard and Rowlinson, 1994 and 2000; and Spencer, 2000). Capital does mechanise and systematise skills in an attempt to increase labour productivity and to minimise the risk of sabotage. Not only is the separation between conception and execution never absolute but it is continually evolving, and redefining what is and what is recognised as skill, including the articulation with the specifically value producing requirements of capitalism, from command in the workplace through to the attempts to ensure realisation in the sale of commodities.

Where, though, does this leave knowledge production and use in relation to value theory? Take the example of automobile production. First, a new model includes initial design, building of a proto-type, testing and fixing of defects, as well as market research and so on. Only after this can mass production begin after which other forms of knowledge work will be attached. This and all labour expended before mass production comprise knowledge labour. Whilst diverse in content and (including wage) forms, all such labour produces no value. A key difference between knowledge labour and commodity-producing labour lies in the reusability of the product of knowledge labour (something which is not true, for example, of commercial labour which also adds no value). Instead of producing value of commodities directly or indirectly through transfer of the value of the labour time contributed in a piecemeal fashion (like fixed capital), knowledge labour allows for "intensified labour" (Marx, 1867, p. 435), creating the conditions for enhancing the productivity and/or complexity of collective labour but without being a part of that collective labour in anything other than a formal sense.

Consider this in light of intra- and inter-sectoral use of knowledge labour. For the first, if an individual capitalist makes more productive use of knowledge than the sectoral norm, the commodity producing labour will have a lower individual value and be able to accrue extra surplus value over the norm in the form of higher profit. The comparison between labours in terms of productivity is possible in principle only when they produce the same commodity. In this case, if one has a higher labour productivity than another, this might be because of different use of collective knowledge or because of differences in skills of individuals. Second, though, the sectoral average level of knowledge might be higher than the social average. In this case, commodity-producing labour of all the individual capitalists in this sector acts as intensified labour. The average labour of such a sector serves as complex labour and comprises "intensified, or rather multiplied simple labour", p. 135. For example, labour of jewellers is complex and produces more value for a given labour time than the simple labour of spinners. Complex labour produces more value precisely because it requires significant efforts in education and training, incorporating more knowledge than other simple labours. As seen earlier, labour in capitalism is collective labour and collective skill or knowledge is formed out of cooperation. Even if machinery dominates individual workers, workers use machinery as instruments of production at the collective level. Knowledge produced in its own (non-value) generation process serves, in the labour process, as the knowledge of the value-producing collective worker. Even if individual workers perform simple labour, collective knowledge can intensify that labour and raise value contributed at the sectoral level.

This interpretation of the contribution of knowledge labour to value production is drawn from the highly contested South Korean debate on the value and price of software or information goods (Kang et al. 2007). The central question is how the value of package software is determined, given production simply requires the compiling and copying of source codes. One group of writers has argued that the value of package software is close to zero because production of package software (i.e. simple copy) requires little labour, but the price of package software is a high monopoly price. Another group has proposed a sort of cost approach in which the presumption is that value has been contributed by software design and is shared across the individual packages sold. Based on the theoretical framework outlined in the previous paragraph, Jeon (2008 and 2009) criticises each of these approaches, and argues that labour expended to produce source codes does not create part of the value of software either directly or indirectly, but allows the labour expended for the production of package software to serve as intensified labour. The value of package software is higher than zero because labour expended for the production of package software acts as intensified labour even if the concrete (and simple) labour time expended per unit of package software is close to zero. Thus, labour that produces source codes is knowledge labour, and that producing package software from the source codes is commodity-producing labour. The peculiarity of software production is that company resources are almost completely dedicated to the knowledge production processes.

A very different view is taken of such developments by those who not only exaggerate their significance empirically but also perceive them to define the contemporary period as a distinct stage of capitalism. Thus, the emergence of the theory of cognitive capitalism coincides with the popularisation of the notion of the knowledge economy, in which production and dissemination of knowledge are believed to play central roles in redefining the economy. However, cognitive capitalism is to be distinguished from the knowledge economy. Whilst theories of the knowledge-based economy (KBE) and economics of innovation do address the same recent phenomena, most of the KBE theories are criticised as technologically deterministic (Vercellone, 2004 and 2007). Even if the quantitative growth of knowledge sectors is notable, it is not sufficient to explain or substantiate the establishment of a knowledge economy considering that knowledge has always been important for production (Paulré, 2004). Rather, proponents of cognitive capitalism posit qualitative change in underlying social relations. A new form of conflict within the capital-labour relation is perceived to have emerged, marked by the hegemony of cognitive or immaterial labour and the corresponding rise of rent as the central economic category. Significantly, the theory bears many similarities with the post-workerism of Hardt and Negri. Both contend that at the heart of the profound transformation of capitalism lies the dominance of immaterial or cognitive over industrial labour, not least as the latter has become emptied of intellect content and application of knowledge, at least qualitatively if not quantitatively. Whilst workers are responsible for both conception and execution, conception represents the dominant form of labour for cognitive capitalism.

From this starting point, the following conclusions are derived. First, labour becomes more autonomous from capital than before as workers appropriate the cognitive and intellectual dimensions of their work. Labour produces not only commodities but also communication, collaboration and relationship, being "immediately social and common", and expanding "the realm of what people share in common" (Hardt and Negri, 2004, p. 114). Further, labour becomes more collective than before as production of knowledge depends on the existing stock of knowledge, itself the result of collective effort.

Second, the labour theory of value is seen as invalid or in crisis in the era of cognitive capitalism despite the attempts of capital to continue to impose it. Labour remains the source of wealth, but it does so because labour produces immaterial products including knowledge. Considering that the value of knowledge, if such a thing exists, cannot be measured by the labour time expended to produce it, the labour theory of value allegedly no longer prevails nor is of relevance.

Third, as the extraction of surplus value becomes less feasible, capital is forced to devise new systematic mechanisms of appropriating the products of living labour. Capital seeks to transform knowledge into intellectual property and, accordingly, appropriates surplus as rent. The distinction between rent and profit blurs, and capital is ever more parasitic (Vercellone, 2008a and b; Negri, 2008; and Negri and Vercellone, 2007). In short, new theory is necessary for the new capitalism (Moulier-Boutang, 2006).

Despite its focus on knowledge production, the theory of cognitive capitalism is flawed in several respects. Fundamentally, this is due to the rejection of Marx's value theory through erroneous interpretation. For the theory, cognitive or knowledge labour (conception) and industrial labour (execution) are understood to be two independent forms of labour. They may coexist, but one is seen to be dominant over the other. In this view, the necessary articulation between conception and execution is minimised if not denied. Accordingly, the validity of value theory is argued to depend on which form of labour prevails; labour creates value and is relevant, but only if its industrial form is dominant. Then, the knowledge form of labour is deprived of any theoretical significance in this interpretation of value theory, especially for the way it contributes to value production, and it is confined instead to the functioning of capital and capitalists. When this is taken over by workers and itself becomes predominant, so value theory is rendered redundant as well as surplus value production as capital has nothing to do other than to appropriate rents on the basis of property rights. On the contrary, as seen earlier, knowledge has an important role in value production per se, determining the productivity and complexity of labour. In sum, the theory of cognitive capitalism is wrong because of its dualistic approach, precluding diverse forms of the interaction between conception and execution in deference to the necessary predominance of whichever one over the other. As shown above, it is possible, even imperative, to extend value theory to incorporate the role of knowledge, marking distinctions across the variegated presence and role of knowledge in all value processes – the nature of its contribution to value production or not, and the presence of knowledge (such as intellectual property rights) and knowledge labour in commodity form as opposed to value and surplus value production. In this light, the strongest case that can be made against value theory in light of the knowledge economy would be if it can be demonstrated that (surplus) value production has been reduced to the status of an epiphenomenon, a proposition that can hardly be sustained given the continuing predominance of waged labour in the production process, including the production of knowledge goods, and quite apart from the heavy presence of other types of (waged) labour throughout the history of capitalism (if for functions other than those associated with knowledge as such including those as varied as social control and speculative commerce). In any case, the current financial crisis is itself one of the knowledge economy in which the failure to produce and realise surplus value is at its most central. Possibly the most prominent example of the knowledge economy has been within finance, as much as the software and media industries with which it interacts. And the excesses of finance demand the deployment, not the rejection of, value theory. In effect, the rejection of value theory for the knowledge economy is, as with so many other grand specifications of the contemporary world, to substitute more or less casual empirical observation around recent concrete developments for an analysis rooted in the continuing predominance of capital and capitalism. This is not to deny the expanded role of knowledge, however understood, but to situate it in relation to class and other relations that persist in their basic structures and processes.

## 4 Concluding Remarks

Without having always made this explicit, our discussion of value through two examples – world market and knowledge – raises deep issues of method. How do we address the abstract and concrete, the simple and complex, the historical and logical, the inner content and external form, and so on? Without, explicitly or otherwise, confronting such issues, it is inevitable that value theory should be perceived to lie somewhere between the inadequate and the erroneous. Whether it be the environment, gender, race and so on or the more traditional terrain of political economy around imperialism, crisis and uneven development, such issues cannot simply be reduced to value theory (which abstracts from them) but nor can they be satisfactorily addressed in its absence. Consequently, its continuing development both in abstract and in historical and concrete application remains imperative.

## Appendix: Correction

Hope all is well and we are obviously very pleased to have contributed to and to have seen our contribution to *C&C100* in print. We are, though, disturbed by the way in which you present our piece in your introduction. To quote (Worth, 2001, p. 5):

> Kliman outlines the importance of continuity in value theory ... In contrast to Kliman, Fine maintains that Marx's value theory remains both inconsistent and incomplete as a form of analysis, and that transformations of labour processes, the shifting terrains of labour management, and the uneven expression of capital contained with the global economy make value theory on its own inadequate.

First, of course, reference should have been to all of us as authors. Second, what you say substantively is the exact opposite of our position and as it is presented in the article as can be seen from reading the first few pages. This is that value theory is essential to address a wide range of phenomena and their contemporary manifestations. Inconsistency is denied, and incompleteness and inadequacy are at most seen to be a necessary and desirable part of value theory given its wide and shifting variety of historical forms that need to be addressed as such for completeness. It is, of course, particularly unfortunate that your misinterpretation arises in the context of our piece being sandwiched between those of Kliman and Freeman who together have argued for a particular interpretation of Marx's value theory alongside the accusation of abandonment by those who disagree with them.

We are not sure how to proceed on this. It may or may not be appropriate to incorporate a correction in a future issue. But we await your response on this.

Take care.

CHAPTER 5

# Marx 200: The Abiding Relevance of the Labour Theory of Value

## Postscript as Personal Preamble

This contribution was requested to mark the 200th anniversary of Marx's birth. Once again, with Alfredo Saad-Filho, I took the opportunity to press the case for value theory.[1] The opportunity is taken to forge the connections between value theory and a range of topics: the determinants of the value of labour power across its moral and historical elements (how do mobile phones get to be such?); financialisation; and the potential for the commodity form (having a price, without being a commodity) to exist without being a commodity (as well as being imputed in case of commodity calculation). These takes on value theory are all part and parcel of addressing the role of economic within social reproduction.

## 1 Introduction[2]

Marxist political economy (MPE) experiences a rhythm and evolution in terms of both its prominence and (perceptions of) its substantive content. More recently, MPE has witnessed a revival in the wake of the Global Financial Crisis (GFC), just as it did when the post-war boom came to an end. No doubt the 150th anniversary of the publication of Volume I of *Capital* and the 200th anniversary of Marx's birth will add to this process. However, this is necessarily different from the Marxisms that were prominent before 1917, in the interwar period, after 1956 or post-1968. This is, in part, because influential social theories are moulded by, just as they mould, their own social and historical context. While this is not the place to detail our interpretation of MPE, its relationship

1 I also helped to organise, and presented at, the Marx Memorial Library's conference of celebration, and contributed Fine (2019a) to the Conference Volume (Davis et al. eds, 2019).

2 First appearing as Fine and Saad-Filho (2018). We are grateful to two anonymous referees and editors for their helpful comments and suggestions. The usual disclaimers apply. Understandably, there is a modicum of overlap with the cases made for value theory in the earlier Chapters.

HTTPS://DOI.ORG/10.1163/9789004766266-006

to economic heterodoxies, and why MPE remains relevant for understanding neoliberalism as the current stage of capitalism,[3] it is important to note that the dynamic and content of MPE are unique, uniquely influenced, and uniquely influential.

First, given its attachment to working class social and political perspectives, the revolutionary abolition of capitalism and the transition to communism (each of which has been conceptualised in different ways within the Marxist tradition, and over time), the fortunes of Marxism are, inevitably, tied to the strength, balance and composition of progressive forces across the globe. Over the past forty years, these have been unfavourable for several well-known reasons: the rise of neoliberalism and financialisation under US hegemony, however understood; the global restructuring of production; regressive shifts in economic policy; the collapse of Soviet-style socialism; the transformations in China; the hiatus and limitations of national liberation movements; the fragmentation of left political parties; the shrinking membership and influence of most trade unions, and so on. The commendable emergence of new movements, such as feminism and environmentalism, have not compensated for the decline of more traditional forms of struggle, and they tend to have a mixed relationship to MPE.[4] Consequently, there has been a noticeable erosion of the impulse to Marxism in the 'age of neoliberalism', despite a recent upsurge.

Second, Marxism adopts a holistic or systemic approach, placing it outside the orbit of neoclassical economics. This is not only because of the latter's methodological individualism of a special type but because of its constituting the economic as a fetishised category in its own right, independent of its social and historical context. The latter also distinguishes MPE from much heterodox economics, with MPE's grounding in production equally distinctive from Keynesian approaches.

Third, MPE has become increasingly confined within academic life and scholarship, where it has been, at least partly, fragmented across traditional disciplinary lines and subjected to standard professional evaluation criteria while, at the same time, continuing to be rejected by mainstream economists for its presumably flawed economics and for failing the tests of mathematical and statistical rigour, and by non-economists for its presumed economism and reductionism. Even within heterodoxy, critiques of MPE often proceed on the

3 For details, see Fine (2012c), Fine and Saad-Filho (2026[1975]), Fine, Bayliss, Robertson and Saad-Filho (2018) and Saad-Filho (2017).

4 See the surveys in the *Socialist Register* of 2012 and 2017, and the relevant entries in Fine et al. (eds) (2012) and Brennan et al. (eds) (2017). Note, also, the parallel decline in the labour process literature.

basis of stylised or even ignorant understandings of MPE's content. In short, Marxism and its political economy are often subject to a careless reconstruction at the hands of each of those who either criticise or deploy it, removing it far from its original content and intent.

Fourth, there are increasing signs of dissatisfaction with the orthodoxy and a growing search for alternatives among those studying economics and the other social sciences, not least with the demands for heterodoxy and pluralism in the teaching of economics. This impulse has been supported by material developments, including the growing realisation that environmental degradation is intimately related to capitalism; the aftermath of the collapse of the USSR and the recognition that capitalism has not furnished a progressive alternative even on its own terms; and the eruption of imperial wars and occupations, even if fought under the guise of anti-terrorism or human rights.

While these distinguishing elements of Marxism, and its dynamics in practice, have often led to its marginalisation, MPE has also withstood the tests of both hard times and intellectual prejudice. For example, because of its emphasis on modes of production, class and the historical, and its attention to considerations of power, conflict, and the systemic, Marxism is genuinely interdisciplinary, with Marx himself offering the richest of contributions across an impressively wide range of fields within (and beyond) the social sciences. These not only provide a fertile body of work upon which continuing scholarship can draw but also the opportunity for the rediscovery and renewal of interpretations of the classics of Marx and Marxism under changing circumstances. This allows MPE to sustain an insightful, critical and constructive presence within and across disciplines and topics, and to retain its broader appeal. This is true for objects of study ranging from the economic to the ideological, and from the most detailed at the local level to the fate of the contemporary world.

MPE has much to offer in two further directions. One is in the critique of all versions of economics, recalling that Marx's own magnus opus, *Capital*, is subtitled *A Critique of Political Economy*, with himself dissecting, in the *Theories of Surplus Value* and elsewhere, the degradation of political economy into the vulgar economics that prevails today. Further, MPE establishes a presence within, influence on, and critique of, each of the social sciences as well as specific topics straddling disciplinary boundaries (the state, globalisation, and the political, the sociological, the historical, the geographical and the anthropological).

Despite these advances, in at least one respect MPE is in the doldrums, especially by comparison with the earlier period of major economic crisis. For the 1960s and 1970s witnessed an extraordinary lively set of debates around the fundamentals of MPE, focusing on methodological, conceptual and theoretical issues and their relevance for the contemporary period as part of a wide-ranging attempt to restore the full scope of the theory after the decades of Stalinism and McCarthyism.[5] Nothing similar has occurred currently even though debates around Marx's method and leading issues, such as the transformation problem and the falling rate of profit, are still subject to new airings.[6]

One reason for this relative stagnation is that earlier debates highlighted major points of interest while, simultaneously, flogging any theoretical differences almost to death even if none was resolved to the satisfaction of those at one or other end of the duelling positions. The long period of relative stagnation following the breakdown of the post-war boom suggested that capitalism could engage in business as usual even if on a sluggish basis. The GFC shattered this perspective, as it brought to the fore the prominent role played by finance in contemporary capitalism. Since then, critical thought has turned towards the nature of contemporary capitalism, as reflected in the rise of such concepts as neoliberalism, financialisation, globalisation and, if rarely in MPE, social capital. Inevitably, the result is to raise the question of the economy outside economics, and to seek guidance from political economy.

Yet, at least until recently, much social theory missed these important developments in contemporary capitalism. Our contention is that that failure was not because MPE has been inappropriate for, or incapable of, addressing these new developments. On the contrary, it is vital for that purpose, as will be illustrated by reference to two core concepts, interest-bearing capital (IBC), as the foundation of financialisation, and the value of labour power (VLP).

This is explored below in seven sections. This introduction is the first. The second examines the structure, meaning and relevance of Marx's theory of value (MTV) for contemporary capitalism. The third reviews the Sraffian critique of MPE, in order to highlight the structure and goals of Marx's analysis. The fourth reviews Marx's theory of the VLP, in view of the most significant views in the literature, and their implications for a dynamic understanding of the VLP. The fifth analyses the development and significance of financialisation for neoliberal capitalism, in the light of original Marxian categories, especially IBC and fictitious capital. The sixth brings the previous sections together, in the analysis of commodification, commodity form and commodity calculation. The seventh concludes.

---

5 See Fine (1986), Fine and Harris (1979), Howard and King (1989, 1991) and Saad-Filho (2002). It is significant that more recent such surveys are few and far between, primarily because MPE has become more fragmented and spread across positions, disciplines and subject matter.

6 Most recently (Moseley, 2015; and Shaikh, 2016).

## 2 The Theory of Value

The theory of value occupies a central place in MPE. Its centrality is indicative of the rich content with which value theory is endowed, which requires that value theory be rejected as simply constituting a theory of price based on a technical definition of the quantity of labour embodied in a commodity.[7] Instead, Marx's theory of value (MTV) seeks to trace out how labour-time exercised within capitalist production is attached to market forms, and its consequences. That is, value is a social relationship between producers expressed, through the market, as a physical relationship between things (or in various forms of equivalence as monetary magnitudes). From this point of view, value theory traces the relations, structures, agencies and processes by which market forms emerge, evolve and are reproduced, and locates them in their historically- and socially-specific contexts. As this is not a matter of right or wrong, but of material realities, the challenge is one of seeking to reproduce the structures, processes, relations and agencies in thought rather than imposing preconceptions upon it from wherever they may derive.

Focus upon uncovering the market forms within capitalism, rather than taking them for granted, offers the opportunity for general analysis of the mode of production in terms of its economic categories. In this respect, Marx endowed us with a rich body of theory, addressing value in the complex context of economic and social reproduction and the (laws of the) accumulation of capital. It follows that MPE does not proceed from the economy or the economic in the abstract through ideal and universal categories (attached, for example, as in neoclassical economics, to scarcity, technology, endowments and preferences). This approach should suffice to dismiss neoclassical or Sraffian interpretations of Marx (see below), that view value theory as a, generally inadequate, ideal theory of (equilibrium) prices or, even if more favourably inclined to MTV, impose ideal 'fixes' to it, rather than selecting and reproducing material processes in thought in order to trace out the complexity of actual value relations.

It is, then, hardly surprising that controversies over abstract issues such as the transformation problem should prove so bitter, pervasive and long lasting, for they reflect big differences in interpretations of Marx as well as his method. By the same token, if anyone has been lucky enough to get the solution right (and plenty believe they have), there is no guarantee that such virtue will extend into other areas of application.

Consequently, of necessity, MTV is both selective and incomplete, for two reasons. On the one hand, there are multiple determinants in the passage

7 For an exposition, see Fine and Saad-Filho (2026[1975]).

from production through to exchange, use and reproduction. Marx's own pre-occupation, as a reflection of capital within its most advanced stage at his own time of writing, is with the formation of exchange relations as productivity is enhanced through accumulation of capital (both transformation of value into prices of production and law of the tendency of the rate of profit to fall), and the (forms taken by the) distribution of surplus value in the form of industrial and commercial profit, interest and rent. Whilst quantitative relations are involved, the prior if not primary concern is with the appropriate logical derivation of categories, their location in the structure of abstraction, and the nature and structure of causation. Thus, *Capital* Volume I focuses on the production of surplus value, Volume II with its circulation, and Volume III with its distribution and movements as a whole, giving rise to interest, rent and the punctuation of accumulation by crises. In addition, the three Volumes of the *Theories of Surplus Value* critically dissect how corresponding categories are deployed in classical political economy, that is, how capitalism presents itself to Marx's contemporaries and predecessors.

On the other hand, whilst the texts mentioned above are replete with empirical and historical illustration, logically derived analyses – including the difference between productive and unproductive labour, the nature of IBC, and the impact of landed property – can only be taken so far before historically-specific developments must be incorporated. What is productive or unproductive labour, for example, can readily be specified logically, although there may be differences over this, but it does not always locate analytically transport workers or state employees in a state-owned industry once and for all. As with value theory more generally, such conundrums lead some to reject and others to insist upon it. We fall into the latter camp and hope to illustrate why and how, by reference to the Sraffian debates, value of labour power and financialisation.

## 3 Sraffianism: One Step Back, No Steps Forward

In the 1970s, debate over MTV was fought more widely than at any time before or since, engaging those situated within Marxist, heterodox and mainstream economics. Although it also spilled over into debates over falling profitability and the distinction between productive and unproductive labour, at the heart of the debate was the so-called transformation problem, in which it was argued not only that Marx was wrong but, often, that the concept of value as labour time is invalid because, for example, values can become negative in the presence of joint production of which fixed capital and its depreciation is an unavoidable example (Steedman, 1977 and ed. 1981).

From this point of view, the whole edifice of Marx's political economy collapses from the simple reality of fixed capital (ironical in view of the attention that Marx devotes to its role in both production and circulation). From our perspective, exposed at the time of the debate (see, for example, Fine, ed. 1986; and Fine and Harris, 1979), this involves a misunderstanding of value relations, in which value is created by concrete labour in production (and so can hardly be negative) but is expressed through exchange relations. There can be no presumption that each piece of concrete labour can be assigned to a single commodity, or mix of commodities, or a single piece of value.

It is striking how this debate not only failed to persuade many to change sides – either you were committed to equilibrium price theory or not, although some straddled the divide (most recently, Moseley 2015; and see also Fine 2017d) but also how the debate simply died. This might be attributed to the general decline in heterodox political economy, but there is a deeper theoretical reason; the equilibrium approach has nowhere to go in terms of further analysis. For, it is negative both in the sense of denying Marx's value theory *and* in depending upon equilibrium prices for fixed technologies and choice of techniques, which are far removed from the subject matter of MPE (and much heterodox economics as well), in which the dynamics of accumulation and technological change are to the fore.

As Fine (1980c) put it, irrespective of the merits of equilibrium analysis, the Sraffian approach tends to conflate two different meanings of 'determination'. One is the ability to *calculate* what prices will be in some equilibrium world of fixed technology. The other is to question *causation* – what makes prices and values be what they are, and what is their relationship to one another. To say, as Sraffians do, that technology and wages 'determine' equilibrium prices and profits refers to the possibility of calculation, but it says nothing about causation, just as $y = x^2$ cannot tell us whether y is caused by x, vice-versa, or both caused by something else and no matter what are x and y and how they are conceptually located.

This debate damaged MPE by suggesting that MTV is flawed as an equilibrium price theory, whilst offering little to replace it since the presumption of fallacy was based upon assumptions that were as unrealistic and fruitless as those of the mainstream – in this sense, Samuelson (1971) was indistinguishable from Steedman (1977).[8] Yet, Marx's analysis of the dynamics of accumulation is based on value theory, and more concerned with how surplus value is created and with what consequences for economic and social reproduction,

8 Although, of course, the Sraffian system had profound implications for one-sector neoclassical economics and the eponymous production function, as accepted by Samuelson (1966) if not his successors (Fine, 2016).

including crises and new phases of capitalism. Thus, value in a context of equilibrium is simply conceptually inadequate and flawed.

Thus, whilst Sraffianism sought to kill value theory (which it did to some degree, and continues to wound it through the conventional wisdom that MTV is invalid), it did so through a methodology that garnered no further momentum of its own. At most, it offered a combination of distributional struggle between capital and labour over unexplained productivity gains, complemented by implications for and from effective demand. This approach had only limited capacity to deal with the multiplicity of determinants, causes and effects that lay outside the simple algebra of the neoclassical production function – nor or of similarly understood value theory, to which it critically moved on from its origins with the Cambridge Capital Controversy (Fine 1980c). In other words, value theory deriving from Marx was closed off and the other fork in the analytical road led to a dead end, which is ironic, given the significance of Sraffa's (1926) other (neglected) contribution to political economy focusing on increasing returns to scale as opposed to the constant returns in the input-output models of the Sraffian critiques of Marx (and neoclassical economics).

This does, though, raise the issue of the relationship between value theory and more complex economic and social phenomena, such as different capital intensities, that are confronted by the so-called transformation problem. One approach, popularised by Sweezy (1968), is that value theory is an abstraction as a first approximation to reality that must be successively modified to be less approximate as more factors are included (his own inclination being to incorporate the capacity to sell commodities and realise potential surplus, as the next largest step to realism as opposed to equilibrium prices).

From our perspective, this is incorrect. On the one hand, later approximations would invalidate what had come before, rendering it redundant. There would be no point to the initial levels of analysis, given the closer approximation of those coming later. On the other hand, Marx's abstractions are about extracting simple underlying realities from the complex forms in which they present themselves, and show in developing the theory how those more complex forms confirm the reality of the simpler concepts (e.g., value derives from production because that is where labour is exercised). Such relations unfold both logically-theoretically, and empirically-historically in MTV.

## 4 Value of Labour Power

The value and the reproduction of labour power occupy significant positions within MPE. Labour power is (re)produced as a special commodity through structures, relations, processes and agencies that do not fall under the immediate power and controls attached to economic reproduction, i.e., the production and circulation of (surplus) value.

The value of labour power (VLP) has been interpreted and deployed in two different ways within MTV, although each draws upon Marx's notion that the purchase of labour power presumes a process of reproduction outside the capitalist sphere, with reliance to a large extent on capitalistically produced means of consumption funded by wages. One definition of the VLP is in terms of physical subsistence, the wage bundle, or the so-called moral and historical elements that make up a customary standard of living, or (social) norms, with different items of the standard having their own norms – food, housing, clothing and so on. Given the use values that comprise the VLP so interpreted, there would appear to be a corresponding VLP, determined by the labour time socially necessary to (re)produce them. Alternatively, the VLP has been defined as simply a value magnitude, either a sum of money or a share of national income or, identical in principle, a quantum of abstract labour time. This could correspond to a range of different wage bundles according to the consumption decisions of workers.

These two ways of approaching the VLP might appear to be compatible. However, tensions arise when we move beyond static analysis associated with simple reproduction. For, with accumulation and productivity growth, the first definition of the VLP as a fixed set of use values would mean a *declining* VLP by the second definition, since the labour time of production of the wage bundle would fall over time. Or, conversely, if the VLP by the second definition were applied, together with productivity growth, it would correspond to a continuing *increase* in customary standards of living, since more commodities could be purchased as they become cheaper.

No doubt simplifying, for Lebowitz (2006 and 2010), the resolution of the tension between these definitions of the VLP depends upon what he calls the "degree of separation", or the extent to which the working class can overcome its fragmentation across different sites of production and collaborate to appropriate the productivity increases for which they are responsible as (surplus) value producers. This is certainly an influential factor in practice, but it narrows our understanding of social reproduction to just one aspect of economic reproduction, even if adding the element of class struggle. This understanding is limited in three ways. First, the pressures and influences upon social reproduction are played out through complex forms of (class) struggle and alliances, which cannot be reduced to the interplay between the (potentially fragmented interests) of capital and labour in production alone. Second, it thereby disregards other determinants of the VLP and, third, methodologically, why should these processes be located at the same level of abstraction as the creation of value itself, as a class relation of production?[9]

A different angle of approach to the VLP is through the examination of *how* the moral and historical elements are established (whether as a bundle of use values or as a quantum of value) rather than treating this in a hand-waving fashion – oh, the customary just changed! There is nothing in the value relations attached to economic reproduction that allows us to answer this; instead, research must delve into broader aspects of social reproduction. To put it in a crass way, at what point does a mobile phone become morally and socially customary, as well as all other sorts of commodities and aspects of reproduction including health, education and welfare, patterns of working, what and how we eat, travel, inhabit, etc. And who gets what and through what mechanisms?

Accordingly, although there must be a correspondence between social norms and the VLP, those norms are complex in how they are created and transformed across four dimensions. First, the VLP itself, across different workers, sectors, locations, and so on, will reflect different standards, determined by skill, organisational strength, bargaining power, and so on. These determine the nature of the variegated labour markets in a capitalist economy, and how they evolve (Fine, 2017b).

Second, there will be different levels of consumption across the use values that make up the VLP. Some will consume more and different than others, although this will inevitably reflect differences in access to purchasing power as well as cultures of consumption, to be specified. These norms will differ from one use value to another, possibly relatively limited in case of washing machines but more distinguishable in foods eaten and holidays taken. These differences will also be reflected in forms of provision, whether housing be owner-occupied or (privately or socially) rented for example, and across most aspects of (private and public) consumption, their relative merits, and who gets access to what and in what form.

Third, there will be shifting norms over whether provision is through the (capitalist) market or not, with other forms of provision straddling or lying outside economic reproduction such as through domestic production or provision by the state or even charity. In this way, so-called domestic labour can be seen to be not only a vital component of social reproduction alongside health, care, education and so on, but also to constitute the norms associated with the VLP in which the content of each can shift and be transformed, as with commodification and de- and re-commodification. For example, decommodification can derive from the removal of provision either to domestic or to state

9 For a detailed analysis, see Fine (1998a and 2008).

(or civil or charitable) responsibility, or being contingent paradoxically upon developments expanding commodification (as in self-entertainment through purchase and use of electronic devices). Further, state provision may expand markets for capitalist production without being capitalist itself, serving to guarantee realisation as part of social reproduction (with capitalistically provided state-funded services or items of consumption such as medicines).

Fourth, these norms are not determined simply by reference to the working class and its cultures. For the social norms attached to commodity consumption derive in part from the income available to spend, which is correlated but not synonymous with wages, as opposed to other forms of income and wealth. In addition, the formation and influence of norms straddles class boundaries even if their levels and forms are heavily conditioned by class – as with owner-occupation, state versus private pension, access to health and education, and so on (Fine, 2013).

This implies that the determination of the VLP and its transformations are a consequence not of some remorseless and pure capitalistic logic but of class and other forms of conflict. For example, even if there is some abstract interest of capital in reducing the VLP, this still has to be brought about and, inevitably, will involve conflicts of interest between, for example, capitals with higher productivity as opposed to those depending upon cruder forms of exploitation. This means that progressive capitalists may support measures for social beyond economic reproduction, especially in response to, or when struggled for by, an organised working class, potentially with the additional support of progressively-oriented intermediate strata which can also benefit from universal forms of provision.

Further, the VLP, and the economic and social reproductions with which it is associated, are subject to major transformations across stages of capitalism. For example, in the post-war Keynesian boom, there was in the advanced economies a coincidence of growth in both commodified and non-commodified provision, as with norms for consumer durables, expanding levels of consumption more generally, and the rise of the welfare state for health, education, pensions, and other elements of social security and well-being. In contrast, over the past three decades the advance of neoliberalism has meant that the VLP has been determined in different ways, and not just through class offensive, austerity and so on. Rather, under neoliberalism economic and social reproduction has become increasingly governed by financialisation both directly and indirectly.[10]

10 See Fine (2012b, 2014b and 2017b) for (neglect of) relationship between social policy and financialisation.

## 5 Financialisation

The growth of finance and its presence and influence across economic and social reproduction have underpinned a corresponding growth of the concept of financialisation across the social sciences.[11] Financialisation is the defining characteristic of the global economy during the past thirty years, and the economic core of neoliberalism. 'Financialisation' is a relatively new term, which has emerged from, and remains confined within, heterodox economics in general, and MPE specifically. Its absence from orthodoxy is because it is both systemic (i.e. characteristic of the workings of the economy as a whole) and dynamic and, hence, it is not reducible to the optimising, equilibrium and efficiency that are centrally important to the orthodoxy.[12]

Unsurprisingly, financialisation is subject to multiple understandings, both because of the variety of conduits through which finance is connected to the rest of the economy (for example, the proliferation of financial markets, across mortgages and pensions to futures markets in carbon emissions), and because of the ways in which these developments are attached to the evolution of the economy itself. Most analyses of financialisation start from the definition in Epstein (2005, p. 3):

> financialization means the increasing role of financial motives, financial markets, financial actors and financial institutions in the operation of the domestic and international economies.

But this is an amorphous and all-embracing conceptualisation. Anything to do with monetary relations counts as financialisation, just as any aspect of commodity relations would count as commodification, or any labour would count as value as a way of 'improving' on Marx.

From the perspective of MTV, this is mixing up the production of (surplus) value and the forms it takes, even if those forms can take on a life of their own independent of capital(ism). Although extremely positive in inspiring empirical analyses of financialisation, such an all-embracing definition collapses analytical distinctions and tends to preclude the logical and historically

---

11 For its rejection as a buzzword/fuzzword, see Christophers (2015) and Michell and Toporowski (2014).

12 See Christophers (2017) and Dymski (2015). Of course, analysis of finance has a strong presence within the orthodoxy, not least with the efficient market hypothesis as critical point of departure for either what might be termed inefficient market hypothesis (informational asymmetries) or, especially in the wake of the GFC, the deployment of behavioural economics.

systemic analyses attached to MPE. This is to suggest that a systematic analysis of financialisation should return to money, through its derivation in Volume I of *Capital*. In Volume III, at a more advanced level both of analysis and of capitalism itself, money capital becomes a commodity with its price (interest) deemed 'irrational' because it lacks foundation in the value relations of production, as opposed to the supply of and demand for loanable money capital.

Fine (2014a) argues for a narrow definition of financialisation drawing upon Marx's theory of interest-bearing capital (IBC), that is, capital lent for the purposes of reaping rewards out of profit-making capital. In brief, financialisation is the process of expansion, diversification and integration of the various forms of capital in exchange (in financial and other markets), through assets that straddle the roles of money as credit and money as capital, and their subordination to IBC. This includes the explicit or implicit securitisation of streams of revenue, and the creation of corresponding financial assets that can be traded. That is, financialisation is not the diffusion of consumer loans, but these loans may become financialised if they are traded as what Marx calls fictitious capital, alongside the proliferation of the volumes and varieties of financial derivatives.

Such processes have promoted the intensive (within existing spheres of operation) and extensive (incorporating activities where it was previously absent) accumulation of fictitious capital, and increased the scope and prevalence of IBC in accumulation, as IBC has appropriated activities that were the preserve of productive and commercial capital (or not capital at all, as in labour engaged in economic and social reproduction). It follows that financialisation is not a form of (pre-capitalist) usury, and it does not hinge upon the exploitation of (wage) revenue. It is, rather, a contemporary form of incorporation of credit relations into the orbit of fictitious capital (Fine, 2010 and 2017a).

This approach contrasts with the all-encompassing notions that allow for financialisation as the presence of more finance of any sort into contemporary life. Instead, the extent and impact of financialisation depend on how financial activity straddles the boundaries between IBC and other forms of capital in exchange, and how it engages with production. Its conceptualisation requires looking at the relationship between productive and money capital, state policies towards banking and finance, and how they have changed over time.

Four implications of financialisation are especially important. First is the dramatic expansion of the range of (speculative) financial transactions, services, institutions, instruments and markets relative to real activity, and the integration and internationalisation of these markets, encompassing ever more areas of economic and social reproduction that were previously provided by the state (for example, housing, pensions, education, health, and economic and social infrastructure).

Second is the increasing predominance of finance over industry, as non-financial companies earn an increasing share of profits from financial as opposed to productive activities. They come to rely less upon the financial system to fund their operations and more on retained earnings or borrowing on open markets, and focus on profits drawn from (short-term) financial dealing as opposed to seeking long-term productivity gains producing things.

Third is the subordination of economic and social policy to the dictates of the promotion of markets, especially of finance. This tends to shift policy towards conservatism, fiscal austerity and commercialisation, and erosion of the institutions, capacity and ethos associated with public provision.

Fourth, all agents – not least the working class – are increasingly embroiled within the financial system. This is whether in pursuit of profitability or within their daily lives.

For these reasons, financialisation has been associated with relatively slow GDP growth rates at least relative to the post-war boom, despite the extraordinarily favourable conditions for growth and productivity increase delivered by neoliberalism, and the prodigious expansion of finance itself (why does the world need three times as many financial services proportionate to the real economy as previously?).

Even though financialisation is associated with growth slowdown and crises at the macroeconomic level, there have been pockets of growth for those who have sheltered themselves from the more dysfunctional forms of finance, used the state to promote (private) accumulation, controlled wages relative to productivity growth, and found both domestic and international markets to serve. In particular, there have been rising returns to the financial sector, and a rising share of income accruing to the holders of financial assets, leading to widening inequalities of income and wealth. At least in principle, these, and the corresponding structures of determination, can be traced through the application of MTV, bearing in mind the realities of contemporary capitalism.

## 6 Commodification, Commodity Form, and Commodity Calculation

Defining financialisation as IBC allows it to be distinguished from its effects, but the more complex relationships with which it is involved still have to be traced out. For example, IBC can prevail in the presence of commodification (C), where money is loaned for the purposes of appropriating interest out of the expansion of production undertaken by those borrowing money as capital. In addition, when payments are regular, whether deriving from surplus value or not, they can be securitised and turned into assets for speculative trading (most obvious in mortgage derivatives). In this latter case, though, there is no direct expansion of commodity production (most houses will have long since been produced); as a result, reference will be made to the commodity form (CF). What distinguishes financial assets is that they are exchangeable and take on the CF without being commodities themselves in any normal sense.

Three implications follow. First, CF is a logical category derived from and even historically preceding capitalist production. Moreover, many exchanges can take on some of the attributes of commodity exchange without being so, given that money can pay for whatever is available irrespective of whether it has been produced for the market and possible profit (or not even produced at all, as in bribery, gifts, pocket money, etc).

Second, capitalism has a tendency both to impose CF (a leading example would be fees and user charges) and to translate CF into commodity production proper (most notably in the commercialisation and subsequent privatisation of public provision), and to appropriate its activities. For example, expansion in the circulation of value implies ever more revenues available that can be deployed for whatever purpose, not necessarily commodity production. Thus, CF is not financialisation but it can, like C, provide the raw material for it by securitising associated revenues.

Third, capitalist commodity production is distinct from other forms of production even if money changes hands in their provision.[13] This implies that, even in the absence of C or CF, activity may still be governed by monetary considerations,[14] or what can be termed commodity calculation (CC). Within mainstream economics, for example, cost-benefit analysis seeks to impose monetary calculation in decision-making where the market does not provide prices to do so, or if there are externalities or social costs and benefits that differ from how the market prices them. By the same token, there are shifting and contested boundaries over what is acceptably assessed through CC.[15] As with the drive to transform CF into C, the same applies for CC and its transition to C, whether through the intermediate step of CF or not. Despite such tendencies, capitalism also expands the world of CC, in knowing the price of everything but the value of nothing.[16]

13 Debate has been fierce over domestic labour in this respect (and productive and unproductive labour) and concerns what does and does not count as (surplus) value as opposed to (surplus) labour in general.

14 Even as their alter ego, for example, in denying the presence of monetary considerations – as in a wedding at whatever cost, or what money cannot buy.

15 See Radin (1996) and Zelizer (1994).

16 There is a false presumption that C expands *absolutely* at the expense of CF and CC, while they tend to expand together; see, for example, Fine (2012a).

The simultaneous expansions and shiftings across CCFCC are marked most obviously by the rise of the welfare state during the Keynesian period and its privatisation under neoliberalism. Bear in mind that it was traditional to see state provision as both displacing market provision and to provide markets for it! For many analyses, especially of, but not confined to, a Polanyian orientation, this is a matter of commodification, decommodification and recommodification, but such perspectives tend to fail to distinguish between commodification, CF and CC, just as the amorphous definition of financialisation conflates all monetary forms and influences together.

Nor is this merely of academic or definitional significance, as can be seen by bringing together the categories of financialisation and the VLP. For, the distinctions between C, CF and CC correspond, respectively, to fully-established (private) capitalist production, the presence of charges and hence streams of revenue (which may or may not be privatised and securitised), and the absence of such revenue streams but the incorporation of practices dictated by market logic (as in so-called New Public Management, drawing upon the market mimetics of quantify, Q, evaluate, E, and prioritise, P – i.e. cut costs/expenditure).

As was indicated above, both C and CF allow for financialisation, since there are streams of revenues that can be securitised and traded on financial markets. By the same token, the extension of CCFCC into social reproduction is part and parcel of the reproduction of labour power and the determination of the VLP, rather than being limited by capital and its forms. These processes also create those who fall outside their orbit, for example, the hard to employ, house, educate, support with income, and so on. This raises the question of the nature of social reproduction under financialised neoliberalism, both where CCFCC prevails, and where it does not (the rolling back by, and rolling out of, the neoliberal state).[17] For example, at the same time that the privatisation of social reproduction is being pursued (i.e. its commodification, with the attendant changes in the VLP), emphasis has also been placed upon the extent to which domestic labour, particularly of women, has become increasingly necessary to compensate for cuts in social provision due to 'austerity'. Thus, the extension of CCFCC to social reproduction tends to shift social to individualised forms of provision and to create added burdens on women in compensating for the withdrawal of sources of income and other forms of material support.

Money, finance, financialisation and the VLP have always come together within capitalism, for example, because the wage is the money form of the VLP but does not in and of itself provide for its social reproduction. What is

17 See Fine and Hall (2012).

distinctive about the contemporary period, and the role of financialisation within it, is the extent to which the latter has intervened in both economic and social reproduction. This can be seen by contrast with the post-war boom. In this respect, it is worth emphasising how neoliberalism departs from post-war Keynesianism. Significantly, for the latter, debate amongst progressives was pitched between reformism and revolution and the extent to which the socialising tendencies of capitalism could be sustained. In the event, both have proved unreliable guides to the socialisation of (re)production. For neither of these seem now to be in prospect and, neoliberal ideology to the contrary in terms of its emphasis upon individuation and reliance upon the market, socialisation of economic and social reproduction (and state intervention to promote it) have continued apace through the financialisation that, itself, underpins neoliberalism.

## 7 Conclusion

Locating the social and historical specificity of the capitalist mode of production draws MPE into a broader terrain concerning periodisation both within capitalism and between capitalism and other modes of production. Across these issues we find considerable variation of position, hardly surprising given the grand sweep of material that they cover, with differences over method, its application and the historical processes themselves, and correspondingly distinct interpretations and refinements of Marx's own work and the historical record. In addition, the connection of value theory to the economic and the social, and to the dynamics of change, is a central aspect of MPE that inevitably raises questions of method and methodology. Such questions loom large within Marxism and in its disputes with, and distinctions from, other schools of thought.

This Chapter has examined three such aspects of the MTV. First is the nature of value itself, as is revealed through the debates driven by the Sraffian critique of the MTV. They make it apparent that the MTV is not a simple thing, as it traverses methodology, conceptualisation, theory, and the logical and the historical. Accordingly, it cannot be dismissed on simplistic technicalities, as suggested by Sraffianism, whilst also open to varying and deeply contested interpretations in principle and practice.

Second is the determination of the VLP as part and parcel of social reproduction, which involves examination of the household, civil society and the state in relation to economic reproduction both logically and historically. In turn, this requires acknowledging the imperatives of capital accumulation, how they are realised, and the role of ideas and cultures in forming the social norms underpinning social provision. These factors interact with provisioning itself as well as broader economic and social developments and interests, determining the material cultures of social reproduction.[18] This is vital in understanding how the VLP is endowed with moral and historical elements, as well as the contested meanings of the consumed to the consumer.

Third is financialisation. Both it and the VLP occupy very different worlds in contemporary capitalism. From the perspective of MPE, and a holistic methodology, they come together in diverse forms across time, place and activity, in ways which should be traced from values to their forms. Today, in scale and scope if not historically uniquely so, this is apparent in everyday life as has been prominent in the financialisation literature. The connections between the VLP and financialisation are forged across different determinants in reflecting and reconstituting the moral and historical elements involved. The VLP attaches to CCFCC by virtue of its social reproduction in which financialisation is increasingly influential. So distinctive are money and labour power that they might be dubbed (non-)commodities of a special type, but they share a deep and complex attachment to underlying (value) determinants.

What money and labour power are, then, is heavily conditioned by their relationship to the world of commodities both materially and culturally, and these relationships have to be filled out both logically and historically. This is what Marx does for money in the opening chapters of *Capital* I and, having laid out the production and circulation of (surplus) value in the remainder of that Volume and Volume II, he offers a structured analysis of finance as capital in exchange in Volume III, ranging over commercial, merchant, money-dealing, loanable and interest-bearing capital.

The systemic relations among social reproduction, finance, industry and the rest of the economy should occupy a prominent place in political economy. With capitalism so demonstrably having failed on its own terms, even under conditions that are arguably the most favourable for it, the case for socialism needs to be made as never before, and it can rest upon a Marxist analysis both for its critique of capitalism and for the light it sheds on the alternatives. With economic and social reproduction increasingly mediated through financialisation, it has become subject to what has been termed the variegated vulnerabilities of everyday (neoliberalised) life,[19] against which dissent has been as

---

18 Itself financialised under contemporary capitalism; see the special issue of *New Political Economy* (Bayliss, Fine and Robertson, eds, 2018).

19 See Fine (2017c).

commonplace as it has been fragmented, with increasingly volatile outcomes in the political arena.

Given the scale of issues involved across value theory (from price to crisis theory, from economic to social reproduction), we cannot expect our account to command agreement in general, whether by those who are committed to value theory or those who reject it. What we do hope to have done is at least to have persuaded of the enduring value of value as a category that remains appropriate for analysing contemporary capitalism. The abiding relevance of value theory is that it forges attachments between grand theory and complex and diverse outcomes without descending into eclecticism or rigid determinism, as we have sought to illustrate.

CHAPTER 6

# Production vs. Realisation in Marx's Theory of Value: A Reply to Kincaid

## Postscript as Personal Preamble

Following the frenzied value theory controversies of the 1970s, it has been rare for value theory to be debated to any great extent with the notable exception of continual contributions to the transformation problem. One exception is provided by this and the following Chapter, in which my work (alongside that of Alfredo Saad-Filho) is taken to task by Jim Kincaid in critique of two of our books. We were fortunate that *Historical Materialism* allowed us two goes each at the material and one another (with our second go reproduced in the following Chapter without Postscript).

## Our Reply[1]

We very much welcome Jim Kincaid's review article of our books, *Marx's 'Capital'* (Fine and Saad-Filho, 2004, fourth edition,[2] but listed here as 2026[1975]) and *The Value of Marx* (Saad-Filho, 2002) and the complimentary remarks that he has to offer. But the leitmotif of his commentary is one concerning our "limitations", a term he uses often to describe our contributions. The nature of his critique is apparent from his title "Production versus Realisation" in which he claims that we are "productivist" because, according to him, we give undue emphasis to production at the expense of exchange.

Before dealing with this charge in detail, it makes sense to place the two books in context. *Marx's 'Capital'* is in its fourth edition, the first having been published in 1975, with this and the other previous editions solely authored by Fine. The first edition appeared in a Macmillan student series of economics texts and was confined for that purpose to 25,000 words. Its success allowed it to outlive the series by a long way and for it to be successively expanded to its current 50,000 words. The third edition was published in 1989 but Macmillan

1 Reproduced from Fine and Saad-Filho (2008).

2 Unfortunately, here and occasionally in what follows, for page references for confirmation of quotations and the like, this means trying to get hold of the fourth edition of 2004.

 HTTPS://DOI.ORG/10.1163/9789004766266-007

declined the chance of a new edition, with Pluto taking it on instead. From the outset, and currently, the purpose has been to offer a faithful representation of Marx's political economy as far as word length and the nature of the material would allow, whilst also engaging modern 'students', university or otherwise, of Marx's ideas on economics in the hope that they would become attached, not least going on to read the real thing.

*Marx's 'Capital'* has done well in terms of translations and longevity, the latter against a declining interest in Marxist political economy and of active *Capital* reading groups and the like. It is significant that popular presentations of Marx's political economy are notable for their absence and/or failure. There are good reasons for this. His ideas are complex and not readily subject to simple summary; they are also controversial and subject to misinterpretation, not least when forced through the prism of orthodox, and even heterodox and sympathetic, economics; and there is a need to strike a balance between abstract theory and contemporary events, needs and interests.

Across these competing tensions, *Marx's 'Capital'* has achieved some modicum of balance, not least with the final chapter of the fourth edition adding topics such as class, the state, globalisation, the environment and socialism. The move to joint authorship was motivated by the wish to add some fresh air to a text that had previously already been gone over three times before. *The Value of Marx* is altogether different being pitched at the most advanced level. It presumes a reading of *Capital*, and debates upon it, in offering its own interpretation of Marx's political economy and the controversies that surround it. In this respect, it is a partial successor to, and advance upon, Fine and Harris (1979) providing, on a narrower terrain, some novel exposition of its own as is accepted by Kincaid – and dos Santos (2007) who offers a review of a very different kind than Kincaid's. In this respect, *The Value of Marx* is, of course, not subject to the same tensions and constraints as *Marx's 'Capital'* in terms of length and reader accessibility. But Marx's classic too, let alone our attempts to represent it, is seen as flawed by Kincaid for similar reasons although the critique is offered in the more technical terms of how to interpret the law of value and competition between many capitals. Kincaid also finds exchange unduly neglected across both books and focuses specifically on the treatment of the composition of capital, also providing an appendix of his own on the issue.

Against this background, it would have been possible for Kincaid to have suggested that *Marx's 'Capital'*, if not *The Value of Marx*, had been analytically compromised in order to achieve its goal of accessibility. This is not done by him, and appropriately so, for we can assert that principle was not sacrificed for readability. In other words, differences between ourselves and Kincaid are genuine, not least because both books under review and our body of work on

Marxist political economy as a whole are mutually consistent and not compromised either by level or subject matter.[3]

With one exception, this means that differences between us are substantive and not presentational. For the latter, Kincaid deplores in *Marx's 'Capital'* the absence of the derivation of money as in the opening chapters of *Capital*. There is, of course, a healthy debate over why Marx began in this way, and whether it is essential and proves the validity of value theory.[4] These debates certainly do shed light on Marx's theory of money (and of money capital and of the monetary forms of capital) but they are pitched at too high a level for our elementary exposition and are liable to prove too esoteric to the uninitiated. No doubt this reflects our own view that Marx's monetary theory can be appropriately developed without first running through the opening chapters of *Capital* itself. Indeed, this is done in chapters 11 and 12 of *Marx's 'Capital'*, covering interest bearing and merchant capital, in text that has essentially been present from the first edition. On these, Kincaid offers no comment at all (although dos Santos comments on little else![5]) even though they deal precisely with the sphere of exchange that we are deemed to neglect and despite the fact that we offer propositions on the three questions to be answered with which he closes.

Specifically:

1) Our treatment of unproductive labour addresses the issue that it can increase the rate of profit without creating surplus value but that this does not place it in the same position as productive labour – not least because costs of circulation can be unnecessarily expanded at the expense of profitability and the intensification of crises – not some academic point in the era of financialisation (Fine, 2007b).
2) "Productivism", however defined, might neglect money but we do not as is evident from the review of dos Santos in this journal. And the presence

---

3 Nonetheless, our contributions have evolved in depth and breadth over time. Further, Kincaid's attempt to drive a wedge between ourselves and Weeks (1981) is inappropriate as we all share the same interpretation of Marx and have worked closely together for many years. Similarly, whilst there are differences with Harvey over application of method and some theoretical propositions, these are limited relative to the broad swathe of agreement on method itself (Fine, 2006b).

4 For a review see Saad-Filho 2004, Ch. 1.

5 Dos Santos suggests two different and incompatible approaches to Marxist treatments of the financial system, drawing upon Itoh and Lapavitsas (1999), assigning us to the interest bearing capital approach (a loan to initiate a circuit of capital) as opposed to his preferred one of what we would term loanable money capital approach (money advanced to earn interest for whatever purpose it is used). We do not consider these to be incompatible but that the latter is the more complex form taken by the former, just as price is to value.

of, but not subordination to, value form analysis is evident throughout our books.[6]

3) Nor do we neglect reproduction, not least with the innovative depiction of *economic* reproduction in diagrammatic form carried over from the first edition of *Marx's 'Capital'* and its insistence upon attachment to social reproduction (and transformation).

In these respects, Kincaid adopts a peculiar and erroneous mode of critique. He rightly observes that we treat exchange as "secondary", a term he uses a number of times. But he often seems to confuse "secondary" with relative neglect – for exchange itself and also for money, competition and reproduction. These are all extensively covered in our books. For, as Kincaid is aware, there is a difference between the order of abstraction (movement from simple and more abstract to complex and more concrete, value to price for example), the order (and nature) of causation (production prior to exchange), the order of presentation (must we always start with the money form?), and the order of investigation (something that does not appear explicitly in our deliberations because it is overwhelmingly contingent). Kincaid would appear to conflate these and move freely between them in his assessment of our work or, at least, not to recognise that priority to production in abstraction does not necessarily entail a secondary and uniform status to everything else in all other respects.

In short, our original sin in not beginning, like Marx, with a full exposition of money and the value form is no such thing but a judicious analytical and expositional choice on our part. However, it serves for Kincaid as a symbol of our "productivist" bias. This does raise the issue of two different criteria for assessing our (and Kincaid's) contributions – by appeal to Marx and by appeal to strength of argument. As an exposition of Marx, our intention is that the two should coincide, and much the same would appear to be true of Kincaid, and so our differences with him can run along parallel lines of interpreting Marx as well. He wishes to drive a wedge between Marx and ourselves by the charge against us of "productivism". In doing so, he is guilty of misinterpreting both Marx and ourselves. In part, he caricatures a "productivist" position and imposes it on our work even though it does not fit and involves ignoring major parts of our work to make it appear as if it does fit. For money, for example, our supposed reliance upon orthodox theory for its functions suggests to him that we rely on orthodoxy whereas we accept that money is the form and measure of value as a social relation under capitalism, but this is not incorporated into orthodox accounts of the functions of money, and cannot be.

---

6 For an extraordinary neglect of value form in pursuit of a political theory of value, see Knafo (2007) where money and exchange value scarcely appear at all.

In this and other respects, Kincaid (2007) interprets Marx himself from his own "circulationist" bias. Possibly as oversight, he suggests, "The substance of value is abstract labour, measured in units of socially necessary labour time", p. 139. This is simply wrong. Value *is* socially necessary labour time and it is *measured* by money (although only after intervention of processes of distribution and exchange) as every value-form theorist knows. His circulationist bias is apparent in what can only be described as an astonishing departure from Marx in his interpretation of value. Our view, and Marx's, pure and simple, is that value is created and determined in production under the control of capitalists (although value can also be created by non-capitalist forms of commodity production). Value production is certainly conditioned by other factors, ranging from capitalist circulation through to the weather. These are analytically derivative and secondary in practice, and they should be examined for their impact upon the accumulation of capital and the concrete forms through which it materialises and is affected. If this means undue priority to production, we plead guilty (although not to the charge that "realisation processes are not discussed in any detail", p. 145, fn. 20).[7]

In contrast, Kincaid argues that value is not created in production alone. For him, "Unless commodities are transformed into money, the labour expended into making them has created no value", p. 145. Lest this be considered an isolated, accidental or ambiguous view on the source of value, Kincaid asserts that, "it makes no sense to ask whether value is created in the production or the circulation phase of capital reproduction", p. 142. Further, we are told that, "Both use values and abstract value are created during the phase of production. But which of these use values are to count as value, *and for how much value*, depends on processes of social validation which take effect during the exchange phases of the circuit of capital", p. 144, emphasis added.

This position on value lies at the core of difference between Kincaid and ourselves, as is apparent from the following critical observations. First, it is ironic that Kincaid should reject underconsumptionism for it at least accepts that (surplus) value is created in production but is constrained from being realised in exchange (a logical and practical possibility, as demonstrated by Marx's schema of reproduction, but not a necessity). By contrast, Kincaid suggests that (surplus) value has not even been produced if it fails to be realised! For example, he claims that "[b]oth use values and abstract value are created during the phase of production. But which of these use values are to count as value, and for how much value, depends on processes of social validation

7 See, for example, relevant Chapters in Fine and Saad-Filho (2026[1975]) and Saad-Filho (2002, Chs 4 and 5).

which take effect during the exchange phases of the circuit of capital", p. 144, and that, "until realisation takes place as commodities are transformed into money it is not clear which firms have produced value and in what amounts ... Unless commodities are transformed into money, the labour expended into making them has created no value. Until the point of realisation by sale, value has no more than a virtual quality", p. 145. This is unadulterated value-form theory, and it is wrong.[8]

Despite his protestations to the contrary much of Kincaid's discussion of exchange, money and circulation does have an underconsumptionist flavour. This is true of his partially exchange-based definition of value. And it emerges in his claim that, "profits depend not just on surplus value extraction (as productivist doctrine tends to argue) but on adequate levels of effective market demand to ensure the realisation of value by the conversion of commodities into money". This is little more than a tautology inspired by Keynesianism – realisation of value depends upon effective demand but with no account of how effective demand is determined. And, in passing, Kincaid seems to accept inconsistently that (surplus) value may be extracted (created) but not realised (and not thereby created for lack of "social validation"), which is destructive for a theory of exploitation under capitalism through production as opposed to exchange.

Second, then, this does not allow for crises to be interpreted as the short and sharp *destruction* of value as such crises would, for him, represent a failure to have created that destroyed value in the first place. However, for Marx this is very different from a situation in which an isolated individual commodity producer fails to produce a socially desired use value for whatever reason – precisely the focus of Kincaid's attention (and that of value-form theory).

Third, Kincaid's wish both to accept the significance of production and to allow value to be created in exchange is an obstacle to further progress of the Marxist project for political economy of examining how forces and relations of capitalist production are both realised through and affected by exchange. We are unable to read his preferred text of Marxist political economy, Heinrich (2004), but he has to accept that it is disappointing when it comes to "the account it offers of the market and non-market processes which influence the rate of profit", p. 157, fn. 49. And Kincaid himself concludes that as far as he is concerned for the analysis of contemporary capitalism, "I concede that such a value theory is still very much of a site under construction", p. 158.[9] In our

8 For a for a detailed refutation of this approach, on the grounds of both internal inconsistency and inconsistency with Marx, see Saad-Filho (2002, Ch. 2).

9 With his favoured Rosdolsky also not having got too far on site.

view, that is how it will always remain since Kincaid's value-form approach will always hop between the two spheres of production and exchange and seek to hold them together through the deployment of Hegelian incantations where necessary, rather than constructing one out of the other. This is only too evident in his treatment of an exchange rate devaluation, itself taken as an unexplained "hit" with the effect that values are suddenly less in some countries and more in others. Currency movements are seen to determine values rather than vice-versa (albeit through a complex chain of causation from conditions of production to conditions of international exchange that Kincaid has simply bypassed). If the US dollar devalues by ten percent does this mean ten percent of the value of commodities produced in the US has been wiped out as Kincaid suggests or, in our view, that value has been redistributed?

Fourth, as in this instance and more generally, it is ironic again that Kincaid's understanding of value should both incorporate a determining influence of exchange in its creation and be accompanied by a discourse on the dialectics around essence and appearance. For the idea of failure to ratify value as a result of failure to sell is the position par excellence of the vast majority not only of capitalists but also of bourgeois political economy, with neoliberalism as its most perfect expression. Value is what you command on the market, a methodological and theoretical stance with which Marx was determined to break in his critique of classical political economy.[10]

Fifth, Kincaid's insistence on the importance of exchange for the creation of value is overtly inspired by the work of I. I. Rubin (1975 and 1978). Rubin's writings were rediscovered by Marxists in the early seventies as part of their reaction against the excesses of neo-Ricardianism. Unfortunately, in some cases this reaction went too far, partly because Rubin's writings tend to be pitched at an excessively high level of abstraction which emphasises the commodity features of capitalism (e.g., decentralisation at the point of production) at the expense of specifically capitalist relations of production, especially wage labour.[11] This emphasis leads Rubin to affirm that labour becomes social through exchange, rather than through its subsumption by capitalist relations. For example, he claims that, pp. 96–97, 142:

> the labour of every commodity producer becomes social only because his product is equalized with the products of all other producers ... [A]bstract labour ... [is] labour which was made equal through the all

10 For an explicit account of the inversion of essence and appearance in debate over falling profitability, see Fine (1982).

11 For a detailed review, see Saad-Filho (2002, Ch. 2).

> round equation of all the products of labour, but the equation of all the products of labour is not possible except through the assimilation of each one of them with a universal equivalent … [The] equalization of labour may take place, but only mentally and in anticipation, in the process of direct production, *before* the act of exchange. But in reality, it takes place through the act of exchange, through the equalization (even though it is mentally anticipated) of the product of the given labour with a definite sum of money.

In this approach to value, money is critically important as measure and substance of value, while the social relations of production which distinguish capitalism from other modes of production are veiled by exchange (sale). This is *precisely* Kincaid's mistake and, in this sense, his interpretation belongs within the Rubin tradition even though he claims to be attempting to explain "the highly financialised capitalism of today", p. 146. It is impossible to do so through the contemplation of exchange: Marxists have always known that the edifice of financial speculation rests upon processes of extraction and realisation of (surplus) value, which generate the resources that are continuously needed to fulfil the commitments of debtors and speculators, reward the brokers, and pay dividends to the shareholders. These are transfers of value created in *production* – establishment of this claim is the primary objective of volume 1 of *Capital*, and our books mirror Marx's own emphasis on the real (and, therefore, analytical) primacy of production.

These comments indicate the extent to which Kincaid's own approach diverges from our own (and, dare we say, Marx's). But Kincaid's contribution is marred over and beyond this by a blatant misreading of our work that is incomprehensible unless possibly a result of force-fitting our contributions into an invented "productivist" frame wherever possible and ignoring them otherwise. This is most obvious in his account of our treatment of the falling rate of profit. He suggests that our view is little more than that the organic composition of capital rises as a result of capitalist accumulation, and this depresses the rate of profit as it is a law of production as opposed to being attached to exchange. Such an account was to be found in a single paragraph in the fourth edition of our book (Fine and Saad-Filho, 2004, p. 111). But there it was immediately followed by the bald statement in the next paragraph that, "However, this interpretation is incorrect",[12] and a totally different

12 Kincaid's interpretation of us as "productivist" is indistinguishable from our own critique of what was termed "fundamentalist" by Fine and Harris (1976b). From this and other relevant work over the intervening period, it is incomprehensible how our approach could be so designated.

interpretation is offered with the following elements. First, the law is not an empirical law (making predictions about the rate of profit) but is concerned with the tensions created within production and between it and exchange during the course of capital accumulation. Second, whilst the law and its counteracting tendencies are at different levels of abstraction (with the counteracting tendencies addressing the consequences through exchange of the accumulation of capital in production), they are of equal causal significance so it is not a matter of one predominating over the other but of how the tendency and the counter-tendencies interact with one another to give rise to more complex and concrete outcomes (including crises). Third, this interpretation of the law is shown to be consistent with Marx's treatment of a range of issues across *Capital*, each of which has usually been seen as controversial but separate from the others. These include the so-called transformation problem and the theory of rent. What they share in common is a particular understanding of the composition of capital in Marx, to which we now turn, as it is extensively addressed by Kincaid himself.

Kincaid criticises our emphasis on the importance of the composition of capital for the explanation of accumulation, the transformation of values into prices, the law of the tendency of the rate of profit to fall and the theory of rent, and our distinction between the organic and value compositions of capital (OCC and VCC). These are sweeping claims, but they are not supported adequately. For example, Kincaid never explains why our emphasis on the composition of capital is misplaced. Instead, he immediately drifts into a conceptual argument about the OCC and the VCC, while ignoring completely their relationship with the technical composition (TCC). Kincaid's claim that our treatment of the composition of capital is unsatisfactory deserves a more detailed answer than can be offered here. However, two issues should be clarified, the measurement of the TCC, OCC and VCC, and the significance of the distinction between the compositions of capital for Marxian analysis.

The TCC is the ratio between the mass of material inputs and the living labour necessary to transform them into the output. This concept is essential for the definition of labour productivity and, therefore, for studies of technical change and accumulation. Since the TCC is the ratio between a heterogeneous bundle of use values and concrete labour, it cannot be measured directly. However, Marx explains that it can be assessed through the OCC, or the value of the means of production (including depreciating fixed capital and circulating constant capital) that absorb one unit of living labour (whether paid as labour power or unpaid as surplus value) in a given firm, industry or economy. Although the OCC is intuitively clear, it can differ across sectors or change over time for two reasons: differences or changes in the TCC (e.g., differences or changes in the labour productivity in *this* industry), or differences or changes in the value of the means of production used up (that reflect the circumstances in *other* industries). In spite of this, for Marx there was no ambiguity. The OCC is a value-reflex of the TCC, and it does *not* change if the TCC is held constant, whatever happens to the value of the elements of capital.[13] In order to distinguish clearly between different technologies and the use of inputs with distinct values, Marx introduces the VCC, or the ratio between the value of the circulating part of the constant capital (including the depreciation of fixed capital) and the variable capital (paid labour) necessary to produce the output (c/v).

A static contrast between the OCC and the VCC is useful to distinguish between technical and value differences across production processes. For example, if two firms use identical technologies to produce different products using inputs with distinct value (e.g., copper and silver jewellery), their TCCs – and, therefore, OCCs – are identical. However, their VCCs are different (in this case, because silver is more expensive than copper). In other words, value differences between the constant and variable capital consumed in distinct industries are captured by the VCC but not the OCC. In contrast, differences in the technologies of production affect the OCC but they may not be accurately reflected by the VCC.

Having cleared the conceptual ground, we can examine the process of accumulation of capital. Technical change is usually introduced in individual firms, which raise their TCCs and, consequently, their OCCs and VCCs (although the three compositions change simultaneously across different sectors in real time, in logical terms the TCC changes first, and this shift is reflected by the OCC and, subsequently, the VCC for particular sectors). For capital in general, its TCC and OCC tend to rise with technical progress and, all else constant, commodity values tend to fall. However, because of the conflicting forces of competition, including mechanisation and declining commodity values, the VCC of capital in general can either rise or fall through time. The outcome depends upon the sectors affected by technical change, the speed of the diffusion of innovations, the structure of the systems of provision of commodities, and so on. However, in general the values at the beginning of the circuit ('earlier values'), at which

---

13 "[I]f one assumes that the organic composition of capitals is given and likewise the differences which arise from the differences in their organic composition, then the value ratio can change although the technological composition remains the same ... The organic changes and those brought about by changes of value can have a similar effect on the rate of profit in certain circumstances. They differ however in the following way. If the latter are not due simply to fluctuations of market prices and are therefore not temporary, they are invariably caused by an organic change in the spheres that provide the elements of constant or of variable capital" (Marx, 1987a, pp. 383–86).

the inputs are purchased, are higher than those at which the output is sold ('later values'). Marx argues that the OCC reflects the TCC at the *initial* (higher) values of the component parts of capital, *before* the new technologies affect the value of the output, in which case the social OCC rises in tandem with the social TCC. In contrast, the VCC reflects the TCC at the *final* (lower) value of the elements of constant and variable capital, determined by the modified conditions of production and newly established in exchange (Saad-Filho, 2002, Ch. 6).

In other words, the OCC is measured at the time of production, while the VCC is determined in exchange and calculated on the basis of the values newly established by the currently predominant technologies. It was in this context that Marx examined the law of the tendency of the rate of profit to fall.

The distinction between TCC, OCC and VCC helps to illuminate the potential implications of accumulation. Technical change raises the TCC, the OCC and total input values (because the output increases). However, the VCC, unit output values and future input prices tend to fall. How the actual process of adjustment happens – especially for large blocks of fixed capital – is crucial, because the sudden devaluation of large masses of capital can lead to financial upheaval and crises. Marx's analysis does not impose immediate or necessary outcomes, but it indicates that the process of accumulation synthesises the contradictions of capital both in production and exchange, and it offers the conceptual tools for the analysis of concrete processes of accumulation and crisis.

Related to the previous point, Kincaid also charges us for neglecting fixed capital and turnover time. His view is that the latter has been decreased considerably recently, and this serves as a counteracting tendency to the falling rate of profit. Our neglect of fixed capital is entirely due to space constraints (and, as part of constant capital, dependent on account of the latter as logically prior). Our approach conforms to that offered by Weeks (1981) (and known of before its publication). We do not disagree with Kincaid but he is too one-sided in his treatment. Whether turnover time on average is increasing or decreasing is an empirical question. But what are the forces underpinning these outcomes? Kincaid offers nothing other than a technologically driven reduction to the benefit of profitability.[14]

The circulation of fixed capital across a number of production periods is contradictory and not determined exclusively by technology (not least in a

14 Although, of course, interpreted in these terms, Brenner's overhang hypothesis is the opposite, with low investment and prolonged turnover time mutually conditioning low productivity and profitability.

crisis when failure of effective demand brings circulation in some areas of the economy to a halt). For example, and at a relatively abstract level, there are two forces acting upon fixed capital – one is to circulate it as quickly as possible to accrue value prior to its obsolescence or crisis. The other is to extend its life indefinitely in order that surplus value can continue to accrue despite its own value already having been replaced through passage through sufficient production periods. This is nothing other than the contradiction between value and use value, respectively, attached to the specificity of fixed capital and its circulation and reproduction. The outcome of these tensions is not technologically determined but is dependent upon the rhythm of accumulation and competition. This can only be investigated empirically but it cannot be reduced to a property of fixed capital alone.

In a sense, this is a specific application of the law of the tendency of the rate of profit to fall and of its counteracting tendencies – one of which is for large masses of fixed capital to earn a lower rate of profit – not to maintain the rate of profit elsewhere as such but to sustain the accumulation of capital as a whole (Fine, 1991, for a discussion). The tendency to an increasing use and faster turnover time of fixed capital is part and parcel of the rising organic composition of capital (OCC).[15]

Despite this treatment of the composition of capital, in which the VCC is the competitive form of realisation of the OCC, reflecting competitive accumulation between capitals, Kincaid suggests we treat competition as secondary and are weak on it. At one level, this involves him in being inconsistent since he specifically highlights the contribution of *The Value of Marx* for distinguishing homogenisation, normalisation and synchronisation of value even though these are explicitly concerned with how competition within and between sectors is essential to the formation of values.

Kincaid's own take on competition is through appeal to the "law of value", as if invoking this law is a substitute for theory, or a frame in and of itself for

15 In his appendix, Kincaid claims that we measure constant and variable capital in labour time rather than money (we do not; see, for example Fine and Saad-Filho, 2004, pp. 104, 107), and that we "seem" to get the definitions of constant capital and rate of profit wrong by ignoring fixed capital (we do not; see Fine and Saad-Filho, 2004, p. 138). These aside, Kincaid does himself get the definition of profit rate quite wrong by insisting that it should include the entire stock of fixed capital as capital advanced rather than that this should reduce with the value fixed capital transfers to the output. For, should a capitalist advance £1m in fixed capital, which depreciates uniformly over ten years, then the £1m will have been returned in its entirety by the end of the decade, one-tenth in each year circulating as constant capital. The average advance will only have been half a million. Of course, the discussion here highlights the tensions involved in this circulation and piecemeal return of fixed capital, and that these are focused on turnover time.

incorporating more complex economic moments on an unsystematic (or circulationist) basis. In our view, the law of value concerns rooting more complex outcomes in value relations. In this respect, it is ironic that Kincaid should deplore our neglect of restructuring and crisis. Fine's work from the 1970s onwards on the competitive, nation-state-driven internationalisation of capital (and the British economy) (Fine and Harris, 1985)[16] brought the idea of such restructuring to the fore in the literature and was a significant impetus, not an adjunct, to simultaneous theoretical work of which *Marx's 'Capital'* (and *The Value of Marx*) is a part. Significantly, Kincaid's own text offers no mention of the state, monopoly and world economy in his own account of competition, the world economy itself a pre-condition for world money that he would himself take as a logically prior starting point for an account of value!

Despite these differences, we are grateful to Kincaid for his constructive engagement with our books. Despite our significant disagreements, explained above, we admire Kincaid's commitment to value theory, and welcome the opportunity to revisit and explain in further detail our argument in *Historical Materialism*. We share Kincaid's interest in the development of a Marxian value theory that engages with contemporary capitalism, and our books have offered avenues for doing so.

16 But see also analyses in early issues of the Bulletin of the Conference of Socialist Economists.

CHAPTER 7

# Twixt Ricardo and Rubin: Debating Kincaid Once More

## 1 Introduction

Re-engaging with Kincaid (2008) after Fine and Saad-Filho (2008) prompts three preliminary remarks. First, Kincaid has overlooked most of our response to his previous piece (Kincaid, 2007) other than in some sort of blanket agreement of what we share in common, which can make it difficult to pinpoint where positions have clarified, shifted, or remained the same, as a result of this debate. Second, apart from repeating selected themes, Kincaid's later piece strays from the original object of commentary on our books. Third, and partly as a consequence of these limitations, it may be impossible to discern whether our disagreements with him derive from genuine differences between us, inconsistencies or analytical errors that Kincaid would himself correct once conscious of them, his appeal to arbitrary factors ranging widely across different levels of analysis, or some combination of these. We begin by seeking to clarify differences over value, then proceed to methodology before addressing a number of issues around the accumulation and circulation of capital that these involve. We conclude that Kincaid (2008) suffers from significant shortcomings, including misinterpretations of Marxian value theory and methodology, and of our books (Fine and Saad-Filho, 2026[1975];[1] and Saad-Filho, 2002). Most significantly, Kincaid's *Reply* is flawed in its (implicit) attempt to bridge the gap between Ricardo and Rubin in order to provide the foundation for his interpretation of Marx's value theory which fundamentally differs from both.

## 2 Production and the Determination of Values

Kincaid's interpretation of value theory is simultaneously *Ricardian* and *Rubinesque*, even though the two are the antithesis of one another: the first is oriented towards substance and the second towards form, although each inevitably, and often blindly, stumbles upon or over the prism through which

1 As explained in the previous Chapter, Fine and Saad-Filho (2004) has been listed as (2026[1975]).

HTTPS://DOI.ORG/10.1163/9789004766266-008

capitalism is viewed by the other. The debt of Kincaid upon Rubin is transparent enough to bear little further comment. The more innovative aspect of Kincaid's contribution derives, instead, from his enriched and displaced Ricardianism.

Kincaid is Ricardian (neo-Ricardian if you wish)[2] because he is committed to a labour theory of value for which labour time of production is the only source of value. Thus, for him, "[t]here is no disagreement that value is created only in production", p. 184. But, like Ricardo and a source of inconsistency if not confusion for both of them, as soon as Kincaid *applies* his value theory he begins to question its validity and, also like Ricardo, he compromises, seeking to modify it. For Ricardo, this is a consequence of the failure to distinguish between value and its form as exchange value (as brilliantly pointed out by Marx and, subsequently, Rubin), not least because of his wish to identify value and price (and other price forms) directly with one another. This creates tensions once it is recognised that commodities are produced *and* sold under different conditions, among them differing compositions of capital and circulation time to bring them to sale. And, in case of commodity money, Ricardo is induced to presume that it is produced with some sort of average composition of capital, otherwise further skewing price away from value (and even such a money cannot do this job properly either). In short, Ricardo's *instrumental* labour theory of value is pragmatically but inconsistently modified even as it is applied,[3] with his theory of rent a revealing example as the determination of value is shifted to the margin of production to allow for the category of rent to exist at all, albeit at the expense of relying upon two distinct value theories, one for agriculture and one for industry (Fine, 1982, Ch. 4).

Kincaid does not go so far as to posit a separate value theory for one sector as opposed to another, but he offers a multiplicity of value theories depending on the assorted influences of exchange upon value determination in each of the cases that he examines. Thus, having initially argued that we share a commitment to value (creation) theory, Kincaid immediately dilutes his position: "However I argue that *whether* value has been created in production depends in part on what happens in circulation", p. 184. This is not some accidental

2 We use the term neo-Ricardian to express a commitment to a labour theory of value, as opposed to those (Sraffians, for example) who would reject any form of this theory altogether because of the divergence between values and prices of production and/or otherwise (with Law of Tendency of Rate of Profit often serving as an added target in following Okishio).

3 See Pilling (1980) for an outstanding and critical exposition of instrumental interpretations of value theory, ones in which the labour theory of value is applied to problems (and generally found to be wanting) as opposed to a value theory that reproduces in thought the material relations attached to labour in practice.

modification or even an analytical refinement, since he spends considerable effort developing a conceptual framework in support of this diluted theory. And so he insists that "value, though not produced during the circulation sequence, remains only *potential* or *virtual* until commodities are sold and capital is transformed back into money form", p. 182.

This statement is, necessarily, open to various interpretations, ranging from the idea that circulation decides whether given quantities of "virtual value" were *really* created in production (although, presumably, those "virtual values" would evaporate if the commodity remains unsold, deflate if it is sold "too cheap", or inflate if it is the other way around), through to the notion that production brings into the world those values whose ghostly existence can only be presumed *ex ante*, and which need to be realised (and, only then, quantitatively determined) in exchange for money before commodities and values can have genuinely been created. This is sufficiently perplexing without adding the complications both of the "traditional" transformation problem, which shows that prices generally have only an indirect relationship with labour time in production and, moreover, of what happens under an inconvertible paper money system.

To add to the confusion, in accepting that he suffered from poor expression in his earlier contribution, Kincaid claims that, "I was trying to say only that value is not fully and finally *produced* until commodities are transformed into money in circulation, so in this sense production and circulation are just two phases of a single process. But the sentence can be read as if I thought that value is created in circulation, which is not my position" (p. 184, emphasis added).[4] Indeed, this sentence can be so read – as can the clarification – unless a tortured distinction is being drawn between *production* of value (in part in circulation) and *creation* of (virtual?) value which seems to be confined to production alone.

Once it has been unhinged from production, Kincaid's value analysis loses its residual coherence. For example, we find that supply and demand can *also* determine commodity values: "if commodities are in short supply, relative to demand, prices rise and more hours of actual labour are counted as socially necessary", p. 186. So we find that price determines value rather than vice-versa, not some of the time but most of the time since Kincaid acknowledges, following Marx, that supply and demand rarely exactly correspond, p. 192, n. 30, and money generally never corresponds to value after the latter is transformed into

4 Note, to eliminate confusion, that circulation is being used in two senses, for which context should make clear which is which. One is for the processes of purchase and sale, the other is for the total movement of capital through the spheres of production and circulation.

price of production. However, this confusion is avoidable. Overinvestment, fluctuations of supply and demand, the weather and other factors may cause fluctuations in market prices, the most concrete expression of value; however, they are analytically secondary (alongside circulation) when their significance is ordered in relation to value *production* by capital and its determinants. Thus, while excess supply or an economic crisis can depress profit rates or destroy values, these processes do not affect either the concept of socially necessary labour in *production*, nor the prior reality of exploitation (otherwise the rate of surplus value would vary with the vagaries of the weather and market prices). But the possibility of differences between value produced and value realised because of the misallocation of social labour or economic crises belong to distinct levels of analysis, and should not be seen as co-determinants in the production (as opposed to the mystical creation) of value (Fine and Saad-Filho, 2026[19075], pp. 20–2; and Saad-Filho, 2002, pp. 31–2, 66–70).

Another layer of confusion arises in Kincaid's account of the formation of value within sectors, for which he refers to "an *averaging* process … [t]he labour producing the same commodities at different times and places must be averaged out", p. 186, emphasis added. This is wrong if a simple notion of average is intended, and is misguided otherwise. There is some process by which the value of a commodity is determined by the array of individual production conditions prevailing within its sector, but it is not an "average" unless this is tautologically taken to mean the outcome itself. As Marx makes clear, value is established within a sector by a norm – it might be worse productivity, best, or most common (although that norm appears in exchange form as price). Value analysis cannot determine this norm in the abstract, nor pretend that values must be determined by the weighted average of the production conditions or whatever. However, through its analysis of competitive accumulation, value theory offers instruments for examining the analysis of the (heterogeneous) conditions of production prevailing within each sector, and the emergence of values out of them.

Kincaid subsequently claims that, "it is only in market competition, when commodities are sold, that the relative efficiency of firms in their use of labour is subject to final social evaluation. The standard of socially necessary time is set within each branch of production separately, and by competition within that branch of production", p. 186. This is a telling restatement of the Ricardian-Rubinesque theory, in which value emerges from *individual* (rather than social) conditions of production: it begins with a Ricardian panic if individual values differ within a sector, and concludes with a Rubinesque solution by allowing exchange to sort out the difficulty in terms of what should count as value in the sector. Such an approach is correct only insofar as both competition and exchange are understood as blanket terms encompassing the social relations of production and exchange that influence the creation of a value norm within a sector. But this is to stretch the meaning of these two words to the point of tautology, in order to exhaust all causation other than production itself and, as already argued above, to turn the relationship between value and exchange upside-down or, more exactly, vice-versa.

So, we find that, by construction, it is almost impossible to pin down the details of Kincaid's value theory. Its ambiguities derive largely from Kincaid's ambivalent account of how value is "determined". In this respect, Kincaid is far richer than Ricardo, who more or less confines his inconsistencies to the tensions between value in production (labour time) and value in exchange (price from profit according to capital advanced and turnover time). In contrast, Kincaid's conundrums arise in four different ways: (a) out of realisation in the narrow sense of whether commodities are sold or not and, if not, were they ever values in the first place, and how are their values determined in each case; (b) out of the elements that constitute competition, and how competition influences the determination of value produced as well as realised; (c) out of a concern with value determination when productivity is changing, and, finally, (d) unlike Ricardo's innovative adherence to the deductive method, Kincaid's value theory is housed in references to dialectics, laws and tendencies, which also determine outcomes. Unsurprisingly, readers are overwhelmed with controversy and ambiguity around the "determination" of value simultaneously across these several dimensions and factors.

Kincaid's contribution does not hold to a consistent and coherent position across each of these understandings of determination, with causal factors other than labour time in production leading him to modify the determinants of value depending on the circumstances. The source of these difficulties is both plain to see and, at the same time, obscured by Kincaid's displaced Ricardianism: it is his apparent reliance upon Ricardian deductivism in basing his value theory on *individual labour time of production* as starting point while, at the same time, calling on Rubinesque value-form theory to wipe out any remaining discrepancies *ex post*, through the magical role of money. Like Ricardo, Kincaid seeks to determine value from within production but concludes that it is modified in moving into exchange so that value cannot be so determined. Kincaid attempts to escape from this apparent contradiction declaring that value is only "virtual" within production, and it is determined quantitatively *ex post* by competition, by the monetary equivalence of commodities which are themselves produced under distinct conditions of productivity and compositions of capital and, ultimately, by reference to the amount of money for which they are sold.

The presumption, then, is that value is created in production but then "determined" subsequently through the vagaries of exchange, although this is inconsistent with the starting point of value from labour time of production. This problem in Kincaid's analysis is due to the conflation between production and labour time as the *logical* starting point with production as the *chronological* starting point of the circuit of capital. But, as admittedly recognised elsewhere by Kincaid, the circulation of capital alternates between production and exchange, rather than starting neatly with one and then finishing with the other. Indeed, the movement between the two cannot be treated as being simultaneous across capitals (in competition or otherwise), since some serve as productive inputs and outlets for others. In other words, the notion of value as socially necessary labour time *presumes* that the general conditions of competition and realisation (as well as supply and demand and the weather) have already been incorporated into the determination of value as part of the general conditions of production of *all* commodities. Whilst exchange and competition have a degree of independence in their subsequent movement and impact, they are conditioned by the developments in production that must be elaborated first, and separately as far as possible, from competition and exchange, and provide the logical foundation for their reconstruction in theory in more complex and concrete forms.

This is exactly the opposite of Kincaid's partly deductive, even empiricist, methodology. He suggests that we can only measure value after it has been realised in exchange, since "[i]t is not possible to measure directly how much value has been created, and by which capitals, until the commodities come to be sold", p. 185 This raises the issue of the extent to which value *relations* and *processes* (not just quantities) exist and can be quantified; after all, factories are observable with numbers of workers, working hours, a flow of output and so on. In this case, what is the status of Kincaid's remark? Is it one about evidence – no solution to the murder until it has been committed? Or is it a theoretical statement about the nature of value? Perhaps, for Kincaid, it is somewhere in between, but for theoretical purposes we not only recognise that value has been produced prior to exchange all the time, but we also presume that its quantity is known. As Kincaid himself acknowledges, this is part and parcel of Marx's own views, not least in his analysis of reproduction in *Capital* 2 and in the transformation of values into prices of production in *Capital* 3. That the *monetary form* of values can only be quantified after sale is little more than a tautology having no bearing on the logical structure, nature and dynamic of value, and so of value theory.

This is to return – one last time – to the issue of determination. Even if we can only "know" value after sale (which is only a partial truth), this cannot mean that the future *determines* the past. If we observe that the ground is wet and that people are carrying umbrellas, we can deduce that it has rained but this does not mean that carrying umbrellas caused the rain.[5] Nor does the ex post evidence of umbrellas having been deployed have any bearing on the causes of rain. It is also a moot point whether the complexity of the exchange system (including, but not limited to, the interaction between supply and demand) further complicates the empirical quantification of value, which helps to explain why there is a mini-industry within Marxist political economy seeking to quantify Marxist categories and sort out the value from the dross. In short, Kincaid's views on the relationship between production and exchange, causation and calculation (both of which might be dubbed determination), abstraction, investigation and exposition (see below), and the significance and timing of availability of empirical evidence are slippery to say the least.

## 3 Methodology

Possibly this is because, in parallel with the Ricardian-Rubinesque (cake and eat it) character of his value theory, Kincaid is also caught between pillar and post when it comes to his methodology (natural or social science?). By way of justification for his favour for modern theories of emergence, "which in recent decades have become a focus of study in a wide range of natural sciences, from cosmology to molecular biology", we are informed that "[e]merging systems usually involve large numbers of agents (molecules, neurons, ants, investors, etc) who act according to local rules, since there is no overall centre of control or planning of the system", p. 193. However, he recognises that "[t]he relevance of work in the natural sciences for political economy can only be approximate and by analogy since there is nothing like money in the non-human world", p. 193, n. 34, despite recent newspaper reports of primitive primate exchange. This is indeed true, although it might be added that there is also nothing like capital, value, exploitation, commerce, banks, states, and human beings conscious of and actively making their own "emergence" but not under conditions of their own choosing.

5 This example is used to address the conflation between calculation and determination in the Sraffian critique of value theory (Fine 1980c, Ch. 6). Note also that the chronologically opposite is also significant – a hurricane warning is in advance of the event but does not cause the hurricane. Incidentally, this places the whole enterprise of Granger causality (the idea that the order in which things happen corresponds to causation) into question.

To Kincaid's regret, Marx lacked not only "the emergence vocabulary of modern natural science", p. 193, but his analysis was also "handicapped by the type of mathematics available to him which dealt mainly with linear functions ... [but] a value theory stressing tendency and emergence could now draw on recent advances in non-linear mathematics to model the chaotic dynamics of capitalist reality", p. 191, n. 26. Thus, we have finally discovered the reason why "it was in Hegel that Marx found a conceptual language for expressing the pattern of dialectical necessity", p. 193. These propositions are symptomatic of the fetishism of mathematics that has encompassed some branches of (mainly Anglo-Saxon) value analysis in recent decades. But they lead to an analytical dead end because, in capitalism, outcomes (values, profit rates, and so on) are *not* determined through the aggregation or averaging out of individual variables from which a social outcome "emerges" in ways that can be modelled mathematically. It is, rather, the other way around, as we have demonstrated in Fine and Saad-Filho (2026[1975], Ch. 1) and Saad-Filho (2002, Ch. 1).

These difficulties are, ultimately, due to the uncertain analytical status of the concrete in Kincaid's approach. They render equivocal his use of the term "essence". For example, he initially proposes that, "it is of the *essence* of capitalism that it is a *monetary* economy", p. 182, first emphasis added,[6] and this term is deployed, again, in asserting that "[c]ompetition is of the *essence* of capitalism, no less than exploitation", p. 195, emphasis added. If all that is being said is that money, competition and exploitation (just as banks, exchange rates and so on) are inevitable in capitalism, there can be no objection but nor does this provide any analytical purchase. If, on the other hand, money, competition, exploitation (and, perhaps, exchange rates, since "the role of exchange rates in the valuation of capital must figure as a *crucial* element in Marxist value theory", emphasis added), are presumed to share the *same* "essential" stature whether in reality or in the reconstruction of the concrete in thought, then there would be a departure from the most basic propositions of Marxism concerning what is the (causal) essence as opposed to the form of capitalism (whilst acknowledging, as in all serious dialectics, that form is not merely a veil to be pierced, but is itself part of reality with real effects).

These ambiguities around essence (and form) are relevant at three levels. First, Kincaid seeks to distinguish "between what is assumed as an abstract theoretical simplification, and the *real* processes of exchange and competition which operate in practice to create tendencies towards what has been posited

6 Leading him to continue immediately, "and that any introduction to Marx's *Capital* should try to explain why Marx thought it crucial to explain the nature of money in capitalism as a basic element in his exploration of fundamentals at the start of *Capital* vol. 1".

in theory", p. 192, emphasis added. This is not an acceptable formulation of the relationship between the real and the abstract. For, although the tendencies identified in theory must legitimise the concepts on which they have been based (value categories), it is wrong to see these concepts as simplifications in the sense of not being real. Rather, they are the more abstract, but no less real, foundations of the complex outcomes developed theoretically and observed empirically.

Second, Kincaid strongly believes that, being "essential", money and the commodity form must be the starting point for *any* Marxist exposition of capitalism. This is simply misguided. Order of exposition is different from that of investigation, abstraction and, most importantly, causation in the real world and, partly as a result, there can be no fixed and ideal form of presentation independent of audience and context. Further, it is also incorrect that money is the key to value. Under capitalism, it is exactly the other way around, with value offering the key to the analysis of money – as well as other (transhistorical if not always universal) categories such as labour, commerce, profit, rent, interest and exchange rates.

Third, Kincaid's circumlocutions around the analytical status of money are of abiding symbolic significance to his Rubinesque use of money as the analytical fix for addressing all manner of exchange outcomes (as suggested in section 1). Specifically, he is wrong to suggest that we disregard money in our introductory text until the treatment of banking capital. For money appears explicitly at an early stage from the analysis of simple commodity production, C-M-C, onwards and, in Saad-Filho (2002), money is examined in all chapters of the book at increasing levels of complexity, starting from the relationship between money and abstract labour, and reaching inflation in inconvertible monetary systems.

## 4 Value Is as Value Does

As we move from the abstract (value in production) to the concrete (exchange), there are three options. Ours is to trace how value is reproduced at more concrete levels. But Kincaid's is to modify/reject value (Ricardo) and/or to wave the magic wand of money to establish what value has been produced (Rubin). This difference in our stance and methods inevitably informs other differences between us at more concrete levels (or as we journey around the circuit of capital and beyond) as we will illustrate.

First, Kincaid's notion of competition is limited, tending to be confined to exchange relations ("competition of firms seeking workers in the labour market, competition in the markets for interest-bearing capital to secure money to finance production", p. 183). In contrast, in our work, competition is perceived primarily in terms of capacity to produce and/or appropriate surplus value – that is, the levers underpinning the restructuring of capital and the production of surplus value, as opposed to differential advantage in or through exchange. The critique of Rubin and his followers including, in this instance, Kincaid, is that their analyses (mis)incorporate competition and the sphere of circulation at too high a level of abstraction. This undermines the categories of value theory that they are deemed to form rather than reproducing them in more complex form as the analysis becomes more concrete and specific (money and competition are subsumed and fundamentally transformed by the relations of exploitation that define capitalism, giving historically specifically significance to exchange, price and sale within this mode of production).

Kincaid's conception of competition is flawed not only because it is limited to the relations of exchange. He also conflates competition with the circuits of production and reproduction of capital. They are distinct although both encompass many capitals. This may explain why he, not us, offers little account of the competition to be found in *Capital* Volume 1, where it is heavily present given the logic underpinning the production of absolute and relative surplus value, commodity exchange under capitalism, the treatment of the forms of wages, and so on.[7] Similarly, the idea that competition appears fully formed in *Capital* Volume 2 is misplaced as this book is more about the relations between many capitals as structured production processes prior to consideration of capitals in competition in the sphere of exchange (integration of *Capital* Volumes 1 and 2 at a more complex level in *Capital* Volume 3). Kincaid's complaint concerning our neglect of "the circuits of production *and reproduction* of capital which fills out much of *Capital*, Vol. 2", p. 182, is particularly inapposite given how fully it is covered, not least diagrammatically and in original fashion harking back to the first edition of *Marx's 'Capital'* itself (Fine, 1975a, quite apart from Fine, 1975b).

Second, despite Kincaid's enriched Ricardian tensions, his work barely touches Ricardo's own concern with the value/exchange value syndrome which was later transferred to Marxist theory through the so-called transformation problem, which Kincaid only mentions in passing. Significantly, the transformation problem has generally served as the staging post for those arguing against Marx's theory of value, since it appears to raise the tensions

7 A virtue of Lebowitz (2003 and 2006) is to bring together issues of production and competition (to appropriate surplus) out of his treatment of *Capital* 1, in positing the relative exclusion of class struggle on which see Fine (2008) for a dissenting view.

between production and exchange in the simplest possible way: how to convert given values into prices, with given wages, static technology and equalised profit rates. Stumble at this stage, and there really is no point in going on.

Kincaid does not stumble although it is not clear whether this is an avoidance or because of his reliance upon the magical (Rubinesque) qualities of money. Instead, he questions our work through the prism of his own form of Ricardianism. This brings on a panic attack of frightening proportions,[8] in terms of the externally introduced factors making for (exchange-related) outcomes for, "under the intense pressure of competitive restructuring, financialisation, ecological limits, and new centres of accumulation",[9] it is not simply the value form, competition, and circulation that must be incorporated but also, amongst other factors, "accumulation by dispossession; privatisation; the commodification of nature, of the resources of non-capitalist societies and of the personal and cultural spaces and products of the life-world", p. 199. These appeals to the immediately concrete and complex are no less dramatic than his earlier appeal to the "modern scientific study of emergence", mentioned above. Ultimately, and not lacking in scope and ambition, Kincaid declares that "to provide an adequate account of current mutations in global capitalism requires a change in the conceptual angle-of-vision of the currently dominant version of value theory", p. 201. So now we know it is not just our value theory that is deficient for its putative "productivist" tendencies (a label imposed upon us that Kincaid simply abandons in his later piece).

Third, Kincaid suggests that our analysis comes unstuck around fixed capital since it is particularly susceptible to variation in value determination in light of developments in exchange *subsequent* to its installation. This is a Ricardian slip which overlooks the specific nature of fixed capital and its contribution to the production of value. What distinguishes fixed capital is not its physical properties as such – a plastic bag can last forever without ever becoming a piece of fixed capital – but its peculiar position as part of constant capital and in its circulation; fixed capital lasts for longer than one production cycle. As a result, whilst value relations are taken as given upon the start of the production period, by necessity of definition (and presumption that value relations

8 Thus, there are scatter-gun references to any number of scarcely compatible approaches from Bellofiore, Bensaïd, Bryan and Rafferty, Carchedi, Duménil, Farjoun and Machover, Harvey, Kliman, Lapavitsas, Mandelbrot, Moseley, Perelman and Roberts, in order to incorporate such diverse topics as derivatives, emergence theory, exchange rates, fractal geometry, intrinsic value, the Korean economic crisis and, not least, world money.

9 See Fine (2003) for the way in which the (increasing) complexity of capitalism leads both proponents and opponents of value theory to argue their positions by reference to the same factors.

will be redefined in following periods), the remaining value of fixed capital is yet to be known. This is not because circulation has yet to take place for this or later periods but because production conditions in this sector, and in the sector producing the inputs (including those producing the elements of fixed capital themselves) are transformed as technologies and productivities change unevenly across the economy.

Fourth, Kincaid suggests, incorrectly, that "Marx ... includes transport to the point of sale as part of the production process. Thus, the production of a can of beans is only completed when it is placed on the supermarket shelves", p. 184, n. 5. This is a Ricardian stance, with an ahistorical view of productive labour (that can lead, as in the domestic labour debate or the production of skills debate, to an infinite Sraffian regress in counting any labour at any time in the past as having contributed to the value of the commodities into which they have ultimately found their way). Transport labour may or may not be productive of value, but this can be examined only once the distinctions between production and exchange and between productive and unproductive labour have been made. Further, whether or not this labour is productive does not depend on the act of transport itself. What counts is under what capital the transport activities are organised; for example, is it retail capital, in which case the activity does not produce value, or is it a separate (capitalist) transport sector, in which case value is produced? Or is it some combination of the two in which case we have to determine which predominates and how as socially necessary labour time? This is just one aspect of competition in the restructuring of capital, but it has implications for the determination of the norm within a sector as the process by which values are established. These complications point to the need for an account of value firmly grounded on the relations of production, again broadly conceived and not just as a quantity of labour time, and it is essential to avoid making arbitrary allocations of activities to production (or exchange) as a presumed determinant of sectoral norms and hence of sectoral value itself.

Fifth, we note that Kincaid's critique of our analysis of the composition of capital, which was so prominent in his previous piece, has been largely abandoned in his rejoinder. We also note, however, that he defines the composition of capital incorrectly as the ratio of constant capital to *labour* as opposed to variable capital, p. 186. This may be of importance given the central role that the technical, organic and value compositions of capital occupy in our own approach, straddling the dynamics of production and circulation as accumulation proceeds. We also have no idea why he should suggest that we perceive the composition of capital as an "empirically determinable ratio", p. 186, n. 12, as opposed to a set of key but highly refined concepts in locating the causes and consequences of capital accumulation, including Marx's treatment of the transformation problem and the law of the tendency of the rate of profit to fall (see above).[10]

Sixth, quite deliberately, our contributions in this debate have been cursory over concrete empirical issues such as the restructuring of the South Korean economy or the significance of exchange rate movements. Since we have not offered analyses of these, it makes little sense for Kincaid to claim they are inadequate or to volunteer alternatives in his piece. Whilst what is sauce for his goose might be considered sauce for our gander (why should he offer concrete analysis in such a debate), our concern has been to advise of the narrow confines of his empirical work, not least for jumping from highly abstract first principles into detailed accounts of state policies and movements in exchange rates. It is therefore a legitimate difference about methodology, leading Kincaid to regret that, "What is questionable ... is the gap which separates such empirical material from the underlying value argument. In this book [Fine and Saad-Filho, 2026[1975]], as elsewhere in much of the current value theory literature, there are a number of crucial disconnections between abstract theory and concrete commentary."

But, as already indicated in our earlier response, our own inclination is to examine the restructuring of capital as a whole in its historical context, and without presumption that exchange rate and other movements are somehow directly to be derived from relatively abstract production categories (in contrast to Kincaid's own "productivist" straitjacket interpretation of our work that does appear to have been abandoned in his rejoinder). The whole structure of international and domestic finance is built upon the circulation of capital as a whole, across a range of functions and assets, and across states, in which an increasing array of financial markets are insulated from *direct* attachment to production. But this does not mean that such effects should be analysed in isolation (as if the sub-prime crisis were independent of the housing market, itself independent of broader patterns of accumulation and their causes and effects). Nor is the independent movement of exchange categories the antithesis of value theory but its consequence. Ironically, this is revealed at the most elementary level at which Kincaid would have us begin our exposition – with the derivation and development of the money form. For Marx's analysis of

10 Respectively, tendency for profit to equalise across sectors with differing or changing productivity (rather than equilibrium pricing for unchanged technology), and contradictions between the law as such and counteracting tendencies (rather than empirical predictions of falling profit rates) (Fine, 1983b; Fine and Saad-Filho, 2026[1975], Chs 9–10; and Saad-Filho, 2002, Ch. 7, for fuller expositions).

money demonstrates that commodity money under capitalism tends to be displaced by independent symbols of itself, as paper or credit, apparently contradicting the starting point of the commodity form of money.

## 5 A Concluding Note

In short, and possibly the most important element offered here in terms of broader lessons for others engaging in value theory, Kincaid's wide-ranging survey of theoretical and empirical topics in value theory falls between two stools. First, as was indicated above, his approach to value is both Ricardian and Rubinesque, and it suffers from weaknesses associated with both (mis-) interpretations of Marx. Second, and more generally, there are two principal traditions of critical engagement with Marx's value theory. One is *intrinsic*, and it seeks to reinterpret, correct or to reject it by inner argument relating to its logic – as in any number of examples around the transformation problem, the falling rate of profit, productive labour, crises, and so on. The other is extrinsic, and it responds to historical and empirical transformations in capitalism itself by perceiving existing value theory as incapable of incorporating them satisfactorily, in which case it must be either reconceptualised or abandoned.

Kincaid, unsurprisingly, stands on both sides of the intrinsic-extrinsic divide, seeking to reinterpret and amend the logic of value theory *and* to offer a new "angle-of-vision" to capture the apparent novelties of contemporary capitalism. However, each of these approaches is methodologically flawed, since Marxian value theory is about reconstructing the class-based production processes of capitalism, through to their consequences in the broader economic and social fabric, and suggesting how they can be transformed through mass action. Value theory is *not* about using externally imposed (arbitrary and often incompatible) theories or standards of logic or evidence to check the conceptual or empirical validity of Marx's account of capitalism. Too many Marxists have been engaged in needless, and sterile, self-flagellation for too long over inner logic and outer complexity, and, as indicated by the strength of our response to Kincaid, who succumbs nowhere near as far as others, we have no intention of allowing committed value theorists to become the whipping boys of such self-imposed conundrums.

CHAPTER 8

# On the Composition of Capital: A Comment on Groll and Orzech

## Postscript as Personal Preamble

The Chapter that follows is almost unique as far as I know. It concerns a debate with Groll and Orzech over the definition, meaning and significance of the organic composition of capital (OCC) in Marx's political economy, a term that recurs again and again across the literature in the different contexts of the transformation problem, the law of the tendency of the rate of profit to fall and the theory of absolute rent. These are to the fore in Volume 3 of *Capital*. But the OCC 'first' makes its appearance in Volume 1 of *Capital*,[1] where it is introduced to capture the specifically capitalist mode of production in the narrow sense, not of capitalism as such but as its systematic source of productivity increase (contingent upon accumulation, the working up of more and more raw materials/constant capital into commodities through the use of machinery, displacement of living labour and production of relative surplus value – all covered in detail in Volume 1). These processes in production, and their preconditions and consequences in economic and social reproduction, are in part addressed throughout the other Volumes of *Capital* (and the *Theories of Surplus Value* and elsewhere). In this light, it is difficult to imagine a more vital concept for understanding Marx's political economy than the OCC. Yet, the uniqueness of my debate with Groll and Orzech derives not only from the apparent paucity of other contributions on the issue but also from the limited reference to the debate by others let alone participation in it.

My own position on the OCC had been laid out long before that of Groll and Orzech and is available in the substance of the Chapter that follows. The reason I chose to respond to their original contribution is because, rarely as already pointed out, they do make a clear distinction between the OCC and the value composition of capital (VCC) – although hardly relating them explicitly to the rising technical composition of capital (TCC) that underpins each of them. We agree that the distinction between the OCC and VCC is essential

1 I place first in inverted commas because there is not a linear progression by time in Marx's published works so that 'later' versions of concepts by Volume or whatever may reflect earlier conceptualisations. See below.

HTTPS://DOI.ORG/10.1163/9789004766266-009

whereas the vast majority of the literature conflates the two conceptually and even terminologically (most commonly by using the VCC and calling it the OCC). But we disagree over how to distinguish between the OCC and the VCC. In a nutshell, for them, the VCC reflects short-run, cyclical variations in prices around the OCC, whereas for me the VCC rests at a more abstract and simpler level, see below.

Significantly, Groll and Orzech (1990) do respond to my critique but it can be hard to find as it is not indexed as such, appearing after and as part of my own reply to them. I was not offered the option of continuing the exchange. I do so below if primarily to bring to the fore the differences between us on the issues that matter (something I found hard to tease out but hope I have done so for others). Their response is a spirited and wide-ranging defence of their position – a complex mix of the new, some clarification and the muddy. Two common, general and overlapping issues are to the fore: what is Marx's position (and how and how much did it change) and what is correct. As Groll and Orzech observe, the first of these issues can be difficult to disentangle and, considering I am no Marxologist, I tend to leave it to others. For the second issue, however, I consider that it is the overall thrust of Marx's work and its relationship to his methodology in general and its application to political economy in particular that is paramount. It is also clear that Groll and Orzech tend to agree with this.

Early in their response Groll and Orzech suggest, as I do, p. 156:

> Fine argues that "Marx's definition of the distinction [between OCC and VCC] depends upon dynamics and the structural distinction between production and exchange." We believe that no such structural distinction exists in the Marxian model.

This borders on the mind-boggling – we cannot even get past whether production and exchange are structurally distinct from one another!

However, all is not lost. For we are told that what I take to be structural distinctions are those of spheres, "There is therefore no 'structural distinction' but rather a mutual relation between the spheres", p. 158. Emphasis is placed on the unity of these spheres as a totality. I have no quibble over this (the unity and the totality) and the only difference seems to be terminological – sphere versus structure. I would use them interchangeably if with a sneaking preference for structure (more general in 'shape' than sphere).

So, their rejection of my structures does not seem to be a major difference despite what is the misleading terms on which they do it. How they bring about their unity is, though, of significance and difference with me, best seen through their use of the distinction, prominent in my explanation, of "old" and "new" values. For me, the measure of the OCC is at old values since, confined within production, it is the mirror (to use Marx's expression) of the increasing TCC. If old values are not used, then the OCC will reflect not only the new value in the production under consideration but also all of the other values that are changing (reducing) throughout the economy (for both constant and variable capital). Groll and Orzech disagree on the grounds that the new value associated with the rising TCC is already established within production, "we argue that Marx introduces the changing productivity in the stage in which the new technique is introduced and that it is OCC which expresses the change", p. 159. I totally disagree, and there is a compelling and easy way to see why. For Marx surplus value is the consequence of the production process and, as such is not predetermined as it depends upon how much surplus labour can be extracted by length of the working day and intensity of work for example. As a result, the production of relative surplus value (which underpins the rising OCC) only establishes how much surplus value has been produced (at what lower values) after, not before, the production process has been completed even if before, embodied in commodity capital, entry into exchange.

So, for Groll and Orzech, incorrectly in my terms, the OCC is already the VCC before it leaves production. As a result, they are reduced to distinguishing between the OCC and the VCC as occurring exclusively within exchange itself, as already observed, "we translate the progressively higher OCC ('progressive development for the social productivity of labour') into progressive exchange conditions to correspond to the changing production conditions and their requirements. It is these requirements that are expressed by OCC, whereas VCC expresses the deviations from them", p. 159.

Now, and this is crucial from my point of view, this is not just a matter of definitions of at what point you measure and apply new and old values. For Groll and Orzech proceed as if the structures/spheres as a totality are immediate in their unity, happen simultaneously or, to put it more fairly and accurately, are realised smoothly in the translation from rising TCC in production to formation of OCC in exchange. This is not a matter of at what point values change (we agree on that and, for them as well as me, new values are established as soon as they are produced, no matter how they are measured) but is a matter of how those values are realised through time and motion across the spheres. Indicative of their approach is the following, "When they [compositions of capital] appear in distribution or exchange, they are expressed in terms of the socially necessary labor needed for their reproduction", p. 157. Now every Marxist political economist knows this to be incorrect if they take account of value form (as exchange value) let alone acknowledge the transformation problem. Values appear as exchange value not as socially necessary labour The very last thing to express changing compositions of capital is socially necessary labour (or value) – this is what is expressed not the expression. The expression of changing compositions of capital in distribution and exchange for me is the VCC (and this is not fluctuations around the OCC). It appears as if Groll and Orzech see the rising OCC as unproblematically realised within exchange leaving the VCC only for more incidental fluctuations within the sphere of exchange alone.

In short, as is made clear in what follows, for me, the distinction between OCC and VCC is made to indicate the structures and processes by which changes in production (and values due to rising TCC/OCC) are formed in exchange, and these are not immediate across the economy as a whole, unlike the changes in values themselves at the point of production within a firm or sector. This can be pinned down in some greater detail. As laid out especially well by Saad-Filho (2002), there is competition within a sector to establish individual values, but its impact upon the composition of capital in other sectors (and vice-versa) is contingent upon the (later) sale of the commodities produced as constant or variable capital. This cannot occur at the same time; it is sequential (and contradictory) into and within the sphere of exchange. Nor, of course, given the vagaries of exchange, can outcomes be guaranteed (as at most partially recognised by the distinction between OCC and VCC by Groll and Orzech as being exclusively confined to market fluctuations). So, it is not just a matter of timing but of those (denied) structures and processes through which, in my terms, the OCC becomes the VCC (with the two coinciding in the supposed "long run" for Groll and Orzech, an anomaly since the OCC is continually changing as is to be continually reflected in the VCC from my perspective – and there is no long run). As it were, the distinction between OCC and VCC is not made to reflect short-run deviations but the contradictions between them is the analytical key to the source of those deviations.

In other words, the effect of the approach of Groll and Orzech is to set aside the structures and processes by which the accumulation of capital is achieved through economic reproduction. It is as if none of these, and associated contradictions and tensions highlighted in Volumes 2 and 3, is of significance, with corresponding misinterpretations of the transformation and falling profitability (see other Chapters). And, by the same token, as with all the other literature that fails to distinguish OCC and VCC at all, within their reply the presence or not of absolute rent is deemed to depend contingently upon whether the OCC is lower in the agricultural sector rather than this being the result of accumulation in the presence of landed property (as a barrier to rising OCC as surplus would be appropriated as rent not profit).

## 1 Introduction[2]

Groll and Orzech's (1987) article on Marx's theory of the decline in the rate of profit brings to the fore the complexity of the treatment of the composition of capital in Marx's political economy. However, their ability to review previous discussion of this matter in a single page of text (their Appendix, note A) signifies the extent to which Marx's theory of the composition of capital has been not only misunderstood but almost entirely neglected.

In particular Groll and Orzech are to be congratulated for making clear that Marx distinguishes three compositions of capital: the technical (TCC); the organic (OCC); and the value (VCC). In the literature the distinction between the last two has been more or less absent. Most of Marx's analysis that has been the focus of attention has concerned OCC (as in the transformation problem and the law of the tendency of the rate of profit to fall). Indeed, VCC hardly ever figures at all – at least in name. For, paradoxically, VCC has more often been used under the name of OCC. Such a confusion follows from the failure to distinguish between VCC and OCC and has meant that the two have been used interchangeably, usually denoted by OCC (and C/V in algebraic terms – constant divided by variable capital). This implies a double confusion: over the substantive difference between the two compositions, and over the terminology employed. The two have been mixed up both in name and in content.

Groll and Orzech do not fall into these errors, and their own interpretation displays and employs a distinction between OCC and VCC that is extremely clear. TCC is simply the physical capital-labour ratio; OCC is this expressed in value terms; and VCC is the variation in the latter due to systematic (cyclical, for example), or, presumably, unsystematic variations in the prices of commodities (most notably, of constant or variable capital). This appears to link the distinction between OCC and VCC neatly to the structural separation between the spheres of production and exchange, respectively, although OCC does incorporate exchange relations insofar as they are not the consequence of cyclical or unsystematic price movements.

However, I will argue here that, although Groll and Orzech correctly recognise the distinction between OCC and VCC, they get it wrong. The next section reveals three major problems with their view. Following that, a critical appraisal is made of their interpretation of falling profitability, which is based on their (false) understanding of the distinction. Finally, I challenge

2 First appearing as Fine (1990a). I am grateful to two anonymous referees for many helpful comments which have been invaluable in my attempts to present difficult and fine distinctions as clearly as possible.

their idea that Marx changed his own views on falling profitability in later life and rejected the analysis in Volume 3 of *Capital* in favour of a final version in Volume 1.

The remainder of this section offers an alternative interpretation of the distinction between OCC and VCC as a background to the subsequent critique of Groll and Orzech. The implications of this alternative have been fully explored elsewhere (see the reference list and especially, Fine, 1983b).

Marx's definition of the distinction depends upon dynamics and the structural distinction between production and exchange, but in ways which differ from the interpretation of Groll and Orzech although it is to be welcomed that, at least, they recognise and attempt a distinction between the two. It is axiomatic in Marx's theory of production that as accumulation takes place, values will be changing through the production of relative surplus value (use of machinery to displace living labour). For Marx, VCC measures TCC in emerging values, the ones that will be established through exchange on the basis of the changing conditions of production. By contrast, OCC measures TCC on the basis of values prevailing at the time of production (without taking account of the change in values that this causes).

According to this definition, the separation between production and exchange is incorporated at an 'earlier' stage than Groll and Orzech suggest; for them, VCC expresses market disequilibrium around given values (even if these are changing). Rather, the process of forming those values is captured by the interpretation offered here, as a continual interaction between the prevailing and emerging values (not between values and their more or less appropriate expression as prices). This is prior to but does not preclude the cyclical or other variations in prices which Groll and Orzech seek to capture. In short, VCC captures the process of translating changing production conditions into changing exchange conditions rather than, as Groll and Orzech suggest, translating given production and exchange conditions into other exchange conditions. What is wrong with their approach?

## 2 The Composition of Capital Consistently Defined and Applied?

First, it is worth noting that Groll and Orzech do not consider that Marx modifies his definitions between the earlier and later works; with this I essentially concur. However, on that basis, it cannot be accepted that VCC has anything to do with relatively independent price movements. For, as the definition itself implies, VCC has to do with the values of the constituents of capital and so is defined independently of price movements. "For instance," Marx says, "certain work in copper and iron may require the same ratio of labour power to mass of means of production. But since copper is more expensive than iron, the value relation between variable and constant capital is different in each case, and hence also the *value composition* of the two", emphasis added.[3] Hence the value composition is definitionally unrelated to cyclical or short-term movements, as Groll and Orzech erroneously require.

Second, their interpretation is not consistent with the full range of applications of OCC (in Volume 3). For OCC figures centrally not only in two of the issues that Groll and Orzech mention – the transformation problem and the falling rate of profit – but also in Marx's theory of absolute rent, an application which they inexplicably fail to acknowledge. Elsewhere (Fine, 1979), it has been shown that Marx's theory of absolute rent proves entirely arbitrary and indefensible unless OCC is interpreted as reflecting production conditions prior to the formation of prices of production,[4] that is, prior to the interaction of production with exchange. This analysis cannot be reproduced here, but according to Groll and Orzech's interpretation of OCC, absolute rent would appear to have to be a short-term monopoly rent contingent upon market fluctuations, something totally at odds with Marx's theory.

Third, Groll and Orzech's interpretation is itself confused and inconsistent. To some extent this is veiled by their use of a variety of conceptual distinctions in which OCC is successively linked to the long run, the qualitative, the "producto-technical," the secular, and new values, while VCC is associated with the short run, the quantitative, market fluctuations, the cyclical, and market values. The issue is not the use of these terms as such but that they must be linked coherently to each other by reference to a well-defined and consistent understanding of the structure and processes of the capitalist economy.

It is not clear that this can be done on the basis of the simple "unity of opposites" Groll and Orzech suggest. For with the value system associated in the long run with OCC, this suggests that the process of value change through productivity increase is irrelevant for the cycle and the short run. Yet Marx's

---

3 He continues: "The value composition of capital, in as much as it is determined by, and reflects, its technical composition, is called the organic composition", as will be discussed below.

4 In particular, there is no way of explaining Marx's propositions that landed property may lead to a lower OCC in agriculture and a price of production that confines the level of absolute rent to the difference between it and the implied relatively higher value of agricultural commodities. Unfortunately, Groll and Orzech do not appear to be aware of the discussion of the compositions of capital in Fine (1979 and 1983b) and Fine (ed.) (1986).

theory of accumulation suggests continual productivity change and hence the necessary relevance of OCC for the "short run".[5]

More precisely, these confusions inevitably lead to a specific inconsistency around the understanding of the transformation problem. Groll and Orzech interpret this as follows, p. 597:

> The divergence of the market cost evaluation from the producto-technical evaluation represents for Marx the non-adaptability of 'production-relations' to the 'production forces.' Taken as a cumulative process, this lack of adaptability in the long run takes the shape of Marx's 'basic contradiction,' while in the short run it creates the so-called 'transformation problem'.

In other words, the transformation problem is a short-run problem dealing with the divergence of market cost (price?) evaluation from values. While there has been a longstanding debate over the transformation problem, at no time has it ever been considered to have anything to do with short-term cyclical movements. Even more significantly, if the transformation problem were associated with the short run, that would mean that it is, by Groll and Orzech's own account, concerned with VCC. But that is completely at odds with Marx's posing of the transformation problem, since that is done entirely in terms of the significance of differences in OCCs across sectors of the economy.[6]

## 3 Falling Profitability

Groll and Orzech's treatment of the falling rate of profit divides into three parts. The first, what they call the technical approach theory (TAT), is nothing other than the Okishio theorem in the simple case for which all commodities exchange at their values. They note the similarity in their Appendix, note B, but what they lack in generality, in assuming commodities exchange at their

---

5 In looking at the falling rate of profit, Groll and Orzech do integrate OCC with VCC in the short run. To the extent that this answers our criticism here it does, however, lead to inconsistency in their basic definitions of the differences between OCC and VCC. As it were, (long-run) OCC is changing over the cycle in the short run along with the VCC! I return to the falling rate of profit below.

6 I have argued (Fine 1983b) that the failure to distinguish VCC and OCC and the use of the former in the name of the latter renders most of the debate on the transformation problem irrelevant to Marx's own treatment. See also Carchedi (1984). Paradoxically, Groll and Orzech distinguish VCC and OCC but, in associating the transformation with the short run, assign to it the problem of prices for differing VCCs.

values, they interpret as a divergence from Okishio insofar as their interpretation is cyclical and for disequilibrium.[7] In light of the confusion revealed above, the status of such a claim is far from clear insofar as TAT is based on (long-run) OCC. Why exchange at values is the appropriate basis on which to explore cyclical movements is left unexplained.

Groll and Orzech's second approach focuses on the short-run, cyclical movements in the prices of variable and constant capital, what they call the value approach theory (VAT) in correspondence with their interpretation of VCC. Here, they first of all produce the (neo-)Ricardian/Okishio/Sraffa proposition that the rate of profit falls if wages rise. They also claim that the rate of profit falls if the price of constant capital rises, so that the rate of profit falls if both prices rise.

This cannot be so (in the absence of a financial sector to allow, in orthodox terms, for outside real balances). For as these are the only two prices in the economic system, if they both rise in the same proportion, then the rate of profit must remain unchanged, as it is a ratio of monetary quantities. Their mistake derives from the fact that surplus value is treated as some sort of constant magnitude as prices change.[8] But it too must be revalued. In the case of constant capital, for example, ceteris paribus, as its price rises what one capitalist gains another loses since they exchange with each other. Consequently, changes in the price of constant capital over the cycle which are not due to productivity changes have no direct effect on the rate of profit as a whole.[9]

The preceding paragraph may be based on a misunderstanding of Groll and Orzech. Marx himself, for example, argues (Volume 3, Chapter 6, section 1) that the rate of profit can fall if the price of constant capital rises, since anything that increases C in the formula S/C + V will decrease the fraction as a whole. But this requires that the increased price of C has only been calculated for those buying capital goods and not for those selling them (which would, however, decrease S to the extent that the increased cost of constant increases V).

7 The status of the Okishio theorem is a central aspect of the debate over Marx's theory of falling profitability. For an attempt to locate the Okishio theorem as the polar opposite of Marx in the context of disequilibrium in production and exchange relations, see Fine (1982). Like Okishio, Groll and Orzech yield the law of the tendency of the rate of profit to rise.

8 Groll and Orzech do appear to recognise this problem in their footnote 37 in "the case in which the price of the output moves in concert with input prices (and the rate of profit therefore remains unaffected), but all inputs are outputs at some stage in their life and changed prices mutually compensate between buyers and sellers."

9 Of course, this is not to suggest that price movements are irrelevant over the cycle, only that they cannot be the systematic initiating cause of a general crisis of profitability. In any case, their importance may be greater for their effects on the (here absent) financial sector and 'animal spirits' more generally.

More generally, the effect of the changes in the price of constant capital has to work its way through to the price of wage goods, V, as well (which equally would tend to decrease the rate of profit if wage consumption is maintained). The important point here, however, is that these issues arise systematically out of differing and changing OCCs across the sectors of the economy and are not problems arising out of exchange-based movements alone. Significantly, Marx's example is motivated by external factors on the price of constant capital, such as foreign trade and customs duties, neither of which is directly relevant to the issue of long-run or cyclical movements in the rate of profit arising out of the accumulation process.

The third approach of Groll and Orzech to the falling rate of profit is to combine the previous two. TAT, associated with OCC and, in light of their Okishio-type theorem, with rising profitability, is joined to the (questionable) VAT of VCC, which with increasing wages and other input prices relative to production costs, gives rise to falling profitability. Groll and Orzech then simply add the two effects together and assert that VAT dominates TAT and implies a falling profitability. This is to compound the confusion insofar as short and long run are being brought together unproblematically to yield a short-run theory.

## 4 Did Marx Reject Volume 3?

Groll and Orzech's theory of falling profitability is then associated with Marx's own (presumed) mature position as laid out in Chapter 25 of Volume 1 of *Capital*,[10] which is seen, together with their own 'law' of the machine (production), as rejecting the analysis of chapters 11 to 13 of volume 3. By their own admission, their evidence for this is flimsy: a later footnote to Volume 1 says little more than that larger capitals can individually make greater profits than smaller ones if they intensify methods of production rather than simply extend them.

However, in the context of Marx's theory of accumulation, this note goes less far than the law of the machine, which Groll and Orzech amply confirm to be present throughout Marx's earlier work. For the law adds that the labour costs displaced by machinery should be greater than the cost of the machinery itself. So, at the end of the day, the theory of Marx's rejection of Volume 3 depends upon his suddenly realising that what he had known all along required him to abandon a large part of his work. This seems most implausible given that Marx is required to embrace the analysis offered by Groll and Orzech, which has

10 Later editions of which postdate *Theories of Surplus Value* and Volume 3 of *Capital*.

itself been shown to be full of problems. It is more reasonable to accept that the distinction between the compositions is crucial but that Groll and Orzech have got it wrong.[11]

Thus, while Groll and Orzech appear to defend Marx by arguing that he ultimately corrected his analysis by throwing over much of Volume 3, an alternative view can be suggested. Marx does employ the distinction between VCC and OCC consistently across the whole of *Capital*, and this work represents a coherent unity rather than a process of development, rejection, and change.

11 In my earlier contributions cited here, it is shown that Marx's work does constitute a consistent entity across his 'mature' political economy throughout a range of applications in which OCC and VCC are distinguished. See Oakley (1983) for a bibliographical account of Marx's work which reveals the coherence across the three Volumes of *Capital* and the three Parts of *Theories of Surplus Value*.

CHAPTER 9

# Transforming the Transformation Problem: Why the 'New Interpretation' Is a Wrong Turning

## Postscript as Personal Preamble

In retrospect (and to a large degree at the time), the New Interpretation (NI) of the transformation problem can be seen to capture a number of general features of many contributions to Marxist value theory whilst adding a few wrinkles of its own. First, it seeks to prove Marx to be correct or at least to validate his analysis. Second, due to some degree of intellectual honesty, it finds this impossible to do without some degree of modification of Marx. Third, it appeals to value form analysis but does so through confining itself to a two-level analysis of value as the abstract at the top (or bottom, depending on which way up you see things) and price and profit as the more concrete/complex at the bottom (top), with no intermediate levels of conceptualisation. Fourth, effectively, it sees the transformation in terms of an equilibrium solution to the relationship between values and prices. Fifth, by the same token, the analysis is static, more specifically with the organic confused with the value composition of capital (see other Chapters), posing the transformation as static redistribution of surplus value for differing value compositions rather than (as for Marx) for differing rates of increase in productivity across sectors. Sixth, its own wrinkle (idiosyncrasy) is to focus upon aggregate identities between total value and total price and total surplus value and surplus profit (rather than seeing total price as the form taken by total value and total profit as the form taken by total surplus value). It proudly provides these identities through redefining the value of labour power ex post in monetary terms (even though Marx could not be clearer that the value of labour power precedes production and the extension of the working day beyond that value is the source of surplus value prior to any further exchange taking place). Seventh, otherwise, it is far from clear what real problems, structures, processes or features of the capitalist economy are captured by the NI as opposed to posing an artificial solution to an artificial problem.[1] Last, and by no means least, and unsurprisingly, the consequences

1 The same is true of the temporal single-system interpretation (TSSI) of the transformation. In what world do we have an iterative sequence of adjustments to (equilibrium) prices whilst all else remains the same. In other words, the analysis is static apart from an ideal sequential

HTTPS://DOI.ORG/10.1163/9789004766266-010

are that the NI becomes a self-contained contribution with no further implications for the study of the capitalist economy in theory or empirically.

## 1 Introduction[2]

The New Interpretation (NI), previously known as the new approach or new solution to the transformation problem, has been the most striking development in Marxist value theory during the last two decades.[3] The NI is inspired by the 'Rubin school';[4] it draws on social rather than technical relations, and maintains that labour becomes abstract (and is socialised) only through the exchange of commodities with money.[5] Therefore, money is the immediate, direct and exclusive expression of abstract labour. The NI takes this view one step further, arguing that such representation of value by money prevails at the level of (some of) the aggregate magnitudes of the capitalist economy.

This interpretation is appealing for those committed to value analysis for several reasons. First, it has links with the previous value debates, especially through the Rubin school and the transformation problem. Second, it is supportive of Marx, retaining value as an underlying abstract and, in some respects, causal category. It preserves, with some modification, key properties of Marx's transformation (ever perceived to be the Achilles heel of value theory), especially the aggregate equalities between price and value (of net produce) and between profit and surplus value. Third, it seeks to put value theory on sound technical foundations, that were perceived by many to have been shaken by 'errors' in Marx's transformation. Fourth, it incorporates money into the analysis, where previously for the transformation problem it had been notably absent, other than as a gold sector setting absolute prices. Fifth, it has inspired concrete analyses, forging an empirical connection between Marx's theory of exploitation and profits and wages.

This paper reviews the analytical foundations of the NI in order to clarify its methodological implications in the wider context of alternative approaches to Marx's value theory. This is not simply a disinterested service to the reader.

construction of value to price adjustments over an artificially created sequence through time. For some coverage of the TSSI, and its critics, primarily leaving aside the point just covered, see Potts (ed.) (2015).

2 Originally published as Fine et al. (2004).

3 Seminal contributions include Duménil (1980, 1983–84 and 1984), Foley (1982, 1983 and 1986) and, at a later stage, Lipietz (1982, 1983 and 1984).

4 Rubin (1975 and 1978); see also Aglietta (1976) and de Vroey (1982 and 1985). For a critique, see Saad-Filho (2002, ch. 2).

5 Note the resonances with Kincaid; see Chapters 5 and 6.

We believe that the NI's intention of re-asserting the social foundations of the labour theory of value, while disposing of the transformation problem and deriving empirical macroeconomic results, is valuable. Nevertheless, the NI is highly questionable from perspectives other than that derived from Rubin. This is demonstrated through detailed criticism of its structure and content, especially its conceptualisation of the value of money and the value of labour power, and the sequencing and dynamics of the capitalist economy.

We show, moreover, that the NI precludes consideration of a range of issues that are vital to radical political economy. That is not to suggest that the complex factors impinging upon value formation, for example through accumulation and technical change, cannot be introduced into the NI. They can, but only after aggregate value and price relations are posited without reference to (the already assumed) value theory. Put differently, the NI collapses the capitalist economy into a simple, two-level dialectic of value and price, mediated by money. Further analytical progress could be achieved, such as developing an account of capital as a structured and dynamic system of accumulation, but only independently of the NI's own contribution. For the latter, one of the most complex outcomes, i.e., price formation, is already pre-determined. Our general conclusion is that the NI is to be welcomed for the issues that it raises, but not for the manner in which it has dealt with them, for which we offer alternatives. In each case, there is a difference in method, with our emphasis being upon the progressive dialectical movement from more abstract to more concrete and complex economic categories, in contrast to the more immediate movement between value and exchange value in the NI.

This Chapter is structured as follows. Section 2 presents a formal summary of the NI demonstrating the significance for it of the labour expression of money (LEM), of reliance on the net product, and of the peculiar definition of the value of labour power. Section 3 criticises the NI concept of the value of money, suggesting that it obscures the real processes underlying determination of prices and the role of money. Section 4 critically reviews the NI concept of the value of labour power, and argues that NI (as well as Sraffian) views are insufficient to explain its determination. Section 5 reviews broader methodological issues surrounding the NI, in terms of its capacity to contribute to an understanding of accumulation and crises. Finally, section 6 offers a conclusion in terms of value theory as an alternative rather than as a complement to the NI.

## 2 The NI: A Simple Formal Presentation

The NI, by virtue of its origins in the transformation debate, has been heavily associated with elaborating the relationship between values and prices. But, as is now fully recognised, the NI is not concerned with individual values and prices. The point can be simply captured by presenting the NI through a set of equations that are totally independent of individual values and prices, with two exceptions, those of labour power and money.[6]

This is important for understanding what are taken to be two critical equalities in Marx's presentation of the transformation of (surplus) value into (profit) and prices of production – that total value equal total price AND total surplus value equal total profit.[7] In general, the (critical) literature has stumbled over whether both of these equalities can hold in general without inconsistency. An apparent virtue of the NI is to allow them to do so. It is important, then, to see how this is achieved in the NI.[8]

Assume total profit (P); total net revenue, total revenue minus non-wage costs, (R); money wage rate, (w); total amount of living labour, L; total surplus value, S; and the ratio L/R (the LEM, symbolised below by m). Three equations follow immediately: profit is net revenue minus wages; surplus value is living labour minus the value represented by wages; and the value of net product equals living labour:

$$P = R - wL \tag{1}$$
$$S = L - wLm \tag{2}$$
$$Rm = L \tag{3}$$

Equation (3) implies that the labour-equivalent of the money value of the net output equals total living labour. Although this equation is a tautology, given the definition of m,[9] it is taken by the NI to be the analogue of Marx's proposition that total value equals total price (though applied to net rather than gross output). Multiplying equation (1) by m, and substituting for Rm from (3) gives:

$$Pm = L - wLm \tag{4}$$

6 To the best of our knowledge, such a simple formal presentation is novel within the literature, since it leaves aside sectoral equations. For the record, the original draft of this paper preceded the more recent papers of Foley (2000) and Duménil and Lévy (2000).

7 This paragraph has been added for clarity for those less familiar with literature on the transformation, taken for granted in the original.

8 Note this is not a problem for us as aggregate price (of production) is understood as the aggregate value in price form and, by the same token aggregate profit as the form of aggregate surplus value. Accordingly, the aggregates are preserved even if their forms are transformed – from aggregate (surplus) value to aggregate (profit) value.

9 We thank Gary Mongiovi for pointing this out.

In other words:

$$S = Pm \tag{5}$$

Profit is the money form of surplus value, as claimed by Marx's other proposition. Thus, it appears that value theory has been vindicated, since both of Marx's much-disputed propositions in solving the transformation problem can be made to hold in a completely general framework.

The reason why the above presentation of the NI is simpler than others in the literature (e.g., Lipietz, 1982; and Mohun, 1994) is that it makes no reference at all to *individual* values, prices or production conditions, which are 'an irrelevant detour' in specifying the analytical content of the NI. In other words, first, the NI is compatible with any set of pricing equations, whether based on equalised rates of profit across sectors, (as is standard in most treatments) or, indeed, any other pricing principle, as long as these satisfy (1) to (3). In spite of this, much of the related literature is concerned with different pricing models, and these can be generalisations of the Sraffian approach to take account of, for example, joint production (Ehrbar, 1989), imperfect competition (Reati, 1986), and value-price ratios for any pricing system (Szumski, 1989 and 1991).

Second, by implication, the NI does not involve a solution to the transformation problem or, to put it another way, it is compatible with any pricing solution. It is simply an "Interpretation" whose formal content is a tautology arising out of the way in which the LEM (or the value of money, L/M) and the value of labour power (wL) have been defined. Here we appear to be pushing against an open door as far as the proponents of the NI are concerned (Foley, 2000, p. 20):

> In the late 1970s Gerard Duménil and I, independently of each other suggested a reconstruction of Marx's labor theory of value emphasizing the relation between money and labor time that preserves the rigorous quantitative relation between paid and unpaid labor on the one hand and the aggregate wage bill and aggregate gross profit ... on the other. This approach was rather uninformatively described as the "New Solution" to the transformation problem, and, after Duménil's observation that it actually abolished the "transformation problem" as such, and thus was not really a solution to anything, equally uninformatively as the "New Interpretation."[10]

10 See also Duménil (1984, p. 347).

Similarly, Mohun (1994, p. 407), whose article offers a particularly clear presentation of many of the issues, recognises that:

> Clearly there is an infinite number of conceivable price systems compatible with this understanding of theory, each price system being a different redistribution of labour-times, and each a price representation of abstract labour, or a form of value.

Nevertheless, his own exposition descends to the level of individual values and prices (if not production conditions) even though this is entirely unnecessary as such given any solution is compatible with the aggregate equations and equalities.

Despite being neutral with respect to pricing (other than aggregate conditions), the NI is not without economic content, for it includes an implicit understanding of how the workings of the capitalist economy should be analysed (see section 5). Indeed, our most telling methodological comment upon the NI is its *immediate* identification of production categories (labour and value) with those of exchange (wages, profits and money). This explains why Duménil (1984) has been so savage in rejecting Lipietz's (1984) suggestion that the NI is compatible with the Sraffian solution where the wage is based on a given bundle of goods.[11] As is apparent from equation (2), the value represented by wages is derived from a monetary magnitude (subject to a conversion factor, the LEM or value of money, see section 3). This is incompatible with the view that the value represented by wages is given by the value of a certain bundle of goods, showing that the NI has important implications for the understanding of the value of labour power (see section 4). In short, as will be shown below, the NI is not analytically neutral in method and theory despite merely manipulating definitions to preserve Marx's aggregates for values/prices and surplus values/profits for the transformation. As such, it is open to the criticisms that follow.

## 3 Value of Money

The definition of the value of money by the NI (the inverse of the LEM) provides a theoretical instrument for the ex post transformation of monetary quantities into value equivalents, especially of wages into the value of labour power. This section shows that, by defining the value of money in this fashion,

11 The same ferocity is also directed at Szumski (1991) by Duménil and Lévy (1991).

the NI precludes analysis of the process of determination of the value of money and its interaction with other socioeconomic factors.

Traditionally, in Marxist analysis, a money commodity (e.g., gold) is assumed to exist, whose unit value, $\lambda^g$, is determined by the labour time socially necessary to produce it (other forms of money are discussed below). The value of gold plays an essential role in expressing abstract labour time embodied in the output as price. However, unlike the LEM, the role of gold in price formation is neither immediate nor direct, but rather mediated by several economic factors, two of which are especially important.

First, if we assume homogenised labour across the economy, the value of gold is determined by the material conditions of its production, including the value composition and turnover rate of gold-producing capital.[12] Differences between the value composition, or turnover rate, of the gold industry and of those for the rest of the economy create a discrepancy between the 'intrinsic' value of the monetary unit and its expression in circulation. For example, if the value composition or turnover rate of gold-producing capitals are above average, commodity values are expressed in prices generally lower than those prevailing when value composition and turnover rate are below average. Therefore, it is wrong to express commodity values directly as price by simply multiplying them individually by $1/\lambda^g$ – the value of the money commodity does not operate identically with the LEM.[13]

Second, two attributes of money in the sphere of exchange are fundamental to the way in which it mediates the expression of value as price, its quantity (M) and velocity (V). If we assume that the entire gross output is sold for money (no trade credit or financial transactions), the relationship between the monetary aspects of exchange, the material and value aspects of production, and the price aspects of exchange is given by:[14]

$$MV = \frac{\lambda . x}{\lambda^g} = p.x \tag{6}$$

where $\lambda$ and p are the (1xn) value and price vectors, respectively, and x is the (nx1) gross output vector.

12 For discussion of the content and analytical significance of the differences between homogeneous, abstract and normalised labour, see Saad-Filho (2002).

13 This is clearly explained by Foley (1982, pp. 39–40). See also Lapavitsas (2000) and Saad-Filho (2002, Chs 5 and 7).

14 Lapavitsas (1996 and 2000); see also Lavoie (1986).

Any interpretation of value theory must provide an explanation of the relationship between monetary and 'production' factors in the expression of output value as price. Marx, as is well-known, rejects the quantity theory of money (QTM), on the grounds that the material and value characteristics of production determine the monetary and price aspects of exchange. With velocity assumed fixed by institutional, historical, and geographical factors, Marx presumes that the quantity of circulating gold is constantly readjusted, through hoarding and dishoarding and the production of gold, in order to conform to the shifting material and value characteristics of production, the latter also dictating changes in prices. Hoarding and dishoarding are concrete ways in which money mediates the expression of the value of aggregate net output as price, and allow it to happen in accordance with the material conditions of production. If, for example, gross output rose, all else equal, the resulting increase in $\lambda.x$ would be expressed as an increase in p.x (p unchanged) through an increase in M, the latter elicited from hoards. In contrast, for the QTM a rise in x would lead to an increase in $\lambda.x$ but there would be a fall in p exactly compensating the rise in x, since M would have remained the same (no hoards supplying an increase).[15]

This simple example shows that money's functions and the institutional framework of the monetary system are concrete ways in which money mediates the expression of value into price for output as a whole. It is misleading to assume that money can express value as price directly and without mediation: the monetary regime matters greatly, even under our extraordinarily simplifying assumptions. In the example used above, if the monetary regime allowed M to be appropriately adjusted, the increased $\lambda.x$ would leave individual prices unchanged; if, on the other hand, the monetary regime prevented M from changing, individual prices would fall. The same value of output would be expressed as higher total price in the former case and unchanged in the latter. Had we measured the LEM after the event (assuming that net output behaved identically with gross), it would be unchanged in the former but higher in the latter. But the difference would contribute nothing to our understanding of the process of expressing value into price.

It also follows from equation (6) that there is a complex relationship between, on the one hand, the value of the money commodity, $\lambda^g$, and on the

15 Readers familiar with the history of economic thought will recognise here Ricardo's (1951b[1816]) analysis of the price implications of a rise in the volume of commodities in circulation. Since our presentation uses vector terms, there are some inevitable problems of interpretation of expressions such as 'rise in x' or 'rise in p'. The economic conclusions are, however, clear.

other, the ratio λ.x/p.x, that is the value commanded by units of money in exchange (which is exactly analogous to the LEM in this context). Analysing the relationship between these two values depends on assumptions made about money's functions and the monetary regime. In the example above, when the Quantity Theory approach is adopted, the value commanded by gold appears to rise while value embodied in gold remains the same.[16] Such a disparity has important implications for monetary theory. It means, for instance, that capitalists who happen to find themselves in possession of large amounts of the money commodity, as well as capitalists who produce it, make windfall gains, while capitalists with payments obligations make corresponding losses. The characteristic conclusion drawn by the Quantity Theory in this case, namely that there will be imports of the money commodity, can be understood as a particular resolution for the disparity between these two values of money.[17] If, on the other hand, the Quantity Theory is rejected, neither the value commanded by gold nor the value embodied in it appears to change. But for that to be the case, a very different functioning of the monetary system and of its articulation with accumulation has to be postulated, one that relies on regular money (dis)hoarding.

It is misleading, then, to assume, as the NI does, that money directly expresses the value of output as price and without mediation. As already noted for the above example, had we simply measured the LEM before and after the event (assuming that net output behaved identically with gross), it would be unchanged in one case but higher in the other. This calculation, based on the definition of the value of money simply as the value commanded by money in circulation, detaches both money and its value from the monetary and financial processes that link money to the general movement of capital accumulation. How deeply unsatisfactory that is becomes obvious when non-commodity forms of money are considered, such as credit money and state fiat money. The functions of these forms of money in and out of the sphere of circulation, especially hoarding, cannot be taken for granted but must be analytically (and historically) elaborated. Analogously, analysis ought to be undertaken of the mechanisms and institutions (the monetary regime) through which the circulating quantity of these forms of money is determined, for which the NI is hardly useful, if not assuming away the issues involved in adopting an as if

16 As Marx (1987b, pp. 403–409) pointed out in discussion of Ricardo's analysis of the interaction of gold and commodities in the sphere of exchange.

17 For a full analysis of this process in terms of the intrinsic and the exchange value of the money commodity, see Lapavitsas (1996 and 2000).

perfectly functioning and rigid relationship between the production and circulation of (surplus) value as (profit) and price.

For the circulating quantity of state fiat money, for instance, retains an arbitrary element to the extent that the state can manipulate it. In contrast, the quantity of credit money is determined largely through the operations of the credit system and their interaction with the process of real capital accumulation (especially the advance and repayment of loans). Furthermore, given the proliferation of the forms of credit money, there could be differences of determination of quantity among banknotes, deposits, bills of exchange, share trust accounts, and so on. Thus, the processes and relations through which non-commodity forms of money come to command value in circulation differ qualitatively and quantitatively for each of these forms, as well as between each of them and commodity money (if one exists and is operative in exchange).

It is intuitive that such variations in the mediating role of money could have significant implications for the expression of the value of output as price.[18] If the value commanded by money in exchange depends on the functioning of the monetary regime, it is very important to establish its precise relationship with the value embodied in the money commodity (if one exists). Divergences between the value commanded by money and the value embodied in the money commodity, for example, are unlikely to be eliminated by purely monetary processes. Sudden disruptions of exchange, monetary crises, recessions and fully-fledged economic crises, in which the money commodity could play an important role as means of payment and means of hoarding, are some of the turbulent ways in which money in practice mediates the expression of value as price.[19] Political economy ought to be able to account for sudden and forcible realignments of the value of money. If the value of money is defined in aggregate as in the NI, it is a definition that must be discarded as soon as the real processes of capitalist accumulation are addressed rather than being set aside for the convenience of the NI.

In this respect, the NI could not be more deficient. Foley (2000, pp. 21–2) states that:

> this definition of the monetary expression of labour time [MELT, the inverse of the LEM] … does not depend on any assumption about the

18 A fuller analysis of these issues along lines suggested here can be found in Itoh and Lapavitsas (1999, ch. 2); see also Lapavitsas (2000).

19 Marx's (1987b, pp. 391–417) analysis of pure price inflation can be interpreted in this way. He shows that reconciliation between the value embodied in, and the value commanded by, money is neither a smooth nor costless process. Moreover, it is a process that may have important distributive implications.

> particular monetary system operating in the economy. In particular, it works well for a commodity money system like the gold standard, or for state-credit based monetary systems like those of the late 20th century. This point underlies the fact that the *definition* of the monetary expression of labor time in this way does not commit us to any particular theory about the *determination* of the MELT ... [the] determining mechanisms are quite different, but in each case money can be viewed as functioning (in part) to express labor time quantitatively.

This does not go beyond tautology, as is revealed to some extent by equations (1)–(3), and is essentially orthogonal to value (as labour) theory. For the value of anything in money can be expressed by the inverse of the unit of the quantity of money with which it is priced. This sharply reveals the NI's exclusion of the real processes that establish the money form of value through hoarding, dishoarding, credit, etc. This separation of definition from determination is completely arbitrary, and the analytical power of the NI, in this respect, is negligible. Moreover, introducing these more complex factors after the NI has already been laid out is equivalent to rubbing it out and starting again with a new LEM, and then doing the same again and again as soon as an even more sophisticated approach is taken to the monetary/financial system and its interactions with the accumulation and circulation of both capital and commodities (including money).

In short, the NI can be interpreted as constructing a theory of money (and hence of the monetary expression of value) purely for its own convenience in resolving the transformation (as it perceives it) and its two aggregate conditions. As a result, the nature, forms and functions of money are set aside as if all exchange is harmonious even before any consideration is given to the complexities of the forms of money as capital.

## 4 Value of Labour Power

We have shown, in section 2, that for the NI the value of labour power is given by transforming the monetary payment of wages through the LEM, while surplus value is the value left over from living labour after the deduction of this value represented by wages. Alternatively, the value of labour power is the worker's share of the net product, while the rate of exploitation measures their inability to command the entire net product. This definition diverges from that traditional conception, in which the value of labour power is given by the value of a fixed bundle of wage goods, usually justified by reference to 'social, moral, institutional and historical' factors.

The difference between these two definitions is significant. They are appropriately, if not always, seen as being mutually exclusive because they represent different ways of understanding how the workers are remunerated.[20] The fixed bundle of wage goods represents the value of labour power in advance in these but not monetary terms; in this case, the money wage is determined only after prices have been established. This approach can be criticised on three grounds. First, it leaves unexplained from where the wage bundle comes, how it changes with society, history and custom, and what if individual workers do not buy the standard bundle? Second, it implies that labour power is the only commodity to be purchased at its value after the transformation, which is arbitrarily unjustifiable theoretically – other than as a device to suit the goal of satisfying the two aggregate equalities between surplus value and profits and net value and prices. Third, it induces a conflation between the workers and the goods they consume. In this case, it is arbitrary to suppose that workers are exploited, because the model leads to identical results if corn, iron or energy are considered to be 'exploited' in place of labour.

In contrast, the NI definition is *ex post*. The value commanded by labour power varies with the price system, only grinding out a corresponding quantity of labour time after production and exchange have been completed, and prices and working class consumption established. This approach is seductive, both because it avoids the limitations of the traditional analysis, and because it corresponds to actual processes in the capitalist economy, specifically, that wage bargaining is undertaken in money terms. However, the NI definition is limited in two important ways. First, no direct account is taken of social and historical elements in the value of labour power, other than the shifting balance of forces between capital and labour; for example, how does the money wage relate to the economic and social reproduction of the workforce, of which the customary standard of living is one component?[21] Second, the value represented by

---

20 See Bellofiore (1989), Foley (1982), Gleicher (1989), Laibman (1982), Lipietz (1982) and Mohun (1994). For Duménil (1984), the money approach to the value of labour power is essential for the NI, and it is incompatible with the Sraffian solution for prices. Duménil and Lévy (1991, p. 363) assert their position most clearly: "The rate of exploitation must be assessed in terms of redistribution value. The specific bundle of commodities that workers buy from their wages is irrelevant … The issue is that of the potential purchasing power of their product, i.e., of the total net product which they created. This is equivalent to saying that the rate of exploitation must be determined in nominal terms, whereas the conventional measure of exploitation refers to labour originally embodied in the bundle of commodities that workers buy."

21 See Wells (1992) for the idea that the value of labour power is ground out by a combination of the roles of the state, households and consumerism.

wages bears no relation to the value of the commodities consumed, given that prices and values diverge from one another.[22]

These limitations arise because the NI leaves undefined the relationship between the value of labour power and the value of other commodities. This raises the question of the commodity character of labour power itself, with potentially destructive consequences for value theory. Moreover, the NI cannot probe beyond one of the effects of exploitation, the inability of the workers to purchase the entire net product.[23] This is the same aspect of exploitation emphasised by 'Ricardian socialist' economists in the early 19th century, and derided by Marx as being an insufficient explanation of capitalist exploitation (Saad-Filho, 1993).

The analysis above shows that both interpretations are riddled with contradictions because they seek to translate the value of labour power directly into a concrete outcome. They are, in fact, flat mirror images of one another, each failing in its own way to acknowledge that the notion of value of labour power is not appropriately attached initially either to a quantity of money or to a quantity of goods. The direct relationship between the value of labour power and a quantity of either goods or money, in these approaches, precludes an account of how the value of labour power is determined except by external agency (non-market custom or market wage conflict, for example). The special nature of the commodity labour power – which is neither capitalistically produced nor reproduced directly – allows for both interpretations, but neither for a choice of both nor a synthesis between them, as they are mutually exclusive.

In our view, the value of labour power should be understood as a simple abstract concept; as a *value* rather than as a use value or exchange value magnitude, whose more complex form as money wages and commodity purchases is constructed out of the historically and socially specific consequences of accumulation. Fine (1998a) has developed this understanding of the value of labour power in some detail in the context of labour market theory. Its constituent elements are reported here insofar as they bear on the positions adopted around the NI.

First, the value of labour power is neither a quantity of money nor goods, but a quantity of *value*. The value of labour power is determined at the aggregate level through the exchange between capital and labour as a whole (i.e.

22 Foley (2000, p. 30) concedes this point: "Saad-Filho [1996] persuades me more by his criticism of the New Interpretation for being excessively reductionist ... I think this criticism has some merit. For example, there may be a real role for a concept of the value of labour power independent of the *ex post* realised wage share in a fully developed Marxist theory."

23 See Foley (1982, pp. 42–43 and 1986, p. 15).

as social classes), prior to the process of production. This is because, at the most abstract level, advancing the value of labour power is a precondition for the production and realisation of surplus value and, subsequently, the performance of labour and exploitation in production. Second, one of the consequences of accumulation is to raise the level of productivity through the production of relative surplus value. This has two effects. It tends to raise the rate of surplus value and lower the value of labour power (through providing wage goods with less value expended), but it also tends to increase the commodities that can be purchased with a given value of labour power as wage goods are cheapened. Thus, the accumulation of capital on the basis of a given value of labour power tends both to redefine (lower) the value of labour power and (increase) the wage bundle.

So far, we might appear to be concerned with elementary propositions concerning the sharing of productivity increases between capital and labour. But this is to jump to an outcome, i.e., more money wage or more consumption, without examining the processes by which such outcomes are achieved, as is typical of the two unmediated approaches outlined previously. Third, then, there is an issue that cannot be addressed by either of the mutually exclusive standard approaches, namely how do new customary standards become established? A start can be made by recognising that consumption norms are differentiated between distinct sections of the population. They are not an average as such, even with some above and some below the norm. This norm is more appropriately understood in a more complex way; for the levels and incidence of consumption are determined as the outcome of continuing socioeconomic processes which grind out customary patterns of consumption. Fourth, what those patterns are and how they are determined is very different from one commodity to another. Food habits, housing, entertainment, and so on, are not only differentially consumed but the patterns and levels of consumption are the consequences of very different structures and processes of causation.[24] Nonetheless, each of these elements in the wage bundle is subject to change as a consequence of accumulation, with the exact outcome dependent upon the complex determination of the value of labour power across these constituent elements.

The previous paragraph can be seen as a critique of the wage bundle approach to the value of labour power. It has its counterpart in the critique of the money approach. For the value of labour power should not be seen as an average quantity of money, with some workers paid more and some paid less.

24 For a general argument along these lines, see Fine and Leopold (1993) and Fine (2002), and Fine et al. (1996) and Fine (1998b) in the specific context of food.

Rather, corresponding to the structures/structuring of employment, there are established patterns of remuneration both within and across enterprises, sectors and occupations. The value of labour power is the basis on which the accumulation of capital interacts with, and influences, such structures and payment systems, and overall levels and incidence of remuneration. Interaction and transformation occur through the socioeconomic processes explained, for example, in *Capital* – deskilling, reskilling, collective labour, formation of trade unions, and so on. The restructuring of labour markets, wages and conditions of service is the other aspect (apart from consumption) of the redefinition of the value of labour power at a more complex level.

In sum, we claim that the value of labour power as a determinant of the price system cannot be legitimately constructed independently of the contradictory tendencies associated with the accumulation of capital, for which a complex analysis ranging over the dynamic structures of both consumption and employment is a precondition. In a nutshell, the value of labour power is an abstract category whose more complex and concrete reworking depends upon addressing the specific nature of different commodities and the differentiation of the workforce. The NI, specifically, excises the mediation between the value of labour power and prices. By posing the value of labour power as a level of wages, the NI is guilty of chaotic abstraction in the ordering of concepts, as analysis moves between the spheres of production and exchange (and from abstract value to differentiated workers, consumers and objects of consumption). This is not a matter of the more complex variation of the value represented by wages around the value of labour power over time in accordance with, for example, balance in the labour market. Rather, it reflects a direct identification of the rate of surplus value with distributive shares between profits and wages rather than the dialectical building up of such distributional shares out of the more abstract categories attached to production and its shifting conditions with and within the accumulation of capital.

## 5 Structures, Sequence and Dynamics

As is implicit in the analysis of the value of money and labour power, one of the key characteristics of the NI is that it understands the capitalist economy in terms of a definite structure (production of value as opposed to its sale and purchase in exchange) and sequencing of activity across those structures. Whilst this might appear to be an elementary insight, it opens up the important consequence that, in contrast to most equilibrium approaches to the transformation problem, especially the Sraffian, the determination of values and prices does not take place simultaneously. For the NI, as was shown in section 4, the value of labour power is only determined in exchange after production has taken place, and after the money wage and the value of money have also been determined.

In spite of this important development for value analysis, the solution advanced by the NI forces an analytical wedge between variable and constant capital. In the absence of technical change, the NI preserves the value of constant capital in the passage from production to exchange, but the same is not true of variable capital. For the NI, the value of labour power is transformed because it contributes living labour that has to be evaluated after the event within exchange. Moseley (2000) has made this point the focus of his critique of the NI, claiming that it represents a major logical inconsistency. According to him, if the LEM were used to transform constant as well as variable capital there would be no analytical problem with the NI, and Marx's own transformation procedure in *Capital* would be confirmed as complete and consistent, p. 312.

Foley (2000, p. 24) acknowledges this difficulty and attempts to bypass it claiming that he is not averse to using the LEM to render "the money flow of purchases of intermediate outputs ... [into] the labor time equivalent of the flow of constant capital." However, he admits, pp. 24–5, that there is "[n]o plausible interpretation of the labor time equivalent of the constant capital or invested capital (since these measures will in general be equal neither to the historical labor embodied in the means of production, nor to the labor that would be required to reproduce them with contemporary technology.)"

The issue runs deeper than this (in)consistency within the NI. If only variable capital were transformed through division by the LEM, the homogeneity of the labour expended during production would provide a logical and real foundation for the analytical procedure adopted by the NI. However, the NI would be open to charges of inconsistency. In contrast, if the release of dead labour during the same period were also transformed using the LEM, severe problems would emerge in spite of Foley's conciliatory statements. There is no logical or economic reason for treating labours expended at different periods in the past, in the several vintages of constant capital that have passed into the value of the current output, as immediately, directly and generally equivalent with each other, as well as with labour expended in the current period, via division by the ratio of the flow of living labour to the price of current net output.

Deploying the LEM would completely disregard the real problems of achieving equivalence between dead and living labour. This is one of the most profound problems of capitalist accumulation, and an endless source of disruption, upset and disequilibrium. Different vintages of capital influence the competitiveness of capitalist enterprises and affect their product price. Competition brings technical change, which leads to sudden readjustment of capital values through the cheapening of their elements as well as 'moral depreciation' (Saad-Filho, 2002, Ch. 5). These forcible and violent changes of valuation of capital are left entirely out of account when the value of constant capital is derived through the simple division of the price of constant capital by a value 'transformer'.

The NI's analytical choice of operation on the net rather than gross product is a direct consequence of its treatment of labour power. It claims that using the gross product would involve double-counting of constant capital on each occasion that it was passed through exchange from one producer to another (Duménil and Levy, 1991).[25] This is, however, simply a red herring. For the double-counting only becomes an issue because of the need for the NI to define value and price in aggregate and confront them with one another in determining, *ex post*, the value of money and the value of labour power. In that context, preventing double counting requires that only living labour be counted.

Attention to the issue of double counting has, in some respects, been both misplaced and misleading. For, much more important than the technical issue of double counting for unchanged values are the implications for the NI of changes in values during capital accumulation. In this case, the value of each commodity potentially changes in the passage from the purchase of labour power to the sale of output. Both constant and variable capital are devalued as commodities become cheaper: whatever the value with which they enter the production process, they could leave with a different value. In this respect, there is no distinction between dead and living labour, although only living labour adds new value.[26]

The misplaced focus upon the choice between net rather than gross product is a symptom of the NI's approach to Marxist political economy. In general

25 "What is redistributed in the economy is the value created during each period, i.e. the value of the net product of the period. In the aggregate, productive workers expend in a given period of time a certain amount of labour which defines the added value during the period. This value is embodied in the net product of the period. The redistribution of value ... must be interpreted on this basis, and not on that of the gross product of the period which leads to double-countings for inputs produced and consumed productively during the period or inherited from previous periods" (Duménil and Lévy, 1991, p. 363).

26 See Marx (1981, pp. 259–261). In other words, neither double counting nor the divergence of input values from their prices can be used legitimately either for or against the NI. Proponents of the latter tend, however, to seize the evidence that Marx recognised these issues as signifying his unwitting support (despite his unambiguous and frequently repeated stance to the contrary).

terms, the NI seeks to confront problems in economic theory in order to carry out empirical work. In contrast, we claim that political economy ought to confront real processes in order to appropriate them in thought. At a more specific level, the NI's methodological stance has implications for the analysis of the contradictions of accumulation. For the NI, structured and sequential re-evaluation is already incorporated within what is effectively a static economy. Consequently, the dynamics of accumulation can only be added by superimposition of transformed production conditions. The result is liable to be either a form of dynamic Sraffianism or a resort to post-Keynesianism: take one static model on the basis of given technology, confront it with another and speculate about their differences. Alternatively, take one model and change the distribution of income, the state of expectations or the structure of the banking system, and imagine the consequences. Analyses of this type are insufficient to explain the complex and contradictory tendencies attached to the accumulation of capital and how these are represented in and through exchange.[27]

Finally, the NI accepts that price is a relatively concrete expression of value. This carries the implication that analysis is pitched at the level of many capitals in competition (although the NI does not specify the nature of that competition). Nevertheless, across the NI there is a chaotic mixture of levels of abstraction. Some are pitched at the most concrete level since they hold for each individual capital, while others are derived at the level of capital as a whole, but often for the totality of exchanges, which only exists at the most complex level.

These points can also be addressed from the perspective of appropriate abstraction in the context of sequencing or moving over the circuit of capital. Equation (1) seems to imply that, for the NI, all forms of payment – sales, profits and wages – can legitimately be treated as if they were simultaneous (see below). This assumption may appear realistic for an individual capital, although the treatment of wage payments as simultaneous with commodity sales is peculiar.[28] In addressing capital as a whole, however, the situation is more complicated, because the revenues of all sectors of the economy should not, in general, be treated as if they were simultaneous. This assumption would, of course, involve a violent abstraction, since individual industrial cycles are

27 For contributions in this vein, see Ernst (1982), Bellofiore (1989) and Naples (1989) whose sequenced disequilibria, however, arise on the basis of given production conditions.

28 Note that the timing of payment is not so much at issue as the timing of the exchange. The purchase of labour power must precede production even if payment is made with a lag (although only accidentally relative to the selling of the commodities produced).

necessarily sequenced relative to one another. Similarly, equation (3) not only splits out living labour alone as defining the value represented by money, but it does so by collapsing what are necessarily sequenced labours into being simultaneous. In the case of living labour, further abstraction is required to strip away the constant capital that is also realised when commodities confront money.

The use of abstraction to render sequenced activities simultaneous is inevitable in any theory and, as such, is not objectionable. However, the NI involves chaotic abstraction. It moves seamlessly between value and price, and surplus value and profit, without regard to whether this conforms to the simultaneous movement from capital as a whole to individual capitals. Specifically, capital as a whole is restored at the level of the price system whenever this is convenient, even though the analysis has already moved to the more concrete level of individual capitals. The method of abstraction is also highly simplified with direct mediation between value and price, without the filling in of the intervening processes of determination. It is precisely such chaotic leapfrogging in abstraction that leads to the absence of the other considerations that we have brought to the fore – accumulation, technical change, the complex forms and functions of money, and the social and historical determination of the value of labour power (Gleicher, 1989).

In sum, the NI brings macroeconomic processes to an abrupt halt once the value of labour power has been defined through the wage revenue. In a capitalist economy, the value represented by wage revenue is transformed once again after it has been spent. In other words, the economy starts with production and ends with exchange before, presumably, starting with production again. However, the NI disregards this transition. The problems this creates are glossed over through reliance on aggregate static conditions, as in equations (1) and (3), and in the lack of concern with the complexity of how values are transformed into prices. As with other assumptions about what values get transformed, how and when, the exclusive focus of the NI upon the passage from production to exchange is arbitrary. While collapsing levels of abstraction across the value/price relationship, the NI fixes its sights on a sociology of exploitation in which selective aspects of Marx's procedure of transformation are subject to piecemeal (and arbitrary) survival.

## 6 Conclusion

Two important features of the NI have endeared it to its supporters. First, it appears to offer support to Marx, albeit in a modified way given the direct mediation between value and price and the substitution of net for gross product in the aggregate identity between net value and price. This only goes to show that appeal to Marx embodies a slippery rationale and needs to be handled with considerable caution. Second, because of its understanding of the value of labour power and the value of money, the NI allows, subject to data and conceptual refinement, for the immediate empirical measurement of Marxist categories not least because the rate of surplus value is construed to be identical to the ratio of profits and wages. However, once these measurements have taken place, it is far from clear what significance they have, since they omit the contradictory processes by which the complex categories give rise to the data (and the complex and concrete processes that have given rise to them).

This limitation arises because the NI deploys a notion of abstract and concrete, or essence and form, which has only two layers – value as the essence, and price as the form with nothing in between other than use of money. Translation between them is immediate and unproblematic, since using the LEM assumes that money represents value in a direct, unmediated, and ideally abstract manner, thus allowing the derivation of macroeconomic relationships. The neutrality of equations (1) to (3) with respect to price formation shows that the material structures, processes and relations through which value becomes price are largely irrelevant for the NI, except as far as (aggregate) quantitative outcomes are concerned. It is as if the simple elaboration of the commodity form at the beginning of *Capital* is sufficient to address wages and profits, without prior attention to the production, distribution and circulation of (surplus) value, technological change, conflicts over the labour process and their influence on accumulation, etc. In effect, the NI seems to imply that the bulk of the three Volumes of *Capital* are only marginally (and unsystematically) relevant for the analysis of how the social relations attached to labour become translated into price relations between commodities. However, to collapse the mediated expression of value as price into the simple division of the total hours worked over the price of the total net product is to dissociate the formation of wages and profits from the complexity and significance of the real processes involved. In a sense, the NI is a theory of the commodity form applied directly to the wage-profit relationship, without otherwise elaborating the laws of capitalist production.

The way in which prices are built up out of abstract labour is extremely complex and requires a theory that appropriates that complexity. Constructing such a theory is not simply a matter of gathering together all the factors involved. For they have to be ordered in relation to one another, and the abstractions employed should be justified by demonstrating that they correspond to material relations, structures and processes, rather than being ideal abstractions speculatively constructed in the mind to solve problems of their own, or others, making. Consistency requires that the more complex categories of thought reproduce the simpler categories at a more concrete level, rather than undermining them.

For, what is the point of a theory of value and price that takes no account of accumulation and of shifting productivity? How do we know that the NI, with its emphasis on redistribution as the means by which value becomes price, is compatible with what are, arguably, much more fundamental structures and processes within the capitalist system? Whilst some contributors to the NI literature seem to be uninterested in such questions, others tend to presume that their approach is compatible with a full analysis of accumulation although such compatibility is rarely, if ever, demonstrated in practice. Such a conclusion is strikingly illustrated by Duménil and Lévy (1993). Consideration of value theory is confined to an appendix of just two pages that bears no relationship to the remainder of their book, despite the coverage suggested by the title. In particular, their work includes the most abrupt and peculiar of dialectics, p. 48:

> The transformation problem is not a problem of the derivation of prices of production from values. The knowledge of values is not helpful in the computation of prices of production. Actually, the relationship between values and prices is fully independent from the fact that profit rates are equalized.

In this case, Marx's value theory is merely a sociology of exploitation, pp. 48–49:

> This does not mean, however, that the labour theory of value is irrelevant to the analysis of capitalism. On the contrary, it is crucial to the theory of exploitation … The capitalist mode of production is simply a new variant of a class society based on the appropriation of surplus labour … The concept of value is, thus, a necessary component of the theory of exploitation under capitalism, whose analysis was a primary purpose of Marx's work in *Capital.*

No other purpose is demonstrated for value theory.[29] Instead, as in other works within the NI, the dialectical mediation between value and price, which has been excised at the outset, is reintroduced after the event. That can take the

---

29 The same emphasis on value theory as confined to a theory of exploitation is explicitly revealed in Duménil and Levy (2000).

form of Sraffianism or the presumption that institutional and historical factors or state policy determine the price vector or other economic variables. The essentially exogenous nature of price determination allows more or less arbitrary attachment of a variety of economic principles, on the one hand, and the more or less direct estimation of Marx's aggregate value categories through national income statistics and input-output data, on the other.

Although the NI represents an important advance over Sraffianism, in which price and value are simultaneous concepts derived from conditions of production and distribution, whatever advance has been made carries a very heavy cost. Whilst raising crucial issues for value theory around the form of value, the value of labour power, the value of money, and the structure, sequencing and dynamics of the capitalist economy, the NI resolves none of them. Rather, it proceeds only by setting value theory aside and confining it to a (static) theory of exploitation.

CHAPTER 10

# Neither Equilibrium as Such nor as Abstraction: Debating Fred Moseley's Transformation

## Postscript as Personal Preamble

There is much to commend in Fred Moseley's Marxist political economy. But, even at the expense of sounding like a stuck record (and not for the first time, such is the nature of being a stuck record), I cannot condemn too strongly his association of it with (long-run) equilibrium whether in the context of the transformation problem or otherwise.[1] It is simply alien to Marx's methodology, method, conceptualisations, theory and concrete analyses. There may be a place for equilibrium in criticising its use by others from a Marxist perspective and from within their own perspectives, thereby exposing limitations and pointing to alternatives. But this cannot be the reproduction of reality in thought as is required by Marxism's own approach. More specifically, as I have endlessly insisted throughout this Volume, treatment of the transformation problem requires a proper distinction between the technical, organic and value compositions of capital without which it is reduced to a static problem of (equilibrium) value-price relations (however well-formulated) as opposed to value-price relations as productivity is changing (through production of relative surplus value).

## (Dis)Engaging Equilibrium[2]

*Capital* and other works of Marx are at no point based on equilibrium. This is my underlying difference with Moseley, and I take it to be an invisible thread running through methodology, conceptualisation, history, theory, conjunctural analyses and political economy. Those interpreting *Capital* through the

1 A case might be made for equilibrium if interpreted as a balance of forces in tension as opposed to a state of rest.

2 First published as Fine (2017d) in critique of Moseley (2017), but also Moseley (2016). See Fine and Saad-Filho (2026[1975]) for discussion of all points made in general, and also Fine et al. (eds) (2012), Fine (2012a) and Saad-Filho (2002). See footnotes for reference to my (joint) work on specific issues. Thanks to Alfredo Saad-Filho for comments. He remains responsible for all errors.

HTTPS://DOI.ORG/10.1163/9789004766266-011

prism of equilibrium can generate insight but it will be both limited and compromised by lack of dialectical understanding of the contradictory dynamics of capitalism.[3] Nothing could be more abstract than equilibrium but it is the enemy of Marxist abstraction.

Moseley makes much of abstraction. Yet it is not only dynamic but also not a simple thing. It involves a number of different elements. It does go from the abstract to the concrete, combining together in the proper order the influence of a cascade of many factors. But it does much more than this, moving from the simple (value, for example) to the complex (price). Abstraction, as the only road to science, can also involve specification of the structures of causation (what determines and explains what, and how); this does not necessarily coincide with movement from the abstract to the concrete nor from the simple to the complex (class struggle, for example, straddles all of these) (Fine, 2008). There are also different ways of ordering exposition (what do I lay out first, second, third …) and different ways of undertaking investigation (where do I start my analysis, restart and critically reconstruct as I proceed). Moseley seems to take abstraction as if one-dimensional, going up or down in a lift. At most he might be interpreted as two-dimensional abstraction, macro/micro and value/monetary. This allows him to bring abstraction and equilibrium together (although even this could be avoided) but the two are incompatible with one another for each of *Capital* and capitalism as totalities.

Yet, then, as Moseley rightly insists, capitalism is a single system, a totality. It is inconceivable for anyone to read *Capital* I closely, without coming to the conclusion that it is both micro and macro simultaneously and integrally so, and that there are different orders attached to the different types of abstraction deployed. *Capital* I begins with the commodity and money and derives capital and the production of (absolute and relative) surplus value with capitals in competition. Without the latter, there is no possibility of value being abstracted as socially-necessary labour time, SNLT, (since competition is the disciplining process that makes a reality both in production, as abstract labour time, and in circulation for which social use value is vital for exchange value).[4] In short, use of, or from, abstraction means developing increasingly complex categorisations, critically reconstructing those simpler concepts that began exposition and supplementing them both logically and historically (so that the commodity with which *Capital* I begins is very different by the time we end with *Capital* III, since it now incorporates surplus value as profit, rent

3 Moseley (2017) uses the term "long-run equilibrium" twelve times!

4 See Fine and Saad-Filho (2008 and 2009), and for the continuing imperative of value theory, Fine (2001b) and Fine et al. (2010).

and interest, as well as the impact of supply and demand, credit relations, and productivity-increasing, and crisis-inducing, accumulation).

These separate elements in abstraction are in part logical but they are not hermetically sealed, neither sequentially nor logically, and certainly not historically.[5] So you cannot put on your undergarments before your trousers (and you cannot even conceive of underpants before you conceive of pants) but ordering them can also be arbitrary from an expositional point of view (which I describe first bears no relation to the chronologies of robing and disrobing). These interminglings, and complexities, of the elements of abstraction could be laid out ad infinitum in all aspects of life. Wilkie Collins[6] moves from the murder to the identification of the murderer, whereas the suspected murderer is presented to the court at the outset. Exposition depends upon context and purpose although not thereby legitimately free to range without regard to logic and reality (no one put their trousers and underpants on at the same time without extreme difficulty).

We should not forget the dynamics of surplus value production in Volume I by moving to equilibria in interpreting Volumes II and/or III. In political economy, the 'actual' can only legitimately be the actual reproduced in thought. Nonetheless, thought can also create imaginary 'actuals' that can have an actual existence by way of exception. An individual can put their underpants on before their trousers as does the fictional Superman. But this does not make Superman anything other than fictional. It is what might be termed an actually empty abstraction, no worthier of consideration than whether garlic actually repels vampires. Thus, debating the positioning of Superman's underpants, does not make the fictional into an actual character, even if such an actual (fictional) Superman can indeed wear his underpants outside his trousers. Concepts have logical properties but, in political economy, they must be shown to reflect rather than to invent their object of study. So, wherever Moseley refers to actual he is unable to say the actual reproduced in thought because of his reliance upon 'actual long-run equilibrium' that can never be anything other than equivalent to a fictional Superman as opposed even to a real man pretending to be so.[7]

---

5 Neither the nature of value itself nor its forms are invariant, themselves being transformed in the passages from elementary exchange to contemporary capitalism (Fine, 1980b).

6 'Inventor' of the mystery novel and close friend of Charles Dickens.

7 Moseley (2017) uses the term "actual" 64 times, four of these attached to "long-run equilibrium"! Indeed, "In Marx's theory of the production and distribution of surplus-value in the three volumes of *Capital*, the actual capitalist economy is assumed to be in long-run equilibrium." This is surely incorrect.

Political economy involves not only identifying "levels of abstraction" (even upstairs-downstairs if you must) but also investigating logically and causally the forces and drivers of change, as well as countertendencies, the interactions of which drive the dialectics of contradictory complexity all of which evaporates with Moseley's appeal to actual long-run equilibrium. Even if long-run equilibrium can be interpreted as the natural price of classical political economy, it is a term derived from, and to be critically reconstructed. The purpose of *Theories of Surplus Value* is to tease out critically the implications of so-called (fictional) natural price for, necessarily partially, capturing the realities of capitalist non-equilibrium accumulation. On this, Ricardo is logically superior to Smith in commitment to a labour theory of value, but Smith is superior to Ricardo in seeking to understand the price form in the context of changing productivities and the growing division of labour, closely related to but different from changes in the organic composition of capital, see below.[8] At most, in scientific value theory, 'natural price' is the momentary value (defined by evolving rather than equilibrium SNLT). This is especially illustrated by what is happening to the price of electronic chips – with a natural as long-run equilibrium price. Not only is there never anything "natural" about any price (it is the product of specifically capitalist or other conditions), the very notion brings capitalism to an indefinite if imaginary halt, capitalism's total antithesis in practice. Unsurprisingly, it leads classical political economy into theories of the stationary state, a sort of end of history.

Note, however, Moseley's correct reference to, and even a section on, "Sequential determination" (if only he would interpret it as logical *and* historical and, correspondingly, contradictory). But, in his hands, this term essentially becomes vacuous since it is tied to long-run equilibrium, with the sequential merely formal (circular without change) and the determination non-existent (nothing changes to be determined in equilibrium other than equilibrium itself). Thus, "Marx's logical method ... is theory ... based on the logic of *sequential determination* of the key variables, not simultaneous determination (as in Sraffian theory and the Sraffian interpretation of Marx's theory)." But, contra Moseley, there is no antithesis between sequential *and* simultaneous determination, and the two can come together when tied to equilibrium as with Moseley (just as with our planetary system for example for which night follows day in sequential equilibrium)!

---

8 See below for compositions of capital but, otherwise, Fine (1982 and 1983b) and Milonakis and Fine (2009). In his book Moseley (2016) hardly surprisingly spends considerable effort to persuade that Marx is committed to natural as long-run equilibrium price.

Despite reliance on equilibrium, in addressing the transformation problem, Moseley is acutely insightful in insisting that inputs, i.e. constant and variable capital, do not need to be transformed as they are already value in money form when they are purchased with money capital advanced, thereby reproducing in thought that point along the actual circuit of capital.[9] This is sequentially followed by the production of surplus value (and the preservation of constant capital) but this is not a process within equilibrium. Subsequently, the transformation of values into prices of *production* and of the produced surplus value into profit is precisely this transformation and nothing more nor less. Neither aggregate value nor surplus value can be altered by the transformation since price/profit are the forms taken by them in exchange. The issue is to trace the real/actual manifest relations by which labour exerted under conditions of capitalist production are realised in exchange, something entirely different from equilibrium price-making. And, more specifically, the transformation is concerned with, is a process of abstraction of, one problem and one problem only (although many, many more processes do go into making market price); namely, what are the effects on the redistribution of surplus value produced according to sectoral differences in organic compositions of capital across sectors, see below. Or, to put it another way – by reference to the previously mentioned attempt by Smith to form a theory of price in context of a growing division of labour – how do differences in the rates of productivity change across sectors affect the processes of equalisation of rates of profit and price formation. Rather than addressing this 'problem', the descent into equilibrium is precisely the error into which Moseley falls, thereby departing from the benefits of his acute insight almost as soon as he has made it.[10]

Proper, not arbitrary, understanding of the (organic) composition of capital is key.[11] Significantly, in his article, Moseley does not mention the composition of capital at all, a rather bizarre reflection on his professed representation

9 Moseley correctly criticises the 'new solution' for arbitrarily transforming constant but not variable capital (although it does so to preserve in its own framing aggregate consistency across totals of price and value, and of profits and surplus value, respectively). This is wrong, as with nearly all treatments of the so-called transformation problem, because (like Moseley) it invents its own fictional problem, the finding of equilibrium prices, which has no attachment to the actual non-equilibrium processes of capitalist circulation *and* accumulation.

10 On the transformation problem, see Fine (1983b), Fine (ed.) (1986) and Fine et al. (2004).

11 Much Marxist economics defines the (organic) composition arbitrarily even in algebraic terms – c/v or c/(c + v) for example – for ease of mathematical manipulation, let alone conflating the value with the organic composition and using them interchangeably, as is only appropriate but vacuous in the fictional world of equilibrium where there is no accumulation and productivity is not changing.

of *Capital*. In a nutshell, there are three compositions of capital – the technical, the organic and the value.[12] With accumulation, the technical refers to the (changing) mass of raw materials worked up into final commodities by a given amount of labour power; the organic reflects this in the values in place at the time that capital is advanced (and so already in money form, Moseley's astute insight); and the value composition reflects the consequences of differential productivity changes across sectors in the formation of new levels of values (SNLT) and *not* the more or less valuable content of the raw materials as such. At this point, the transformation is not concerned with whether it is valuable gold or cheap copper that is going into production (such differences in value compositions are already accommodated in money form in capital advanced) but the impact of different rates of increase in productivity in gold- and copper-using industries (i.e. different *organic* compositions). This is the reflection of what happens in capitalism in conditions of competition within sectors (Volume I), and the transformation builds upon such macro/micro analyses of Volumes I and II for competition between sectors in the tendency for profitability to equalise between sectors (Volume III's transformation). It stands in sharp contrast to equilibrium treatments of the transformation 'problem' which see it in terms both of equilibrium and value, not organic, composition (with value compositions appearing at the beginning and end of the transformation as equilibrium prices, whereas Marx's transformation is concerned with prices of production derived from the dynamics of the accumulation of capital and correspondingly differentiated productivity increases across sectors).

In a nutshell, Marx begins with the value composition of capital in money (capital) form (correctly perceived in form if not in content by Moseley) prior to the transformation in light of its being sequentially followed by production with the latter's differing organic compositions across sectors.[13] The subsequent reformation of transformed (not equilibrium) value composition is part and parcel of the counteracting tendencies to the tendency of the rate of profit to fall (derived from rising organic compositions). The next step taken, then,

12 See Fine and Harris (1979) and Fine (1983b, 1990a and 1991).

13 I freely admit that, across his evolving work and conceptualisations, Marx is far from clear and consistent in conforming to the interpretation offered here (around the distinctions in the compositions of capital and their different impacts upon price formation – more or less valuable inputs for value composition, as opposed to more or less productivity increase across sectors for the organic composition). But, as Moseley closes, "I would hope that there would be no objection to such a reasonable reconstruction of Marx's theory, which would make the theory logically consistent and would make possible its further development."

from the transformation in Volume III is to address the law of the tendency of the rate of profit to fall and its counteracting tendencies. Each of these, properly understood, derives directly and necessarily from the accumulation of capital but the law is simpler (more abstract) than the countertendencies, and their contradictory interaction are still more complex, not least in giving rise to rhythms in the accumulation processes including crises. In this respect, the transformation is an essential step towards a theory of accumulation interrupted by crises, and not a tangential theory of equilibrium prices with no further implications.

Nonetheless, at the most abstract level at which it can be considered, the distinction between different forms of capital *in exchange* can, and must, proceed by abstracting from the transformation of values into prices – even though some commodities may be more sale- or loan-intensive than others (just as they can be more capital-intensive in production and/or in value of raw materials used). This is because one of the distinctions between commercial capital and interest-bearing capital is that the first is subject to the tendency to equalise profitability with industrial capital whereas the second is not. In this context, the extrapolated use of equilibrium prices would abolish this distinction (other than as a more or less temporary monopoly or premium for liquidity) and identify the rate of interest with the rate of profit, as occurs within much mainstream economics. In such an ideal world, rates of return would have to be equalised. The result would be that interest would be unable to be specified as a category distinct from profit, and the distinction between money as simple credit (used merely to buy and sell) and as capital (as an advance to appropriate profit) would be lost.[14] Whilst Moseley's account does not progress from the transformation to embrace the tendency of the rate of profit to fall, nor the distinctive role of interest-bearing capital, his equilibrium abstractions would be the severest of constraints in doing so – unless equilibrium could suddenly transform itself from a state of rest into the dialectics of accumulation.

There is, then, a seamless trajectory, that cannot be leapfrogged, between the accumulation of capital as derived from the production of surplus value (Volume I) and the contradictory forms it takes as a dynamic process as represented through Volumes II and III of *Capital*. For the latter, it is the circulation and distribution of surplus value as increasing productivity is derived (or interrupted by crisis). Thus, the transformation leads directly into the law of the tendency of the rate of profit to fall and the counteracting tendencies, with

14 This is key to the understanding of financialisation and its relationship to neoliberalism, see Fine (2010 and 2014a) and Bayliss et al. (2017) and Fine and Saad-Filho (2026[1975]).

both drawing upon the role of the organic (and, implicitly, value) composition. Most commentators address the two issues of transformation and falling profitability as separate controversies, but they are intimately related in terms of how rising organic compositions lead to tensions not in equilibrium prices but in the accumulation process. The division between profit of enterprise and interest can be derived without resort to consideration of the organic composition as such since it has no direct bearing on how access to finance for accumulation brings about differential rates of productivity increase (Fine, 1985–86, 1988, 2010 and 2014a).

But it is different with the less prominent but equally indicative theory of absolute rent where landed property intervenes potentially to dull accumulation and lead to rising organic composition, allowing for higher prices than would otherwise prevail in view of lesser productivity increase and appropriation of rent. Voilà space created for absolute rent out of lower organic composition as part and parcel of the theory of accumulation, consistent with all that has gone before (rather than arbitrary monopoly price) (Fine, 1979, 1980a and 1990b). Is it accidental that the transformation as equilibrium seems unable to address any of these issues, let alone crisis and, as such, is the end of political economy just as it is the end of history (what else is equilibrium)?[15]

The paradox of the equilibrium interpretations of the transformation is that they shoehorn into their own frame those other interpretations that do genuinely reflect, however partially, the dialectical logic of *Capital*.[16] They also become a self-contained object of analysis in their own right, thereby precluding satisfactorily taking theoretical, historical and conjunctural analyses further.

15 Note how Moseley's (outline of his) book has no coverage of these issues as they seem to be strictly orthogonal to his interpretation of the transformation (as macro/micro/value/monetary).

16 See Moseley's (2016) account of others as (wrong) equilibrium theorists or simply wrong, as for Fine and Saad-Filho, for not being equilibrium theorists at all.

CHAPTER 11

# Banking Capital and the Theory of Interest

## Postscript as Personal Preamble

Marx's theory of money and finance (and are these even the correct terms?) is extremely difficult to engage for a number of reasons. First, there is, dare I say it, the tortuous opening to Volume 1 of *Capital* in which we have an endless discussion of the various forms of equivalencies between commodities and between commodities and money.[1] What is that all about, and why does it have so little to do with what follows, at least in Volume 1 of *Capital*? The answers are that value is being related to the value form (in exchange or as exchange value) and, after that, the discussion is more or less confined to (surplus) value production, at least until we get to later Volumes of *Capital*.

Second, Marx's monetary theory is not just about the (monetary) determinants of price but involves a whole series of structures, processes, agencies and relations in traversing the production of (surplus) value to the value form. Relative to the varieties of what have now become orthodox approaches to money as its supply and demand, with finance almost serving as a separate field, Marx's theories of money and finance are integral with one another, something that can be counter-intuitive and especially for those more rather than less trained in mainstream economics.

Third, along these lines, a crucial distinction for Marx is between money as such, with all of its properties of means of payment, measure of price and store of value, and money as capital for which it is put to use to make more money. This distinction (for example, to borrow to make a purchase for consumption as opposed to borrowing to initiate an investment to make a profit) obtains both for the individual and for the economy as a whole if not necessarily in conformity with one another (as is acknowledged by Keynes paradox of thrift – the more you save as opposed to spend the less the economy invests, especially in context of unemployment).

Fourth, given the distinction between money as such and money as capital, there are different forms taken by each of them in the production and circulation of value. Much of Marx's monetary theory is based upon (gold as) commodity money but we now have all sorts of different monies and the means to

1 See Fine (2023) where it is suggested that a little elementary set theory on equivalencies would highly ease the formal side of Marx's presentation!

HTTPS://DOI.ORG/10.1163/9789004766266-012

deploy them, not least with the cashless economy, the credit card, the mobile phone, etc.[2] The range of financial assets is becoming even more bewildering, especially in the age of financialisation.

Fifth, Marx's own contributions reflect these increasing complexities with a proliferation of conceptualisations over the different forms of capital in exchange and the relations between them and with (surplus) value production and circulation. We need to finesse the differences across merchant, commercial, loanable money, interest bearing, fictitious capital, and more.

Sixth, within Volume 3 of *Capital*, these are all dealt with at greater or lesser length. But, the work is far from complete, with mixtures of theory, empirical observation, commentary upon others, and so on. Making sense of this material is extremely demanding.

Seventh, as a result of all of these factors, Marx's theory of finance tends to have been neglected, overlooked altogether, or dismissed as outdated. So, we do not have well-established traditions upon which to draw. Instead, bits and pieces of Marx's analysis might be picked up and married with contemporary empirical and/or theoretical developments. This is most obvious in the case of financialisation as a result of which the imperative connection between value theory and money and finance is lost (see debate between Christophers and Fine, 2020).

In the opening Chapter to this Volume, I have explained how I set about seeking to make sense of the three Volumes of *Capital* (and *Theories of Surplus Value*). I had already offered an overview in Fine and Saad-Filho (2026[1975]). What follows is a later and more extended treatment of some aspects of Marx's theory of money and finance.

## 1 Introduction[3]

The purpose of this Chapter is to outline the structure of Marx's theory of interest.[4] It covers a topic that is as important as it is subject to neglect. The current period of capitalism is characterised by all sorts of secular and cyclical monetary disorders but these are the most immediate and consequently the most complex of economic phenomena. Marxism has scarcely begun to

2 Significantly, it is part and parcel of Marx's monetary theory that a commodity money will be displaced by a symbol of itself (as paper money).

3 First appearing as Fine (1985–86).

4 I am grateful to Michael Ball, David Laibman and others for comments on an earlier draft. Reference to Volume III of *Capital* (London: Lawrence and Wishart, 1972b) is given by Volume number alone, e.g., III, p. 293, and similarly for Volume II for which only one chapter reference is made. Reference to the *Grundrisse* is to the Pelican edition (London, 1973).

understand what are the underlying determinants of these developments even if it recognises that their roots lie in the crises of capitalist production. This analytical underdevelopment has its counterpart in the relative absence of attention to Marx's own analysis of the movement of capital in the sphere of exchange.[5] Unfortunately Marx's views have rarely been studied in depth. This may reflect a belief that passages concerning, for example, "The Currency Principle and the English Bank Legislation of 1844" (Ch. XXXIV of Volume III of *Capital*) have little relevance for the capitalism of the 1980s. It may also be due to the fact that Marx's exposition in Volume III of *Capital* is the furthest from completion of any of the material contained within it, as is made clear by Engels' preface to the volume.

This last factor should not, however, be taken to mean that Marx's analysis is underdeveloped. Even if it were presented in its most perfect form, the exposition would remain difficult because of the different elements combined within it. These include the logical and structural characteristics of interest formation; the historically evolved conditions within which these are situated; conjunctural factors; and the criticism of alternative theories of interest determination. It is true that these are jumbled together in Marx's exposition as he is in the process of working out his own theory, but these elements are there and not in such a state of disarray as might appear at first sight.

## 2 Money and Merchant's Capital

One of the themes running through Marx's treatment of capital in exchange is that there is a crucial distinction to be made between money as money and money as capital. Money functions as money when it acts simply as a means of exchange between two agents, hence mediating commodity exchange, irrespective of the position of those agents in the circulation of capital as a whole whether they be capitalists engaging in production or capitalists and workers engaging in consumption. In other words, the role of money as money is understood by reference to the formula for simple commodity circulation, C–M–C. By contrast, money as capital is understood by reference to the individual circuit of capital, M–C … P … C–M', where money is employed for the specific purpose of producing surplus value. Now, there is a definite relation between the two functions, since the exchanges of simple commodity circulation and of industrial production are ultimately connected, most notably

5 For an elementary introduction to the structure and process of the capitalist economy as elaborated by Marx, see Fine (1975[2026]), where terms such as sphere of exchange, commodity capital, etc are explained.

when we recognise that C–M for one agent is M–C for another. Further, both the use of money as money and as capital can involve credit relations as money is lent and borrowed to perform the acts of exchange involved.

For Marx, however, the operation of money as money is seen as part of merchant's capital. Accordingly, it is necessary to begin with some comments on merchant's capital. Marx makes clear at the outset that his treatment of merchant's capital is an abstract one. In practice, the functions of trading and producing (particularly the ambiguous role played by costs of circulation and distribution in functions such as transport) are to some extent intermingled. There is, however, a tendency for a separation between the two functions and it must be reproduced in theory in order to comprehend the specific nature of merchant's capital which is the carrying out of exchange alone (III, p. 267–68):

> We have explained … to what extent the transport industry, storage and distribution of commodities in a distributable form, may be regarded as production processes continuing within the process of circulation. These episodes incidental to the circulation of commodity capital are sometimes confused with the distinctive functions of merchant's or commercial capital. Sometimes they are, indeed, practically bound up with these distinct, specific functions, although with the development of the social division of labor the function of merchant's capital evolves in a pure form, i.e., divorced from those real functions, and independent of them. These functions are therefore irrelevant to our purpose, which is to define the specific difference of this special form of capital. In so far as capital solely employed in the circulation process, special commercial capital, partly combines those functions with its specific ones, it does not appear in its pure form. We obtain its pure form after stripping it of all these incidental functions

Apart from the division between industrial and merchant's capital, an abstraction is involved in the division of merchant's capital itself into its two forms of commercial (buying and selling of commodities) capital and money-dealing capital (MDC). Indeed, Marx opens Part IV of Volume III of *Capital*, the part following that dealing with the law of the tendency of the rate of profit to fall and the first to deal with capital in exchange, as follows (III, p. 267):

> Merchant's, or trading, capital breaks up into two forms or subdivisions, namely, commercial capital and money-dealing capital, which we shall now define more closely, in so far as this is necessary for our analysis of capital in its basic structure. This is all the more necessary, because modern political economy, even in the persons of its best exponents, throws

> trading capital and industrial capital indiscriminately together and, in effect, wholly overlooks the characteristic peculiarities of the former.

With the development of capitalist production, merchant's capital and its two components become the specialised tasks of particular capitalists, thereby creating a division of 'labour' among them. Certain functions which arise from the commodity form of production, become the specialised activity of money dealers. These include bookkeeping, the calculation and safeguarding of a money reserve and the role of cashier (see II, Ch. XIX). Now what is crucial for Marx's theory of merchant's capital, and consequently for MDC, is that it is subject to mobility with industrial capital and, consequently, exhibits a tendency to earn an average rate of profit even though it is not itself the source of surplus value (which can only be created by productive (wage) labour engaged by industrial capital) (III, p. 282):[6]

> Should merchant's capital yield a higher percentage of average profit than industrial capital, then a portion of the latter would transform itself into merchant's capital. Should it yield a lower average profit, then the converse would result. A portion of the merchant's capital would then be transformed into industrial capital.

## 3 Modified Prices of Production

A necessary implication is that the returns to MDC tend to be equalised to the rate of profit on industrial capital. More generally, the intervention of merchant's capital modifies the formation of prices of production, since capital advanced in the buying and selling of commodities shares in the surplus value distributed as profits.[7] The addition of merchant costs (and profits on them) to price conforms to the sale of commodities at (modified) values, even if it appears as if commercial costs and profits are an addition to value for, "It is

6 These notions of the source of surplus value and of the significance of productive as opposed to unproductive labour are controversial within Marxism. For a consideration of various views, see Fine and Harris (1979, Chapter 3).

7 The formation of prices of production (the so-called transformation problem) is controversial. For various approaches to the problem, see Fine and Harris (1979, Ch. 2), Elson, ed. (1979) and Steedman (ed.) (1981). The differences within this debate are not of concern here. It suffices to recognise the distinction between the production of (surplus) value and its distribution as (profits) prices according to an increasingly complex set of determinants. This is because we are not concerned with relative prices but with the relation in aggregate between industrial and commercial selling price.

just an illusion that commercial profit is a mere addition to, or a nominal rise of, the prices of commodities in excess of their value" (III, p. 282), and more specifically: "the merchant's selling price thus exceeds the purchase price not because the former exceeds the total value, but because the latter is below this value" (III, p. 286). In other words, merchant costs and profits are made up by merchants buying at below value and selling at value.

Suppose, initially, that merchants simply use money of an amount B to perform their functions. Using the usual notation, it follows that capital advanced is now C + V + B. The rate of profit r equals S/(C + V + B). Industrialists sell commodities to merchants at an aggregate price:

$$(C + V)(1 + r)$$

Merchants in turn add their profits to form selling price

$$(C + V)(1 + r) + Br = C + V + (C + V + B)r$$

But (C + V + B) r = S, so that it follows that total selling price equals C + V + S, which is total value produced.

The situation is more complex when the merchants have costs other than the simple advance of money. These costs include means of production used in the process of circulation and variable capital advanced as commercial wages. Let these costs be K. Following the procedure used above, industrialists sell at (C + V) (1 + r) and merchants sell at:

$$(C + V)(1 + r) + Br + K(1 + r)$$

in order to earn profit on money advances, B, as before and to recuperate costs, K, together with profit on them. For total selling price to remain equal to total value, it follows that:

$$(C + V)(1 + r) + Br + K(1 + r) = C + V + S$$

This yields:

$$r = (S - K)/(C + V + B + K)$$

Not surprisingly, the additional capital advances K are reflected in the denominator but, as costs, they are a deduction in the numerator from surplus value in the formation of the rate of profit.

In an important article, Panico (1980) also considers Marx's analysis. As I have differences with his approach and interpretation, it will be useful to discuss these as a means of obtaining clarity. For Panico (1980), Marx's analysis is easily interpreted to concur with the formula given above for K = 0. But in III, Chapter XVII, where Marx considers these matters, he appears to skirt around the question in the case where K is non-zero. Panico's own interpretation is that Marx showed (in Volume III of *Capital* and in the *Grundrisse*) that the selling price would not be equal to value when K is non-zero, although Panico restricts this observation to the commercial costs of labour power alone. The view taken here is the opposite, that Marx continues to proceed with the exchange of commodities at their values whatever the level and composition of circulation costs.[8] If this were not so, there would be an inconsistency in Marx's analysis and consequently in Panico's. For, if circulation costs produce a divergence of selling prices from values, then the initial capital advances C and V diverge from their values and the formulation as a whole is erroneous.[9] Panico's references to *Capital* and *Grundrisse* are also flawed by the way in each case in which Marx proceeds. After admitting that all circulation costs must be an addition to form the merchant's selling price, Marx observes that (III, p. 291, emphasis added):

> So far as this [circulation costs] concerns the total capital of society, it means in fact that a portion of it must be set aside for secondary operations which are no part of the self-expansion process, and that this portion of the social capital must be continually reproduced for this purpose. *This reduces the rate of profit for the individual capitalist and for the entire class of industrial capitalists.*

And (*Grundrisse*, p. 548, emphasis in original):

> If one imagines all production carried out by labour alone, then all the larger advances which it requires during its realization appear as what they are – *deduction from surplus value.*

8 But not for the formation of relative prices for which the relative compositions of capital and circulation costs will produce divergence from value as in the transformation problem.

9 Here, there is a parallel with the transformation problem for which the result that commodities do not exchange at their values is incompatible with the starting point of capital advances at value.

There is clear evidence of Marx's support for the formula adopted here for the case K is non-zero. The rate of profit is reduced not simply because of greater capital advances, including merchant's capital B + K, but also because of deductions from surplus value distributed to provide for the real costs of circulation.

## 4 The Specificity of Merchant's Capital

It might appear that this is an insignificant dispute; that the matter is of little importance for merchant's capital, money-dealing capital and consequently for the theory of the rate of interest. This is not so, because it goes to the heart of the distinction between industrial and merchant's capital. For some, there is little point in distinguishing between the two, since each enjoys an equalised rate of profit and employs exploited wage labour.[10] Capital in exchange is treated as a separate branch of the economy, like steel or coal. Marx's own view on this is absolutely clear (III, p. 323):

> Nothing could be more absurd than to regard merchant's capital, whether in the shape of commercial or of money-dealing capital, as a particular variety of industrial capital.

He justifies this position by reference to the distinction between the production of (surplus) value and its transformation into money form by realisation. These are qualitatively different activities and, as the formula illustrates, they have different quantitative effects on the formation of the rate of profit.

Nor is this simply a technical point of getting the formula for the rate of profit correct. Marx's emphasis on the discussion of the development of merchant's capital is predominantly upon the decreased costs of circulation that result from division of labour and specialisation among capitalists. Paradoxically this is seen to be more so the more merchant's capital is both an independent and specialised sphere of operation of capital which, nevertheless, becomes increasingly subordinated to industrial capital. These factors are all progressive for industrial capital: "It [merchant's capital] may help indirectly to increase the surplus value produced by the industrial capitalists" (III, p. 279) through the reduction of circulation costs and time and of the necessary money capital advances. Despite these emphases, Marx often refers to the *limits* within which merchant's capital must operate. These are defined by the

10 This is the position of Gough and Harrison (1975) which corresponds to a particular view of the lack of significance in distinguishing between productive and unproductive labour. Those interested should follow the references in Fine and Harris (1979).

aggregate circulation of commodities (more cannot be sold than is produced, and less may well be sold) and average circulation costs cannot exceed those that would be borne by industrial capitalists undertaking trading on their own account. These are very flexible limits even if competition necessarily reduces *individual* circulation costs to an average through equalisation of the rate of profit between merchants and industrialists.

However, the social costs of circulation on average depend partly on individual costs and also on the total merchant's capital advanced. An excess of, or insufficiently centralised, merchant's capital produces additional costs and lowers the rate of profit both by increasing capital advances and deductions from surplus value to replace circulation costs, although this has to be set against the reduction of circulation costs associated with specialisation in buying and selling. An additional advance of new merchant's capital does not of necessity produce more circulation. The same is not true by analogy for industrial capital which has both commodities and surplus value as its result. This is clearly seen from the formula for the rate of profit, since K represents an aggregate over individual capitalists. An increase in these not only reduces the rate of profit but increases the deduction from surplus value. The same is not true for increases in C and V which, even at lower than average efficiency, raise the surplus value produced but only at the expense of the averaged rate of profit.[11]

## 5 Merchant's Capital at a More Complex Level

A number of different aspects of merchant's capital have been analysed in their pure form, as the reflection of tendencies within the capitalist economy. At a more complex level there is a combination of these different elements. Merchant's capital is necessarily integrated with productive activity such as transport and storage, although this does not render all transport, etc. productive since some may derive from the functions of buying and selling. This appears to be problematic, since it would seem to be impossible to distinguish what is and what is not commercial activity. After all, the same lorry and driver may at the same time be undertaking both speculative and distributive activity on behalf of capital. This problem is not subject to solution at the level of analysis at which it is posed; this, however, does not render redundant the distinction between merchant's and industrial capital. Just as merchant's capital is subject to a tendency to be confined to exchange activity, so it is never purely imprisoned there. It is most easily combined with other activities that are in

11 The average or normal rate of profit may not decline simply because of the addition of an inefficient capital, whereas the averaged must decline.

principle organised as capitalist production, and transport and communication are the most obvious of candidates.[12] Which are these is a matter of historical development. In the sweep of history, it is possible to point to the diminishing role covered by the activities of merchant's capital as it becomes subordinated to industrial capital. But this is by no means a linear progression, particularly in modern times, partly because of conglomeration and partly because of the rapid technical change that can take place in communications with the possibility of the commercial sector as its source or as its base. Nor is this merely of academic interest. It has been shown that in so far as merchant's capital is accumulated, it can expand the costs of circulation as well as reduce them. To the same extent this applies to productive activity that has been appropriated by merchant's capital. The significance of this is particularly felt in crises. For Marx, crises of capitalist production may be manifested in particularly acute forms for merchant's capital and this will be felt by all activities that it covers, particularly when they are themselves over-replicated as a result of association with merchant's capital.[13]

What has just been argued applies equally to money-dealing capital as a part of merchant's capital. It is analysed in its pure form but cannot always be found like this. It is found incorporated both with industrial capital and with merchant's capital more generally. For an understanding of Marx's theory of interest it is also necessary to analyse MDC in isolation from interest-bearing capital, while recognising that the two are intimately connected in practice. But this anticipates an understanding of interest-bearing capital, and this question will be considered later.

## 6 Money-Dealing Capital and the Rate of Interest

If it is correct to treat MDC as part of merchant's capital, then it follows that it tends to earn a rate of return equal to the normal rate of profit. Consequently,

12 An analogous argument may help to illustrate the point of method involved. Recent developments in the theory of domestic labour have emphasised the division between the economic and social reproduction of the wage labourer. But this insight cannot determine which use values are produced within the home; only that there is a tendency, however much realised, for them to be produced by capital.

13 To give an example that recurs, we need only consider shipping. The slightest tremor in trading sends the capitalist fleets into excess supply. It would bear investigating the extent to which the ownership and operation of ships is a precondition of entry into the world of large-scale trading. For example, but no doubt affected by the Suez crisis, one-way trans-Atlantic freights to the continent fell in price from 100 to 25 shillings in 1957.

MDC has no direct influence on the formation of the rate of interest, just as neither industrial nor commercial capital influence it directly. This is a result that is in direct conflict with much of bourgeois economics and also with the immediate appearance of the matter in many instances.

For most modern monetary theory, the rate of interest is at least in part determined by the supply of and demand for money. While the supply of money is often taken to be fixed or subject to government control, the demand for money is taken to depend inversely upon the rate of interest (the cost of holding it). In so far as the functions of MDC depend upon the use of a flexible quantity of money, this quantity will vary with the rate of interest. Consequently, money-dealing capital influences the demand for money and the rate of interest directly. Marx's view is different; he argues that money-dealing capital simply earns an average rate of profit like merchant's and industrial capital. As such it has no special place in the 'money market'.[14]

At an immediate empirical level, the activities of MDC are often treated as if they involve interest payments, most notably through the rate of interest which is paid on deposits for safekeeping and in the (higher) rate of interest which is charged upon the loan of these deposits. A number of clarifying points must be made here. First, the rate of return for MDC contingent upon the difference between these rates of interest should have a tendency to equalise to the rate of profit, since capital is potentially mobile in and out of these sectors. Why should a trader who sells on credit by borrowing to finance the purchases of customers make a greater profit than a cash retailer, once account is taken of interest charges, both to trader and customer? Similarly, the handling of money or its functions is no basis upon which a capitalist is necessarily able to earn interest. Consequently, MDC has nothing to do with the determination of the rate of interest (and at a complex level this is itself seen to be ambiguous since there are different rates of interest, for borrowing and lending, for example). Indeed, the rates of interest have been taken to be exogenous; they have not been analysed. Second, the circumstances in which the normal rate of profit on MDC becomes confused with interest payments tend to be those in which MDC becomes a part of banking capital rather than a specialised sphere of merchant's activity. It is just because banks undertake credit operations that involve interest payments and also operate MDC in which payments take the form of interest, that the illusion is created that money dealing is synonymous

14 Later, it will be shown that, at a more complex level of analysis, the 'money market' may be affected differently by money-dealing than by commercial or industrial capital. Note that for bourgeois monetary theory industrial and merchant's capital also affect the rate of interest directly through their demand for money.

with credit transactions. In other words, whether in conjunction with other banking operations or not, MDC, as a portion of merchant's capital, appears to be a portion of interest-bearing capital.[15] But the latter also remains to be analysed.

## 7 Interest-Bearing Capital

Marx's theory of interest-bearing capital (IBC) is based upon the role of money as capital. As such, it concerns only the borrowing and lending which takes place between the money capitalist and other (industrial or merchant) capitalists (III, p. 353):

> The entire transaction, as assumed, takes place between two kinds of capitalists the money capitalist and the industrial or merchant capitalist.

As such, capital becomes a commodity *sui generis* (III, p. 339) which provides the use-value of self-expansion both for lender and borrower, the former realising the rate of interest and the latter the profit of enterprise which remains from the surplus value appropriated, through the use of the money capital, after the payment of interest. Moreover, Marx emphasises that the price of this unique commodity is "irrational" (III, p. 353), since the level of the rate of interest bears no relation to any underlying production conditions. It depends upon the competitive relations governing the classes of borrowers and lenders.

It follows that to be able to use IBC is to be able to be a capitalist rather than simply to be able to borrow. Consequently, it is not the payment of an interest as such which characterises IBC, but the use to which the loan is put. It must be advanced as money capital to embark upon a circuit of industrial (or merchant) capital. As it were, Marx strips aside all other credit relations and examines those between two fractions of the capitalist class, a division of the class of capitalists which produces a division of surplus value into interest and profit of enterprise. The fraction of capitalists which appropriates profit of enterprise is responsible for the functioning of capital over the industrial

15 There are other examples in which the true nature of economic relations are concealed by their assumed form involving interest relations. In this context, see Harris (1976), showing that credit relations involving workers, with or without interest payments, are the form in which merchant's capital realises variable capital. To be concrete, hire purchase (purchase involving an instalment plan) is a form of trading, not of lending, and is associated with normal rates of profit. See also Bhaduri (1977).

circuit – supervising production and sale. The fraction which appropriates interest functions as the owner of (money) capital, but it is important to recognise that this does not necessarily correspond to ownership itself. For the control of IBC is derived from the centralisation of the hoards of money which are temporarily idle in the hands of their owners but which are rendered active through the banking system. In a sense, the function of ownership of money is embodied in IBC on behalf of society as a whole, irrespective of the distribution of ownership of the individual deposits that have gone to make up the money that is subsequently loaned, (III, p. 368):

> Moreover, with the development of large-scale industry money-capital, so far as it appears on the market, is not represented by some individual capitalist, not the owner of one or another fraction of the capital in the market, but assumes the nature of a concentrated, organized mass, which, quite different from actual production, is subject to the control of bankers, i.e., the representatives of social capital.

In other words, IBC arises out of two factors. The first is the formation of hoards of temporarily idle money (which are supplemented by the accumulation of capital through the surplus value realised during the sale of commodity capital). In this respect, money stands apart from the mass of commodities and represents value in its purest form. Second, money as such represents potential capital, the ability to renew and expand production of surplus value. Here there is a contrast between merchant's, including money-dealing, capital – for which the use of money is through its continuous intervention within the processes of circulation, as most notably represented by its formula, M–C–M' as opposed to IBC, whose formula is M–M' where money stands apart from the circulation and production of commodities.

Despite this, IBC has the closest of relations to capital accumulated in production. It is the analysis of these relations in their pure form which permits Marx to clarify certain aspects of the financial system.

First, access to IBC is a mechanism of competition between industrial capitalists. This is a continual theme throughout the three volumes of *Capital*. Increase in size of capital is the means of competitive accumulation in the pursuit of productivity increases through the introduction of machinery, and expanding use of raw materials at the relative expense of living labour. This role for the credit system presupposes a certain level of development of the economy, one generally characterised as monopoly capital.[16] Apart from the

16 See Fine and Harris (1979, Ch. 7) for a more substantial treatment of this point.

features of machine production, it involves a realisation of the conditions for a tendency of the rate of profit to be equalised precisely because of the mobility of capital engendered by the credit system.[17] Elsewhere Marx makes clear that it is only at this stage of development that commodities exchange at prices of production as opposed to values.[18]

Second, while the operation of IBC is the financial mechanism whereby prices of production are formed through the tendency to equalise rates of profit, it does not guarantee for itself an associated 'natural' rate of interest. What must be recognised is the structural separation between control of money capital and control of productive capital. But their form of integration and the resulting division of surplus value between the two fractions is not thereby quantitatively determined. It would be quite exceptional for the rate of interest to be driven so low that it merely represented a normal rate of profit on capital advanced. For this would require that competition within the fraction of IBC be as intense as across the sectors of industrial capital. But, while competition between industrial capitals is, in part, fought by access to greater quantities of IBC, there are limitations on the extent to which this can occur within the banking sector itself. For the sector would be making loans to finance a potential rival, rather than to increase its own 'productivity', and this would have to result in the complete ineffectiveness of the control of society's idle money capital in the appropriation of surplus value. It is the separation between IBC and industrial capital in this context, and the necessity for them to be integrated during the course of accumulation, that has given rise to the concept of finance capital, notably originating with Hilferding (1981). Interestingly, he argues that the two fractions of IBC and industrial capital tend to be fused into a closer and closer relationship but that a "promoter's profit" results from the dealing in the shares that "fictitiously" represent claims on the surplus value that they will yield. The point, here, is not to question the theoretical or empirical validity of Hilferding's schema but to note how it recognises and specifies a particular form of the necessary relationship between IBC and industrial capital.

It follows that there is competition within the IBC sector but that it is not comparable to the competitive process within the industrial sector since the potential sources of money capital for further accumulation are not systematically available through the credit system but are contingent upon relations with particular industrial capitalists and other holders of idle money. This is not to deny the tendency towards uniformity in rates of interest. Marx

17 This makes nonsense of the view that monopoly is the opposite of competition and the negation of the tendency of the rate of profit to be equalised.

18 See Fine (1979), and for a debate over the issue Catephores (1980) and Fine (1980b).

emphasises how quickly this is realised because of the mobility of money over the money markets and the uniformity of the 'commodity' involved, in contrast to the dull movement by which the rate of profit is equalised across sectors (III, pp. 363–36). But while uniformity for the rate of interest is created within money markets, and within the industrial sector by access to IBC, the asymmetry between them reflects a structural separation between the two fractions and limits the mobility between them. The result is reflected in the formation of (the rate of) interest, not now as a form of profit as is the case for MDC but as an appropriation of surplus value at the expense of profit and over and above normal profit for dealing in money, trade or industry. By the same token, this confirms the fallacy of presuming the existence of a natural rate of interest in parallel with a natural rate of profit (III, Ch. XXII). For industrial (and merchant's) capital, labour times of production (and circulation) determine the rate of profit and with it prices of production. Competition is the mechanism for establishing these. In contrast, for money markets, though, it is competition that determines the level of the rate of interest, not only for it to be uniform within the sector itself but more fundamentally in the conflict with industrial capital over the division of surplus value between interest and profit of enterprise (III, p. 370).

Third, and as is already clear, the existence of IBC represents a division within the capitalist class between those who monopolise the supply of IBC and those who use it as capital in production (III, p. 379):

> Interest-bearing capital as such has not wage-labour, but productive capital for its opposite ... interest-bearing capital is capital as property as distinct from capital as function.

And, further, (III, p. 382):

> Interest is a relationship between two capitalists, not between capitalist and labourer.

But, fourth, this understanding of IBC has a crucial significance for interpretation of Marx's analysis. It is that his observations at this stage about movements in the rate of interest do not concern immediate empirical movements but rather concern those tendencies that reflect the more abstract balance between the fractions of the classes.[19] As Marx observes at the outset (III, p. 358, beginning to Chapter XXII):

19 A parallel at the level of method can be drawn with the law of the tendency of the rate of profit to fall. Where Marx refers to the law as such and the counteracting influences, he is

> The subject … cannot be analysed in detail … We are concerned with the independent form of interest-bearing capital and the individualisation of interest, as distinct from profit.

In this Chapter, Marx runs a number of themes concurrently: the identification of IBC in its pure form, fluctuations in the relationship between the rates of profit and interest and the long-term and cyclical determinants of the rate of interest.[20] However, the use of the term "rate of interest" is something of a misnomer at this stage for two different reasons. On the one hand, Marx is more concerned with the division of the mass of surplus value between interest falling to IBC and profit of enterprise.[21] On the other hand, the relations between IBC and industrial capital cannot be observed directly in the pure form in which they have been analysed. They are only observed indirectly through the operations of banking capital as a whole. It has already been seen that for MDC, profitability may be appropriated through a divergence between the rates of interest at which borrowing and lending take place. Much the same is true for the interest which is appropriated by IBC. What is important to the banking sector and the return to IBC is the difference between the rates of interest at which borrowing and lending take place. For this reason, even when the real rate of interest is negative (i.e., the nominal rate is below the rate of inflation), banks are able to appropriate interest since this is more or less independent of the absolute levels at which the difference between the rates at which borrowing and lending take place through the banking system. Accordingly, the formation of the return to IBC is more complex than the simple relationship between the fractions of capital that it embodies. It involves other forms of capital in exchange, such as MDC, and is effected through different rates of interest even though there tends to be a strict relationship between these (III, p. 365).

concerned with abstract tendencies and not with immediate empirical movements in the rate of profit, as is often supposed and is at times suggested by Marx's form of expression. See Fine and Harris (1979, Chapter 4).

20 For an assessment of these, see Harris (1976).

21 See Harris (1981). Again there is a parallel with the law of the tendency of the rate of profit to fall (see fn. 19) where Marx's analysis of the internal contradictions (III, Chapter XV) focuses upon the mass of surplus value that can be accumulated rather than upon the rate of profit as such.

## 8 The Logical Distinctiveness of Interest as an Economic Category

From this analysis, it emerges that there are four separate characteristics that distinguish IBC from MDC and from industrial and merchant capital more generally. These are:

(i) The use of borrowing and lending (i.e., credit relations) specifically for the purpose of advancing money capital for the appropriation of surplus value;
(ii) The division of surplus value into profit of enterprise and interest in which the latter represents a rate of return over and above the normal rate of profit;
(iii) The division of the capitalist class into two fractions; and
(iv) The power of IBC is derived from its centralising the individualised hoards of money and making them available through the credit system as a powerful mechanism of competition.

Now, it is crucial that all of the conditions must hold for the definition of interest as a separate economic category and this is a question of logic rather than of empirical validity. For example, if (i) were not to hold, then IBC would be identical to the advance of credit in general, i.e., indistinguishable from MDC which earns the normal rate of profit. Consequently, interest cannot be defined distinctively even if it is used by name in practice to represent the form in which the normal profit payments are made. The other three conditions are necessary to guarantee the logical basis for the distinctive category of interest, for otherwise, interest would represent the more or less temporary deviation of the return on IBC from the normal rate of profit. This could occur in any sector where it is favoured by market conditions.

Marx's ability to construct a distinct theory of interest as opposed to profit is a distinguishing mark of his economics. In contrast to classical political economy, Marx is able to locate interest adequately within the analytical structure of his economic thought, thereby deriving interest as a consequence of the competitive relations between two fractions of the capitalist class rather than as an arbitrary 'natural' rate for which there are no determinants other than supply and demand. Equally, within moneyless neoclassical economics, most notably for the Fisherian theory of intertemporal consumption and production, the rates of interest and profit are conceptually identical. Even for Keynesian economics (and for Keynes himself), where monetary factors are specifically introduced, the rate of profit as represented by the Marginal Efficiency of Capital is set equal to the rate of interest. Moreover, while short-term expectations may lead to a disequilibrium value of the rate of interest, underlying Keynesianism is the idea that there is a full-employment natural or equilibrium rate of interest. This divergence from Marx's theory – with many being attracted by the idea that Keynes' liquidity theory is the complement for exchange of Marx's theory of surplus value for production – is intimately connected to Keynesian theory's failure to differentiate between demand, and hence credit, for accumulation and for consumption except for multiplier purposes. Marx not only categorises interest distinctively, he also does so by reference to the abstract tendencies which he has identified for the capitalist economy – for the rate of profit to be equalised, for the credit system to be the mechanism of competition in accumulation, for money to stand apart from other commodities, and for idle hoards to be centralised in the banking system, etc. But, because it is an analysis based on such abstract considerations, the existence and significance of interest as a category can only be determined historically and discovered by empirical analysis. We now turn to see how Marx attempted to deal with such issues.

## 9 Loanable Money Capital

Marx's theory of IBC clearly involves credit relations, the advance and receipt of money in the form of a loan, but in which the loan has a specific purpose, namely, to be used as money capital for accumulation. It is such relations which lie at the core of the determination of the rate of interest. But there are other credit relations, particularly those involved in buying and selling more generally. These have, however, already been dealt with as MDC, i.e., part of merchant's capital. Here the role of credit is to facilitate buying and selling, and this has nothing to do with earning a distinctive rate of interest as such. On the contrary, the existing rates of interest are taken as the point of departure for calculating the terms of loans in order that a normal rate of profit is not foregone by the use of money capital for these credit purposes. These observations only apply to the categories in their pure form. As has already been seen, for money-dealing and commercial capital, these pure forms exist by way of tendency alone. Merchant's capital can appropriate what is in principle an activity of industrial capital such as transport. It is not necessary to repeat this form of argument when account is taken of IBC. This fraction of capital is in a very powerful position to combine its specified functions with those that are normally reserved for industrial[22] or commercial capital, and particularly for MDC. Indeed, this is almost certainly to be the case, since while a bank may

22 This is one way in which finance capital can be understood in so far as IBC becomes more than 'capital as property' and participates in capital as function.

conceivably only lend to industrialists, it is liable to draw deposits from all sections of society and be unable to guarantee that its loans are used exclusively for expansion of production rather than for facilitating buying and selling in general.[23] In short, the money-dealing and credit relations associated with merchant's capital tend to be concentrated in the hands of bankers, so that banking capital (III, Ch. XXIX) combines both IBC and MDC.[24]

This does not necessarily mean that the normal rate of profit is no longer earned on the money-dealing portion of banking capital. This depends upon the competition in this section of activities. But in so far as it becomes the exclusive function of banking capital it will tend to earn the rate of interest as well as the normal rate of profit. In either case, these results will be masked by the interest form in which banks appropriate surplus value. For the bank, "its profit is generally made by borrowing at a lower rate of interest than it receives in loaning" (III, p. 402).

In order to make the distinction between credit operations which expand production and those which simply facilitate exchange, Marx first draws the distinction at the level of money. He contrasts money as money (in its function as means of circulation in the absence of credit, for which means of circulation is identical to means of payment) with money as capital. Having made this distinction in the absence of credit except as IBC, it is a simple theoretical step to extend it to circumstances where there are other forms of credit. The existence of these conceals the distinction between money as money and money as capital because both tend to be worked together and to be subject to remuneration in the form of interest. The significance of the distinction is nevertheless crucial to Marx since the rate of interest "is determined by the supply and demand of money capital as distinguished from the other forms of capital" (III, p. 419). Indeed, Marx observes that the confusion between money capital and money as such is a device used "to make capital out of means of circulation as such through the artificial intervention of legislation, and to raise the interest rate" (III, p. 419). This is just one example of many in which Marx, employing long and varied quotations, demonstrates both the distinction and the mixing between money as such and money as capital and the confusion

---

23 It is worth remarking that while financing accumulation involves facilitating exchange (credit or loan to purchase means of production), the converse is not necessarily true.

24 These are not the only elements of banking capital, which is consequently a more complex category than loanable money capital (on which see below). Banking capital also includes securities, which Marx analyses as part of fictitious capital. See III, Ch. XXIX, "Component Parts of Bank Capital," and not Ch. XXV "Credit and Fictitious Capital," where the latter is notable for its absence.

this creates in the minds of commentators, bankers and legislators as a reflection of the varied activity of banks themselves.[25]

Marx's own procedure is to maintain the distinction between the two pure forms of capital (money-dealing and interest-bearing) and their correspondence to the functions of money as money and as capital. The practical combination of these activities is then understood at a more complex and concrete level of analysis for which the term loanable money capital (LMC) is reserved (III, p. 402–402; see also III, p. 507 and p. 513 for the distinction between LMC and IBC):

> The care of the reserve funds of businessmen, the technical operations of receiving and disbursing money, of international payments, and thus of the bullion trade, are concentrated in the hands of the money dealers. The other side of the credit system the management of interest-bearing capital, or money capital develops alongside this money-dealing as a special function of the money-dealers. Borrowing and lending money becomes their particular business ... The loanable capital which the banks have at their disposal streams to them in various ways ... These funds are thus converted into loanable money capital.

It is in the movements of LMC that the rate of interest is also determined at the more complex level of the supply of and demand for both money as capital and money as revenue as money to expand the circuits of capital as opposed to money to act as a means of payment. Marx develops separate theories for these in their effect on the rate of interest over the course of the cycle (III, p. 447). Here, the rate of interest is determined at the more complex level of movements in the money market, reflecting both the role of money as capital (IBC) and money as means of payment (merchant's capital). Of crucial significance is that there are two Departments of money (I expenditure of revenue, and II transfer of capital; the terminology is Marx's, III, p. 447) which have potentially opposing effects on the rate of interest, the demand for Department II expanding in boom and for Department I in recession when creditworthiness collapses. Accordingly, their overall effect can only possibly be understood if a distinction is drawn between them. This is precisely what is absent from bourgeois monetary theory because of its preoccupation with a homogeneous

25 It is here that Marx's exposition is at its most incomplete, with lengthy quotations interspersed with commentary. This should not serve to cloak the extent to which Marx's analysis is developed. It does, however, make for tedious reading except for those interested in the history of monetary theory or banking legislation and crises.

money supply; it is also absent from banking practice because the two functions of money are combined in practice.

It might be thought that these deficiencies could be remedied, particularly in banking practice with divisional departments having special responsibilities for industrial loans as opposed to overdraft facilities to finance consumption, for example. Such a view would approach the problem from an individualistic agency perspective, as if the banks, individually or collectively, could determine the division between money used as capital and money used as revenue. Marx demonstrates obliquely the fallacy of such an approach. He asks the question: when is an accumulation of money capital an accumulation of real capital (III, p. 476)? Surely, it must be advanced as money capital and banks may play a greater or lesser role in supervising this? But ultimately the real accumulation of capital depends not upon an advance of money capital (for which IBC may be a precondition) but upon the production and appropriation of surplus value. In other words, the division between IBC and MDC is not guaranteed by the activities of the banks themselves; it is a result determined by the extent to which IBC is indeed productive for capital, for otherwise it is converted into MDC by the (failure of the) process of production itself (III, p. 507):

> The accumulation of loan capital consists simply in the fact that money is precipitated as loanable money. This process is very different from an actual transformation into capital; it is merely the accumulation of money in a form in which it can be transformed into capital. But this accumulation can reflect ... events which are greatly different from actual accumulation.

## 10 Money Capital and Real Capital

The closing remarks of the preceding section modify – or, more exactly, reverse – a balance that has previously been present within the analysis. Capitals in exchange have been analysed in their pure forms and they have been seen, in practice, to be combined in more complex forms. The determination of the rate of interest as opposed to profit of enterprise is seen to depend upon IBC since MDC is subject merely to a normal rate of profit. In so far as these two forms of capital are combined to form LMC, IBC plays a determining role in the movement of MDC since it is linked directly with the accumulation of capital. Nevertheless, in the determination of the market rate of interest, the demand for money as means of payment may predominate over the demand for money as capital, during a credit crisis for example, and consequently be the most important factor. In the relations between banking and industrial capital, as presented so far, there seems to have been a determining role for the banks, which constrain and coerce industry through their monopoly of the supply of finance. It is this order of determination that has now been reversed, since it has been shown that the very division of banking capital between IBC and MDC is determined by the accumulation of capital in production. This is not itself a function of the industrial capitalists but is contingent upon the development of the forces and relations of capitalist production. It is these that are analytically summarised at an abstract level in the law of the tendency of the rate of profit to fall. It is the working of this law in contradiction with its counteracting influences that forms the basis on which banking capital is to be analysed as a more complex manifestation of the law.[26]

Highlighting the relationship between abstract laws and their more concrete results does not provide the more concrete analysis itself. How is this to be done? To return to the determination of the market rate of interest (an important factor in analysing the course of crisis), it has been shown that it results from the complex interaction of IBC and MDC with corresponding and possibly contrary movements in the role of money as capital and as means of payment, respectively. This interaction is non-analysable without further historical detail since logically it can only be identified in principle. In parallel with the extent to which merchant's capital appropriates the activities of industrial capital (see above), it can easily be seen that the empirical forms of existence of banking capital combine different functions whose boundaries do not necessarily correspond to the forms of capital identified at an abstract level.

Essentially there are two questions: first, what are the banking activities which correspond to MDC (and thus subject to a normal rate of profit) as opposed to those which also earn a rate of interest; and second, what are the ways in which the separate activities of MDC and IBC are combined? These questions can only be answered empirically according to the organisation and evolution of the banking system, taking account of the banks themselves, the banking legislation under which they operate and the conjunctural circumstances where relevant.[27] This is exactly the path followed by Marx in the

26 That Marx's analysis of the banking system is predicated upon the law of the tendency of the rate of profit to fall has been demonstrated by Kim (1982).

27 It should be observed that the structural determinants of the banking system are as fluid as money itself, precisely because the banks and legislation do not determine the division between money as such and as capital. A crisis in the banking system can represent not only an acute reversal in the two functions of money but also a simultaneous destruction of the forms in which they had previously been combined. An obvious example is the relative destruction of small-scale banking in the United States in the 1930s.

continuing presentation of his theory of banking capital. No doubt the presentation of his analysis still leaves much to be desired, but those who yearn for a more abstract content to the analysis, comparable to the rest of *Capital*, are mistaken. Marx's presentation is necessarily complex and concrete since this is the only level at which it can proceed. Indeed, Marx criticises many commentators for presuming that the monetary crises in Britain can be understood by imposing fixed determinants on the (market) rate of interest, analyses which necessarily abolish the complex and variable interaction between MDC and IBC in the formation of LMC. The same criticism can be levelled at Panico's (1980) consideration of Marx's theory of interest. He correctly identifies MDC as a form of merchant's capital, but he incorrectly presumes that it can be utilised as a portion of banking capital, i.e., as a determinant of the market rate of interest. He employs a Sraffian system, modified to allow borrowing and lending through banks in order that purchases can be made by industrialists on credit. The borrowing and lending take place at different rates of interest and this is a source both of banking profits and an additional surplus. Now, if Panico is concerned with simple reproduction so that banking activity merely facilitates buying and selling, then he is concerned purely with MDC and the difference between the rates of interest should tend to yield a normal rate of profit alone. This does appear to be Panico's intention since, p. 375:

> we suppose that the activity of the bankers consists only of providing for that part of circulation which promotes the transactions between consumers, merchants and producers, by transforming capital from one form (e.g., bills of exchange) into another (e.g., cash) ... We are, therefore, ruling out the fact that bankers also make available new capital for the industrial capitalists.

But, at the level of analysis employed by Panico, for which the market rates of interest (for borrowing and lending) are concretely determined, banking capital is not able itself to determine whether the use of LMC is or is not a real accumulation of IBC and hence potentially of industrial capital. Even a slight extension of the working day would render Panico's assumptions erroneous.[28] Industrialists are using loans from banks to facilitate exchange and these in principle could be used to expand production. Such an interpretation is consistent with the Sraffian equations since these can hold independently of the scale of production.

28 Fixed coefficients of production (including labour expended) are, however, a distinguishing feature of the divorce of Sraffian from Marxian analysis.

If, then, on the other hand, Panico is concerned with expanded reproduction, his subject is banking capital, combining both IBC and MDC as LMC. In this instance, the Sraffian analysis combines IBC and MDC by a simple additive and simultaneous relation. This contrasts with Marx's analysis, for which there is a complex and contradictory interaction between the two which is fluid (rather than exhibiting fixed coefficients).[29] In short, either Panico simply deals with MDC, in which case there is no possibility of entering upon an analysis of the determinants of the rate of interest;[30] or he treats IBC as a simple extension of MDC, for which there would be no rate of interest but merely normal profit. By contrast, the determination of the rate of interest depends upon a specific analysis of IBC. Otherwise, there is merely an illusory determination of the normal rate of profit in the form of interest.[31] Panico certainly diverges from Marx's presentation of the subject. Hopefully Marx's theory has been shown to be in correspondence with the material organisation of banking in the capitalist economy according to the interpretation offered here.

## 11 Conclusion

This has been a lengthy and complex paper, and it is not intended to reproduce its results in conclusion. Rather, some indications of future directions of analysis will be made, noting the extent to which the subject has suffered neglect within western Marxism. At the level of exegesis, Marx's own writings remain extremely important and fruitful, however poorly presented. This Chapter merely outlines the main theoretical considerations involved, but there are others – such as the treatment of fictitious capital. In addition, in *Capital* and elsewhere, Marx's analyses of contemporary political economists and of

29 At the level of method, the Sraffian treatment of the rate of interest here parallels its treatment of the rate of profit. There, the law as such and the counteracting influences are treated as simultaneous and additive factors determining the rate of profit empirically rather than as abstract tendencies in contradiction with each other.

30 This is implicitly recognised by Panico since he has to take the rate of interest on deposits as exogenously given. If this interpretation of Panico is correct, then he has proceeded in the tradition of modern monetary theory. This is to conflate money as means of payment and as capital and treat them simply as the former.

31 This illusion is reinforced by denying the tendency for normal profit on IBC treated as MDC. A monopoly in money allows a higher rate of profit in this sector and this gives the appearance of interest over and above profit. This is, however, a theory that could be applied to any sector of the economy in which monopoly yielded excess profits. The result is to fail to distinguish money as a specifically different sector. This is most apparent from the Sraffian equations where it is only by assumption that banking earns a higher rate of return but that others do not.

specific economic crises deserve consideration. While apparently confined to the minutiae of the nineteenth century, these subjects are exemplary exercises in the dispelling of illusions created by the banking system and in the concrete analysis of the (UK) banking system. More significant are the implications for the analysis of contemporary capitalism. In the explanation of the post-war expansion and the period of stagflation to which it has given rise, Marxist theory has been relatively successful in analysing the 'real' phenomena in terms of the expansion and reorganisation of capitalist production. The insights gained into the accompanying monetary phenomena can only be described as dismal by comparison. There is at best a parody of relatively dated cost-push and demand-pull theories[32] in which inflation, for example, is seen as a result of class conflict, either directly through competing claims for the surplus (as in Rowthorn, 1980) or indirectly through pressure on the state to expand demand and hence the money supply in order to guarantee working-class demands such as full employment (as in Yaffe, 1973). These approaches have a claim to Marxism only in so far as they assign a causative role to class antagonism, but they do so in a way that is profoundly unsatisfactory, linking the most abstract class interests immediately to the most concrete economic phenomena.

A reassessment of Marx's theory of banking and interest suggests rather different perspectives. The empirical forms of existence of MDC and IBC, and their mode of combination as LMC, must be discovered. The major new problem of the role played by state credit must be analysed and, for this, Marx leaves only a few scattered comments, for example: "We shall deal only with commercial and bank credit. The connection between the development of this form of credit and that of public credit will not be considered here" (III, p. 400). The special position occupied by international monetary relations is no less underdeveloped. At the very least, it can be hoped that the Marxist theory of monetary phenomena will take care to distinguish the two functions of money as means of payment and as capital.[33] These problems are more easily stated than embarked upon or resolved, but embarked upon they must be if Marxism is to progress beyond a pale parody of bourgeois monetary theory.

---

32 Bourgeois theory has now 'progressed' beyond the cost-push/demand-pull dichotomy and has introduced the role played by expectations. It is a pessimistic anticipation that leads one to believe that expectations will soon be appearing in the more sophisticated and advanced Marxist theories of inflation.

33 For an analysis of inflation based on these distinctions, see Fine and Harris (1979, Chs 5 and 8) and Fine (1980c, Ch. 4). These fall short of a more complex understanding of the modern banking system. It is clear that Hilferding approaches finance capital by examining the empirical form of combination of MDC and IBC along with other factors. But he does so in a way that is not entirely satisfactory at the theoretical level and by generalising from certain empirical observations.

CHAPTER 12

# From Capital in Production to Capital in Exchange

## Postscript as Personal Preamble

After the publication of the previous Chapter in *Science and Society* (Fine, 1985–86) a response to it came from Panico (1988), not least because I had criticised him in my original for having misread Marx (not least in effectively writing out the distinctive category of interest-bearing capital). What follows is my response to Panico (Fine, 1988) which hopefully can be understood despite being standalone. In retrospect, and possibly at the time, it seems the differences between us originate in his wishing to impose the Cambridge surplus approach on Marx, essentially seeking to marry a theory of interest to a Sraffian distributional framing. As a result, it is hardly surprising that his own contribution is light on value theory, let alone the value form, that there is little consideration of the connection between finance and the contradictions attached to the accumulation of capital, and that the transformation problem should loom large in the discussion. In short, rather than abandoning value theory to get to Marx's theory of capital in exchange, it is integral to a full understanding of it.

In the Preamble to the previous Chapter, I indicate why it is so difficult to engage with Marx's theory of money and finance – not least because of the complexity of his thought in light of the increasing complexity and shifting nature of its subject matter. This is all reflected in the (appropriate) rise of the concept of financialisation over the period of neoliberalism (Fine, 2022 for my latest take on financialisation, and 2024 for its relationship to neoliberalism). The literature on financialisation has, though, itself reflected these complexities without necessarily rooting them in sound foundations in the understanding of capitalism and economic and social reproduction within it, not least with its standard definition being "the increasing role of financial motives, markets, actors and institutions in the operation of the domestic and international economies" (Epstein, 2005, p. 3). Whilst this opens cans of worms around the workings, forms and cultures of finance, and captures the spirit of the neoliberal age, it does nothing to specify the theory by which to frame such developments, let alone one that establishes it within a Marxist problematic of the relationship between the capitals in production and exchange.

HTTPS://DOI.ORG/10.1163/9789004766266-013

## 1 Introduction

I have some difficulty in replying to Panico (1988) for he is honest enough to admit that "no attempt will be made to deal with the analyses and evidence presented by Fine to support his views and interpretations", p. 311. Instead, his contribution reasserts that he is correct and my writings are scrutinised, not surprisingly successfully, for instances of where I disagree with him and hence am proved wrong. Nonetheless, a few major areas of disagreement can be revealed and clarified.

## 2 On the Transformation Problem and the Problem Transformed

Panico makes much of the change I have made in my views on the transformation problem. As we shall see, as he acknowledges I suggest, this is not important for my presentation of merchant and interest-bearing capital (IBC), but it is crucial to his analysis. This is why he is so insistent upon the transformation problem and perceives my presentation of banking capital as a misguided attempt, almost a conspiracy, to defend value theory rather than its development at a more complex level.

But to set the record straight. If the transformation is interpreted as an equilibrium price theory for unequal compositions of capital, then Marx's solution is numerically incorrect but it can be corrected (Fine and Harris, 1979). The problem this involves in calculating prices from values, the so-called irrelevant detour, has no causative significance whatsoever, and can only do so for those who confuse causation with calculation because the word 'determine' is used for both (Fine, 1980c). I now no longer believe that this equilibrium price problem is what concerned Marx. For, if it were, he would have used the term value composition rather than organic composition in posing the problem. In other words, Marx is concerned with the effects on prices of differences in the intensity of capital accumulation across sectors, for which his solution is quite appropriate (Fine, 1983b, reproduced with an account of the transformation debate in my edited collection of 1986). Moreover, this approach establishes a much firmer connection between the transformation problem and the rest of Marx's analyses, particularly of the tendency of the rate of profit to fall (Fine, 1982), and of agricultural rent (Fine, 1979).

## 3 On Aggregate Capital and Capital Aggregation

This is an immodest list of the attempts I have made to show how a particular view of the transformation problem leads to an appropriate interpretation of Marx's work across a wide range. Presumably Panico would see all of these contributions as errors stemming from, and as a misguided attempt to defend, value theory. But the list does not include merchant capital and IBC for which, in Marx's analysis at least, differing compositions of capital do not have any conceptual nor deep analytical significance. What is at issue is the aggregate relationship between (surplus) value in production and (surplus) value in exchange. In this context, I present a solution to the problem of the level of the profit rate in the presence of merchant capital, with costs K other than money advances, from which prices will follow:

$$r = (S - K)/(C + V + B + K)$$

Panico does the same with his preferred solution:

$$r = S/(C + V + B + K)$$

He gives support from Marx for this solution (but fails to admit the support I give for mine). But all of the evidence given by Panico, from Marx (1972, p. 288), precedes much of Marx's discussion of the with or without '–K' problem which Marx never properly resolves – although he asks the question again (p. 289) and again (p. 292) and again (p. 294). Certainly, Marx cannot be satisfied with Panico's solution.

And with good reason, for it fails to answer what is concerning Marx. Where does the K come from to pay back merchants' real costs? I suggest, with support from Marx, from surplus value (Fine, 1985–86, p. 392).

Panico gives no answer and his solution cannot be correct. This is easy to see in two ways. First, subject to equal compositions of capital, which is not at issue, our respective calculations of relative prices turn out to be the same. But what happens in aggregate? Panico could not be plainer: "circulation costs like K thus increase the exchange value of commodities", p. 313. But increase exchange values relative to what? There can be no answer since exchange value in aggregate has no longer been tied to value in aggregate. Moreover, Panico invents an increase in exchange value equal to K precisely because he has thrown this amount of value into circulation without explaining from where it has come.

This problem for Panico arises in part because of his confusion between aggregate circulation and circulation of individual commodities. This is why he fails to understand the above criticism which is presented in an alternative form in my original article. I point out that, if Panico is correct, then the exchange value of output diverges from (is greater than) the exchange value of inputs (and surplus) a clear inconsistency. But so obsessed is Panico with tying my position to a false one on the transformation problem that he interprets my remarks to be addressed to the problem of relative prices and rebukes me for being confused.

## 4 On Interest-Bearing Capital and Capital Bearing Interest

However, just as the transformation problem is irrelevant to the above, so merchant capital is irrelevant to the determination of the rate of interest within and as a defining characteristic of Marx's theory. It is not clear how Panico can possibly dispute this, for the two are treated in separate parts of Volume III of *Capital* (see also Chiodi and Messori, 1984). Thus, the use of merchant capital as a factor in the determination of the rate of interest is due to Panico, not to Marx, even if he wishes to claim his ideas are in the spirit of Marx.

I would spiritedly claim otherwise. In my article, I suggest that merchant and interest-bearing capital are abstract categories in Marx's work and that their combination gives rise to more complex monetary forms which are historically contingent. I argue that Panico's approach, in contrast, is made by a simple additive relationship, a characterisation to which he takes offence.

What do I mean by "simply additive"? Merely that the monetary relationships are understood in terms of an immediate correspondence between the theoretical categories – interest-bearing capital, etc – and the empirical categories such as the rate of interest agreed between borrowers and lenders. That this is so for Panico is explicit in the simple additive way in which extra equations and variables are used in the standard Sraffian system to introduce interest in the first place, and further equations are appended as the monetary system becomes more complex/concrete. Moreover, Panico's method is hardly surprising since the Sraffian system, which is his starting point, adopts exactly the same attitude to the explanation for price and profit in rejecting analysis based on the more abstract and underlying categories of (surplus) value.

This also explains how and why Panico finds Marx's monetary theory useful. For Marx's analysis of monetary phenomena can always be reduced from a complex structure of contradictory categories and levels of abstraction to a system of simultaneous determination. Again, there are parallels with value theory in all of its dimensions – as in the tendency of the rate of profit to fall, for example.

But a number of aspects of Marx's theory will be lost and/or misrepresented. In Panico's case, the relationship between real accumulation and the monetary system disappears except as a mutual determination of distribution. In other words, economic crises (which are a rare creature in Panico's work) are either assumed and then transmitted through the monetary system or the opposite path must be travelled. The contradictory relations between production, distribution and exchange, as intensified by the accumulation of capital, simply become reduced to a distributional struggle. It is not clear how things could be different for a supplemented Sraffian system in which the analysis can be conducted in unit terms for any level of otherwise undetermined output.

The second loss relative to Marx involved in Panico's method is the abstract analysis of the structure of monetary relations which give rise to the historically contingent and concrete forms of exchange and credit relations. In other words, how are we to understand the modern forms of the banking system?

Marx gave considerable insight into such structures for the time when he was writing[1] and, in my article, I argued that such monetary relations are not immediately transparent. For whether a bank loan, for example, serves merely as a means of payment (merchant capital) or as a part of IBC depends only partly on the immediate intentions of the economic agents concerned and more on the relationship that the loan has to the accumulation of capital. Thus, the banking system cannot be simply read off by what banks do but depends on the structure of monetary relations and how it circulates industrial capital and commodities in aggregate.

This all said, there remain considerable problems with Panico's monetary theory, even on its own terms. Central to his analysis is the equation set:

$$(Ap + l)(1 + r) + qi - dt = p$$
$$(K_b p + l_b)(1 + r) + Br + Dt = Qi$$

where A, p, l and r are the normal Sraffian notation and the other terms reflect the material inputs and costs of borrowing by banks from industrialists, t, and vice versa for i. B is the money put in by banks out of their own pockets and the second equation explains the source of bank profits and interest.[2] As we

1 For an outstanding exposition of this, see Lapavitsas (1986).

2 These equations are used in various modified forms by Panico. These exclude the wage rate which is taken as numeraire, as opposed to the other formulations in his work (Panico, 1983,

have suggested earlier, this is merchant capital simply treated additively and, because it does not deal in IBC – the credit relations between industrial capitalist and banks for the purpose of accumulation – but only in means of circulation, these equations erroneously participate in the determination of the rates of interest relative to Marx's theory.

But do these equations participate in the determination of distribution as Panico suggests? Let us, for mathematical convenience and greater generality, rewrite the second equation in matrix form as the per unit inputs and outputs required by the banking sector to circulate commodities for each industrial sector. Then it becomes:

$$(K_b p + l_b)(1 + r) + br + dt = qi$$

where $K_b$ is now a matrix of inputs and $l_b$ is a vector of commercial labours. But we can now combine the two equations eliminating i and t: the q and d in the two equations are the same because each loan is also a corresponding credit:

$$(Ap + l)(1 + r) + (K_b p + l_b)(1 + r) + br = p$$

In other words, the relationship between the rate of profit and the level of wages is independent of the determination of the rate of interest, reproducing Marx's result for merchant capital. This occurs, with only the material inputs and money from the banking sector having an effect, since loans and credits mutually cancel each other out and require no material inputs.[3]

This is true for the economy as a whole, but not for individual sectors insofar as there are differences in the composition of material inputs in production and/or circulation (which lead to greater or lesser credit costs). In short, Panico's reply appears to be so centrally focused on the transformation problem because he believes that the mutual relations between interest and profit, which he wishes to construct, are dependent upon it. But this is not so even within his own Sraffian economics; that he can believe otherwise is a result of confusion between what is true for the economy as a whole as compared to an individual sector.

But this is not all that is troubling about Panico's equations. They are without output scale. If we double all outputs and inputs, then the second equation

---

III; 1984; and 1985, p. 56). In the last work, the term B has been dropped, a point we take up later.

3 In the Sraffian equation system, however, the distinction between merchant and industrial capital cannot be brought out since the former is simply treated as an additional sector to the latter, something that is only valid for the immediate determination of the rate of profit.

is in serious trouble, since all but the bank's own money B can be scaled up. Here we have the old problem of the inconsistency between the homogeneity postulate and the classical dichotomy between the real and monetary sectors.[4] Panico is in trouble because he does not have a theory of where B, money, comes from and how it relates to the real accumulation of capital. Perhaps for that reason, B is set equal to zero in his later work (Panico, 1985, p. 56).

Also, Panico's second equation is inconsistent, because banks make different rates of return on their expenditures $K_b p$ and k and B (for which they earn r) and on their loans Q (for which they earn i). Panico never justifies this except in terms of competition, with bankers potentially becoming industrialists to obtain a higher rate of return if their own falls below r. This should apply, though, to all assets. As far as the banker is concerned, ability to spend is represented by all advances, including Q which could be used to set up their own factory as well as somebody else's. Thus, leaving out the offending B, Panico's per unit equation should be, in per unit terms:

$$(K_b p + l_b)(1 + i) + dt = qi$$

In other words, banks obtain their 'profits' through the interest rate mechanism, without necessarily relying on capital of their own, and this reflects their structural monopoly over the commodity money-capital. Combining this with the first equation yields:

$$(Ap + l)(1 + r) + (K_b + l_b)(1 + i) = p$$

Clearly, r and i are inversely related and we have yielded, in Sraffian terms, Marx's result of the inverse relation between interest and the profit of enterprise.

## 5 From the Abstract to the Concrete or from the Concrete to the Abstract

In the previous section, we have shown that any sensible form of Panico's central system of equations merely serves to reproduce Marx's results – either the independence of the rate of profit on industrial and merchant capital from the rate of interest (when credit merely circulates commodities) or the inverse relation between interest and profit of enterprise (when banking as a structurally

4 First observed by Patinkin (1966). See also Harris (1981), for example.

separate sector is essential to economic reproduction). But because Panico erroneously believes otherwise, he proceeds by constructing another equation to close the system. This is motivated by two separate arguments, although it is not clear whether Panico believes they are the same or not. The spirit of these seems to be as follows.

First, in the equations given above, he claims only to deal with circulation and not with IBC, so that the extension to the latter is the source of another equation. For example, in Panico (1983, III, p. 21), he presumes that there must be a positive relation between the rates of return on real and financial assets so that:

$$r = f(i) \text{ where } f'(i) > 0$$

In Panico (1985), the rate of interest is determined by expectations about future returns. These solutions have the following properties in common. They are simply additive, as explained above. They determine the rate of interest by monetary factors alone, and Panico (1983, II, p. 49) claims this to be Marx's theory – although even a casual reading of Marx would reveal his interest in the connection between a real accumulation of capital and an accumulation of banking capital and how the relation between the two affects the rate of interest.

Second, Panico draws on the distinction between the market and average rates of interest, with the former being the more volatile short-term rate. He rebukes me then for not having noticed that his original 1980 article was concerned alone with the relationship between the rates of interest and profit. But this will not do. For, if IBC is being introduced to determine the market rate of interest, i.e., short-term fluctuations, then the implication is that IBC does not exist in the longer run or we do not have a theory to determine it. In other words, the question of average and market rates of interest is quite separate from the question of the theory of IBC, although the latter is an underlying determinant of interest rates in Marx's theory. This is also indicative of the reversal of Marx's structure of monetary relations relative to Panico's approach. For in Marx, IBC is the underlying and abstract determinant of monetary relations on the basis of value relations that are already determined.[5]

5 Because of the way in which Panico determines the rate of interest at the most complex level and then uses it to determine distribution and prices in the Sraffian system, there are some anomalies. Wages are, for example, at times taken as given whereas they would be affected at this complex level by worker involvement in credit relations.

## 6 The Value of Debate and the Debate of Value

It is with some reluctance that I include this section, which will be more concerned with the tone and context of Panico's reply, for the content of the debate is surely what is more important than the way in which it is conducted. But there are certain distortions and intolerances in his contribution that might be overlooked if they were not indicative of a more generally held view that he seeks to promote. Anyone reading Panico's reply would gain the impression that I am representative of a school that is uncomradely and dogmatic in its approach. To give but one example, and each of the others is similar in its half-truth through distorted use of "quotations",[6] Panico (1988, p. 317, leaving out the references) argues that he [Fine] uses the term "bourgeois" to dismiss economic arguments in his article and in other works, where he goes so far as to claim that authors like Dobb and Meek "embraced bourgeois positions" and found Marx "even erroneous" [italics added by Panico] in the context of the transformation problem. For one of the quotations referred to by Panico, let us see what I say in full (Fine, 1983b, p. 521) in the opening paragraph to an article:

> The divergence of prices of production from values was seen as the Achilles heel of the labour theory of value even before the publication of Volume III of Capital. Subsequently, it has invariably proved to be the grounds on which bourgeois economics has dismissed Marxism, preoccupied as this economics is with the precise calculation of prices, for which a labour theory of value is irrelevant given the role played by other factors of production (and demand). Even within *Marxism* [italics added], there has been associated with the Sraffian school, a dismissal of the labour theory of value on the grounds of the transformation problem.

I do not see how this can be interpreted as anything other than a fair assessment of the state of the debate over the transformation problem, and there is certainly no implication that Sraffians are bourgeois economists. What Panico, as careful study of his other references makes clear, seems to object to is the use of the term bourgeois to describe an economic argument or school of thought – but he falsely presents this term as a device cunningly used to "dismiss economic arguments".

But, if there is any uncomradely dogma to be found, it is surely in Panico's contribution. He makes it clear that the value debate should not only be laid to rest, a point with which I might agree insofar as most of the arguments on

6 I put "quotations" in quotations because Panico employs the technique of quoting one or two "guilty" words around which he constructs his own (mis)representations.

all sides must have been presented by now,[7] but also seeks to "cast doubt on the utility of the disproportionate amount of energy absorbed by the *defense* (emphasis added) of the labor theory of value" (Panico, 1988, p. 310–11). But the only way in which he justifies this view, that those who defend the labour theory of value are wasting their time (and also the time of those who are consequently drawn into attacking it), is by use of the law of large numbers of eminent economists.

Two points need to be made in response to this. First, debate is not settled by numbers; otherwise, I suspect, neither Panico nor I would be wasting the time of bourgeois, if I may, economists. Second, the value debate has been significant and has attracted eminent contributions on all sides. It is not a one-horse race that has already been run and won or lost. Panico's intolerance, however, does not simply arise from his personal outlook but is part and parcel of much of the Sraffian school, with its charges of irrelevant detours and obscurantism and its continuing failure to deal with the criticisms raised by those who support value theory. Instead, they do fall back entirely on the consequences of the logic contained within a set of mathematical equations. It is worth recalling the comment of Lord Horder (1938, p. 6), "We have developed a passion for formulae which mitigate facts and obscure issues".

But on a more serious note, it is important to recognise that Panico belongs to a school of Sraffian economics, associated with Cambridge, which is particularly intolerant when it comes to value theory.[8] For it views the economic world in terms of given size and composition of output, technical conditions of production and a given real wage. From this a surplus is derived and distributed. But this surplus approach goes much further than this, as is made clear by Eatwell (1982) for example. All economic theory is interpreted in the light of its answer to this question of the distribution of the surplus. Quite clearly, this might be a useful classification device in so far as it allows each economic idea to be assessed in terms of whether it conforms to the Sraffian model or not. But it cannot add to knowledge of the economy since it merely categorises economic theory as right or wrong according to a Sraffian model that is the ultimate arbiter (as Panico tends to do with me).

7 Panico might also have noticed that the value debate is far from dead within *Science & Society*, for the issue in which my article appears includes a non-Sraffian contribution and the journal held a debate in 1984–85!

8 I mean, of course, intellectually. But it is significant that in the debate over value theory, 'defensive' contributions are notable for their absence in the *Cambridge Journal of Economics* and *Contributions to Political Economy*. On a more immediate level, a comment by me on Panico's original article was also refused publication. Presumably *Science & Society* is more catholic in its tastes or simply has lower standards!

Nor does the matter rest here. For this view of the world through Sraffa-coloured spectacles has been taken much too far by forcing economics, not only into the categories of Sraffian or non-Sraffian in content, but also in terms of the very questions that are asked. As it were, it is presumed that every economist is asking the surplus approach question and so other questions of interest which may be more central to their thought are ignored.[9] This can lead to the most exaggerated and frequent distortions, as can be seen in the work of Panico (1984, p. 9) since he fully embraces the surplus approach:

> the development of Sraffa's suggestion does not imply any fundamental change in the basic structure of the surplus theory of value and distribution of the classical political economists and Marx.

It is not clear how anyone could hold such a view, except in the light of the surplus approach to the history of economic thought which I have outlined above. For it is implied that all the classical political economists and Marx and Sraffa are pretty much the same – and usually the way this is shown, tautologously, is to correct their mistakes towards the Sraffian system.[10] A more satisfactory position is surely that of Steedman who fully recognises the differences between Sraffa and Marx and argues that one of them has to go, and we know which one for him.

Panico's unique contribution, however, is to take the surplus approach and add to it another of Sraffa's suggestions, that the system be closed by a monetary theory of the rate of interest independent of the real system and as a determinant of the rate of profit. This then also becomes a tablet of stone through which monetary theory of others is reinterpreted. This seems to explain why, as I hope I have shown, Panico gets Marx's theory wrong, makes elementary mistakes in his own theory, considers that my interpretations are solely motivated by a wish to defend value theory and, ironically, why his own contribution is solely motivated by the wish to promote the surplus approach.[11]

---

9 Sraffa was himself guilty of this, even as the most respected interpreter of Ricardo, as has been argued by Faccarello (1982) and Fine (1983a).

10 Panico (1983, I, p. 51) even does this for Tooke's monetary theory.

11 Two final points. First, Panico tends to suggest that my criticisms are limited by my not having seen his work. This includes unpublished and hard to learn of Discussion Papers, an only recently published thesis, which contains the former essentially unmodified, and a number of articles which I may or may not have seen before having drafted my own. None of them would have changed what I had written, although this reply to him should explain why Panico considers they include a development of Marx's theory of IBC, whilst I consider that they do not. Second, Panico twice accuses me of claiming that he is after "additional surplus" from the banking sector. My remark, however, is purely an innocent interpretation in words of his second equation.

CHAPTER 13

# Marx's Rent Theory Revisited? Landed Property, Nature and Value

## Postscript as Personal Preamble

It has on occasion been suggested that Fine (1979) on Marx's theory of rent is a classic. The case can certainly be made. It covers all of the controversies around Marx's account, unifying the treatments of Differential Rent 1 and 2 with Absolute Rent, whilst also dispelling the common misunderstanding both of Absolute as Monopoly Rent and of its arbitrary dependence upon the difference between price of production and value for a sector deemed to suffer lower organic composition of capital. In addition, the piece digs deep into value theory itself – how value and price are formed both within and between sectors – and shows that Marx's theory of rent is underpinned by exactly the same principles as his treatment of the transformation problem and falling profitability (see earlier Chapters). So, there is a neat demonstration of the unity of Marx's theory across the three Volumes of *Capital*.

This explains the context in which the Chapter that follows was drafted – sheer opportunism. As a member of the Deutscher Prize Committee (www.deutscherprize.org.uk/wp/past-recipients/), I had the pleasure of reading Saito (2017) and to see it awarded the prize for 2018. He demonstrates how in his later years Marx became fascinated with the science of using more and more raw materials such as artificial fertilizers to increase the productivity of agriculture. This corresponded exactly to what I was saying about his theory of rent and its dependence upon a rising organic composition, and the chance to showcase my earlier, unduly neglected classic article (albeit this Chapter also shrouded in updating for contemporary relevance upon referees' insistence).

## 1 Introduction[1]

It is now forty years since *Economy and Society* hosted a debate on Marx's theory of rent or, more exactly, landed property, around an early contribution by

1 Originally appearing as Fine (2019b).

Fine (1979).[2] It is an opportune moment to assess the continuing significance of Marx's theory, and how it might be interpreted for present-day scholarship and developments within which the issue of rent is critical. Initially, though, it is important to contextualise the original debate.

First and foremost, this was part of a much broader set of controversies over Marx's political economy that had successively tiptoed their way through and beyond the three volumes of *Capital*.[3] These debates, to a large extent, covered value theory (methodologically and substantively – how are we to understand value and what is it?); circulation and crisis (is underconsumption valid or not, with or without the presence of colonies and monopolies?); the so-called transformation problem (what is the relationship between value and prices of production?); the falling rate of profit (is it subject to a law derived from accumulation?); and, with decreasing attention, almost seeming to reflect the extent to which these topics appear late in Volume III, money, finance and – ultimately – rent.

Second, beyond rounding up the usual suspects in debating Marx's political economy from various perspectives (not only different interpretations of it, but also its wholesale rejection as invalid), the contributors to rent theory at this time reflected the strong influence of Marxism within economic geography, not least in light of the work of David Harvey and Doreen Massey, and a particular interest in the urban in general and housing in particular.[4] These specific concerns necessarily led to questions over the relevance, and the broader applicability, of Marx's theory of landed property and (agricultural) rent.

The current context for assessing Marx's theory of rent is different. Debates over his political economy certainly continue but they are much more subdued, with protagonists tending to adopt one or other of positions that have long been debated, if not resolved. On the other hand, debates over rent seem to flourish as never before, often with scant regard for Marx's theory, not least in the concept of rent-seeking in mainstream economics, or appeals to the rents of technical innovation or those attached to the 'post-workerist' condition. Further, not least in the wake of sub-prime, there is a renewed interest in housing rents, and especially in the role played by (the financialisation of) mortgages.

---

2 See also Ball (1980), Fine (1980a and b) and Catephores (1980).

3 Significantly, some contributions on rent are reproduced with a sheaf of other contributions around value theory, as originally published in *Economy and Society* (Fine, ed. 1986).

4 As representative, see Ball et al. (eds) (1985) with my own contribution addressing landownership and the British coal industry, as discussed below.

The purpose of this retrospective, then, is to revisit the earlier contributions in light of these and other contemporary concerns, especially the critical scholarship and politics around land, rent, nature and ecosocialism more generally. I begin by briefly laying out the complexity of Marx's theory of rent and why it should be open to alternative interpretations. I then suggest, referring to another distinctive aspect of the contemporary scene – the new availability of (commentary on) Marx's notebooks[5] – that (as no doubt all true Marxists will claim) these are supportive of my original interpretation of his rent theory. Finally, I return to the implications for contemporary concerns.

## 2 From Agronomy to Rent in Marx's Political Economy

Marx's theory has long been subject to dispute and varying interpretations. This has resulted in part from the unfinished nature of his own studies and their presentations, primarily in Volume 3 of *Capital* and *Theories of Surplus Value*. But these disputes have also turned on the extent to which Marx's accounts of differential rent 1 and differential rent 2 (DR1 and DR2) do or do not differ from Ricardo's notions of *extensive* and *intensive* margins, respectively; as well as the validity of Marx's own innovative treatment of absolute rent (AR) on newly-cultivated land, and its being limited to the difference between value and price of production in light of the presumed lower organic composition of capital (OCC) in agriculture relative to industry. Specifically, absolute rent is often interpreted as a monopoly rent (MR), which is only limited by the willingness of the user to pay and the capacity of the owner to withhold, and not by some arbitrary deviation of price of production from value as a result of a lower capital-intensity within agriculture. In part, controversy also continues as a result of the casual ways in which Marx's contributions are selectively picked over for various authors' own purposes, with scant regard to Marx's treatments as a whole nor their situation within the broader corpus of his political economy. It is in the latter that key concepts are rooted, such as the OCC, as well as the nature of the accumulation of capital and its corresponding implications for the accumulation, production, distribution and circulation of (surplus) value. In extreme forms, these partial readings treat rent in the absence of dynamics, even within an equilibrium, and as primarily distributional.

5 For an interesting location of the new publications in the context of reinterpreting Marx's political economy in the wake of his two hundredth anniversary, see the collection edited by Faccarello and Kurz (2018).

This last comment, in particular, does not apply to Kohei Saito's (2017) meticulous consideration of the most recently published Marx manuscripts within the *Marx-Engels-Gesamtausgabe* (MEGA) collection, including Marx's natural scientific notebooks. However, although Saito covers Marx's rent theory in passing, this is not his main purpose. Rather, it is to establish Marx's credentials as ecologically conscious of the social co-production of nature, focusing on how Marx treats labour and agriculture. For the latter, in a brief summary scarcely able to do justice to Saito's account, he shows that:

> 1) Marx departs from Ricardo by allowing for both diminishing returns to land for some aspects of production (especially those that depend upon properties of the soil that can be exhausted, rather than reproduced, as a result of undue pursuit of the profit imperative), and also increasing returns, in so far as chemical and/or organic fertilizers can be applied to enhance productivity;
> 2) the impact of fertilizer on soil's properties and on productivity was the subject of intense debate amongst agronomists and chemists while Marx was still in the process of formulating his rent theory. Marx took an intense interest in these debates, following them closely in his reading and note-taking.

Saito puts the second point down to Marx's dual motivation of criticising Malthusianism – and its dependence on the theory of population *and* declining productivity on ever-worsening land – and in allowing for the future (agricultural) productive potential of socialism. But there are also implications for Marx's theory of rent that are, at most, implicit in Saito's account.

Initially, observe that Marx's discussion of rent (both DR1 and especially DR2) differs from Ricardo's, since Ricardo views rent as arising out of the properties of the soil, or at least from the differences in productivity of different lands given the least productive application of capital to the soil should the same land be cultivated with extra capital, rather than being applied to the next worse land. For Ricardo, the existence of landed property determines who gets the rent – not the level of rent, which is a property of the soil itself given the extent of capital accumulation on decreasingly fertile land. In contrast, for Marx, rent is the form taken, under capitalist relations, for gaining access to land as an essential means of production. Conditions of access are necessarily socially and historically specific, governed by law and custom, and – ultimately – individual leases. The latter, however detailed, can hardly lay out levels of rent in case of every future, uncertain eventuality – not least, as revealed by Marx's own review of studies of agronomy, over what makes for the best fertilizer and productivity increases, quite apart from the vagaries of climate and market conditions.

Accordingly, Marx's theory of rent is necessarily an interpretation of the social and natural in light of (dynamic, variably productive) capital accumulation upon the land. In particular, Marx confronts the 'normal' process of accumulation of industrial capital and value formation,[6] laid out in successive volumes of *Capital*, with the intervention of landed property, including both forms of ownership and access to the land and its natural properties. The reproducibility of conditions of fertility (and location) cannot be reasonably assumed within the accumulation of capital. With 'normal' levels of capital applied to the land, there will be differential productivity, with rent accruing to owners of better land. This might seem to identify Marx's first form of differential rent, DR1, with Ricardo's extensive margin, but only on condition that the 'normal' level of capital has been specified (its scale, but also restrictions and compulsions in terms of fixed capital on the land and how the land is to be left after leases end, etc). But these are major conditions as, crucially, rent derives not from the land's physical properties as such but also from how property relations govern its use and on what terms – including the scale of capital, which is determined in the context of landed property as a relation not a thing.

Whilst apparent nit-picking, these qualifications are vital in moving from DR1 to DR2 and in distinguishing Marx's DR2 from Ricardo's intensive margin. For Ricardo, the latter refers simply to the declining productivity of successive applications of capital to land already in use. For Marx, however, larger-scale capitals are not simply more of the same – or, more exactly, more of the same with lesser productivity, as for Ricardo – but are conducive to increased productivity and therefore a source of surplus profitability over smaller capitals or the normal level of capital for the sector should this be exceeded. For industrial capital, the norm will be competitively increased over time by competition within the sector. This may, however, be obstructed in the case of agriculture, in part if Ricardo's declining intensive margin does indeed apply, but also because of the effective presence of landed property – as some, possibly all, of that surplus profitability is taken as rent, DR2. Whether so, and how much, is contingent upon the conditions of access to the land, both in general and in specific leases. Short leases, for example, discourage long-term fixed capital improvements (irrigation, for example) as the benefits accrue to the landowner

6 Much of my earlier contribution on Marx's rent theory is dedicated both to specifying this normal in terms of determination of (surplus) value in light of accumulation and how it is modified by the intervention of landed property. But the details are not reproduced here.

not the investor; and preservation of fertility of the soil is not in the tenant's interest if this is at the expense of more or less immediate profitability.

Note, though, that landed property can also be conducive to accumulation and productivity increases, as shown in the case of the development of British coalmining, as landowners found it worthwhile making fixed investments to attract investment in mines within large estates and so earn larger levels of royalties from the coal extracted (Fine, 1990b). The same clearly can apply to estates with large numbers of tenant farmers. The crucial point, to be taken up later in the context of financialisation, is that the price of land, as well- and long-recognised, is the securitised value of the streams of rents that it (potentially) generates, and which can then be traded as fictitious capital. This may serve as a barrier to accumulation to the extent that landowners appropriate the surplus deriving from accumulation. By the same token, the landowners can have an interest in facilitating the generation as well as the appropriation of the surplus.[7]

Significantly, then, the issue that precisely concerns Marx in his studies of agronomy in general is the extent and effects of the increasing application of fertilizer, as noted in particular detail by Saito (2017). Marx's attention is drawn to agriculture as, in part, an industrial process, converting commodity fertilizer into commodity food, albeit dulled relative to industry by the intervention of landed property to appropriate a portion of surplus profit as rent (DR2) as capital is intensively applied.

It follows that the lower organic composition of capital (OCC) in agriculture as compared to industry is neither arbitrary nor empirically derived as such. Rather, it is a reflection of the potential barriers to capital accumulation on the land as an industrial process, not because of properties of the soil or agriculture, but because of the role of landed property as it appropriates surplus profitability in the form of rent.[8] In short, the tendency to a lower OCC in agriculture is established through Marx's theory of DR2. But how does this relate to absolute rent (AR), the minimum rent paid on land in use? Marx's theory of DR (1 and 2) is built around *intra*-sectoral competition to establish the value of differential productivity of capitals across the lands in use, thereby realising these rents. As indicated above, the competitive process is conditioned by landed property relative to industrial investment as capitals cannot compete

7 This is of relevance for all, not just agricultural landed property, and is mediated by the ways in which accumulation and restructuring of capital are realised, with (monopolised) distribution of output being decisive historically in the cases of diamonds and oil – by de Beers and Standard Oil, respectively (Fine, 1994).

8 Of course, this argument depends upon a clear understanding of the distinction between value and organic compositions of capital (and their relationship to the increasing technical composition). These distinctions tend not only to be ignored but conflated with one another.

intensively without potentially foregoing surplus profit as DR2 to landowners. By contrast, AR arises out of *inter*-sectoral competition to equalise the rate of profit across sectors via flows of capital to and from higher and lower rates of profit. For industrial accumulation, these two processes can occur separately from one another and, as such, the latter falls under the rubric of the so-called 'transformation problem'.[9]

The transformation of values into prices of production given the decisive presence of landed property is again different. For capital to flow into agriculture (or out, if already committed), rent has to be paid according to the general or specific conditions attached to landed property. This can make a significant difference to the process of forming prices of production. Indeed, rather than intra- and inter-sectoral competition being independent of one another, they have an intimate connection forged by the need to gain access to land, whether accumulation is extensive across different pieces of land or intensive in a given parcel of land.[10] Specifically, if capital were to flow into existing land in use, it potentially generates DR2, the surplus profit that could be derived from intensive accumulation and rising OCC, as previously delineated. If, instead, capital flows into new land, of average quality for sake of argument, then the maximum rent that could be charged (AR) is the DR2 that would otherwise derive from intensive as opposed to this extensive cultivation.

It follows that there is a limit, or maximum, to absolute rent equal to the rent/surplus profit that would otherwise be charged for intensive accumulation. So, there is a limit, it is not arbitrary, and it derives from the lower OCC that

9 In general, treatments of the transformation problem use the term 'organic composition', as does Marx, but in fact rely substantively upon the value composition. See Fine (2017d) for a recent discussion.

10 In passing, it is worth noting that this argument is made purely in the context of the OCC, so that it would not necessarily be verified empirically by traditionally conceived and measured capital-labour ratios, since it is possible (although unlikely) that the value of the raw materials worked by agriculture (seed, pesticides, fertilizer, etc; quite apart from depreciation on machinery) might themselves be of high value and so would also be the value worked by agriculture. Marx's argument is simply about the increasing quantum of raw materials being worked, as measured by the OCC, not the greater or lesser value of those raw materials themselves. I am grateful to Shehryar Qazi for pointing this out explicitly, although he sees it as a source of inconsistency in my approach, conflating two levels of competition as opposed to seeing them as integral in case of land. Note that, in my original exposition, I used the device of asking what is the normal land and what is the normal level of capital in use in defining value in agriculture. In practice, as critically observed by Ball (1980) in response, rent of all sorts is just something that is paid as an amalgam whether it be DR1, DR2, AR or even something else such as MR. This is indicative of how the processes of competition are integrated with one another in gaining access to land, but it remains worthwhile disentangling the separate structures and processes involved in rent creation even if a single rent combining them together is paid in practice.

results because of the impediment to intensive accumulation posed by landed property. As shown elsewhere,[11] the limit to AR (i.e. the most DR2 could be due to rising OCC) exactly equals the difference between value and price of production as a result of the lower OCC because of movement onto new land to avoid paying DR2. Everything fits neatly together, with lower OCC arising from impeded accumulation, avoidance of payment of DR2 from intensive accumulation on existing land, and with AR at most payable at the level of what that DR2 would be and made up of the difference between value and price of production!

## 3 Contemporary Relevance

In sum, none of Marx's theoretical propositions appears arbitrary once his understanding of OCC (deriving in narrow terms from increasing use of the raw materials of constant capital on the land) is properly understood and grounded in his theory of capital accumulation, conditioned by the presence of landed property. Marx's notebooks, as closely studied by Saito, establish conformity with this interpretation as Marx was increasingly drawn towards understanding the role of the increasing OCC in capitalist agriculture, and its potential to be thwarted by the presence of landed property.

But is all this merely an esoteric exercise in the History of (Marxist) Economic Thought, confined to nineteenth-century agriculture as the natural and biological sciences were (embryonically and increasingly successfully) being turned towards the problem of raising agricultural productivity, and thereby drawing Marx's attention? There are a number of reasons for the continuing relevance of understanding Marx's theory of rent or at least debating its interpretation in the broader context of his political economy as a whole. One (not new, as I have brought it up many times before; most recently in Fine, 2017d) is that Marx's rent theory is methodologically, conceptually and theoretically integral across his political economy as a whole. More specifically, his treatment of rent through reference to the OCC is consistent with, and draws upon, his other work, not least his theory of the labour process and relative surplus value, his transformation of values into prices of production, and the law of the tendency of the rate of profit to fall and counteracting tendencies. Whilst each of these has been more or less controversial, they have tended to be treated as

11 See Fine (1979) and Fine and Saad-Filho (2026[1975]). Fratini (2018) draws the conclusion that Marx's AR is distinctive from DR1, DR2 and MR but takes this little further; see also Takenaga (2018).

separate from one another. Yet, throughout each, there is a compelling framing of analysis by Marx in terms of what is ultimately a reliance upon the role of the (rising) OCC, properly understood.[12]

But there are broader implications from consolidating value theory integrally in this way, whether by reference to landed property or not. For it points to an understanding of the accumulation of capital in terms of the levels, rhythms and forms taken by economic restructuring and reproduction. First, there is the case of landed property, with its potential to intervene to obstruct accumulation. This points, as emphasised by Saito, to the extent to which Marx also anticipated the integral relationship between society and nature in such reproduction, with the capacities both to enrich and to degrade the soil in pursuit of its productivity for capital. As a result, as anticipated by many supporters of Marx in the society/nature debate, irrespective of the dispute over whether Marx himself neglected nature (or suffered from a nature/society dualism), his methods of analysis do not preclude, indeed are the basis for, addressing contemporary environmental problems in terms of the material preconditions for, and consequences of, how accumulation proceeds. In his study of the latest agronomy of his time, Marx is shown to be acutely aware of the reproduction of the environment as part and parcel of the reproduction of the economy – although it is surely fanciful to suggest that he anticipated or could address environmental crises on the scale on which we now experience them. Indeed, as Benton (2019, p. 87) suggests:[13]

> No-one seemed to have noticed that for Marx the most fundamental source of all other dimensions of alienation was alienation from nature, and that, for him at that time, communism was a vision of reconciliation among humans on the basis of reconciliation with nature.

Second, as should be apparent, Marx's theory of rent (as an appropriation of surplus value) is not a *general* theory of rent, of universal applicability, for two reasons. On the one hand, access to land is contingent upon historical and social circumstances that govern the ways in which appropriation of DR2 (or movement onto 'new'[14] land and appropriation of AR) occur. The theory sets limits, not outcomes, and impediments to accumulation may be more serious

12 And not to be conflated with value composition; see fn. 9, above.

13 And he adds (Benton, 2019, p. 88), "Some more 'orthodox' Marxists read my work as a critique of Marx, rather than a critique *of some readings* of Marx, and an attempt to develop a largely unexplored ecological dimension to his work."

14 'New' might involve change of crop or use, for example.

than levels of rents actually achieved, with the outcomes contingent upon conflict between landlords and tenants. On the other hand, as is apparent, Marx's theory (at least to the extent presented here) is not general because it ultimately derives from a primary focus on the rising OCC as a source of rent. But rent can arise for other reasons attached or intrinsic to accumulation, or from external factors such as urban development onto agricultural land. Rent can also occur from the circulation of value as opposed to surplus value: monopoly rent as distinct from absolute rent. Inevitably, vineyards and champagne spring to mind, but monopoly rents increasingly arise out of what is commonly known in mainstream literature as 'developmental gains', of which there is a huge variety of sources, most notably through financialisation of owner-occupation mortgages (see Robertson, 2014; and Bayliss et al. 2019, for accounts in the context of British housing).

But the securitisation and financialisation of housing rents in the current period inevitably conflates the underlying sources of rents with one another, across differential, absolute and monopoly rents. And these cannot be readily unbundled with any precision since rent is a single payment, and not distinguished in practice by its constituent parts. Yet, it can be deduced that the vast majority of housing rents derive from MR, since the amount of new house-building (as a source of new surplus) is a fraction of the stock of residences, all of which can attract disproportionate price (as imputed rent) increases. The (differentiated) financialisation of mortgages has shifted the appropriation of these rents towards both speculative finance and those fortunate enough to be able to gain from homeownership. On the other side, we see an intensification of housing poverty and – in the UK case – growth in housing benefit within the private rented sector at the expense of social housing (National Housing Federation, 2017). Nor is this primarily, let alone exclusively, a (re)distributional issue, but one of how differentiated financialisation of mortgages has interacted with differentiation of housing supply, and direct and indirect conditions of access to land; itself subject to a tendency to intensified boom and bust – although the UK is a major exception given the peculiarities of its housing system with price increases accruing with relatively limited supply increase.[15] Ultimately, this all reveals the extent to which the accumulation of capital on and around landed property tends to fragment

15 That this is in part due to land-banking by construction companies, as opposed to restrictive land-use planning, is highlighted by Christophers' (2018) study of the privatisation of half of state-owned land in the UK in the recent neoliberal period. For a comparative study of housing in light of financialisation, see Robertson (2016).

and disorganise the potential for resistance and the pursuit of alternatives, not least in an era of globalised, financialised neoliberalism.

Third, then, as emphasised in other work, both economic and social reproduction and restructuring under neoliberalism have been underpinned, directly and indirectly, by financialisation (Bayliss, et al. 2019). This is not simply a matter of the greater or lesser appropriation of surplus in the form of interest and the like, but how this affects accumulation. The bulk of the financialisation literature views it as having sacrificed long-term, productivity and wage-increasing investment for short-term, speculative asset accumulation with knock-on effects on inequality, housing poverty, work, everyday life and so on. This is broadly correct but it is far from universal, most notably in both the urban development and agricultural sectors, each of which can be unevenly subject to excessive accumulation across time and place.[16] It is not simply that the extent of financialisation, and its effects, are variegated. Financialisation can lead to bursts of, and even extended, accumulation, especially where prospective revenues from long-term investments can be securitised in the present. And this is precisely where landed property makes a difference whether it be in mineral exploration and extraction, intensifying rather than dulling fossil fuel capitalism (Malm, 2013), or in the financialisation of agriculture itself, ranging across the whole food system: from land grabs to the diseases of affluence; from cheap, poor quality foods to price spikes on speculatively-traded primary commodities; and now with more suffering globally from malnutrition through over- than from under-eating (Bayliss and Fine, 2021).

In short, Marx's theory of landed property is not just a technical specification of quantities of rent, based on arbitrary assumptions and of limited applicability. Neither is it an arcane debate within the history of economic thought. Rather, it offers a method, grounded in value theory, for understanding how contemporary forms of accumulation attached to financialisation of land and the goods and services that flow from it, underpin economic, social and material reproduction with corresponding consequences which range from the environment to our everyday lives.

16 Whilst this might be thought to reflect Harvey's (1985) notion of the shift to the tertiary sector, and even Aalbers' (2016) quaternary sector, these are relatively *ad hoc* conceptualisations, and such shifts are contingent on the much more general incentives and capacities for financialised accumulation, not least in energy, food, new technologies. and so on, as opposed to the tertiary and quaternary, however tightly specified.

# References


Aalbers, M. (2016) *The Financialization of Housing: a Political Economy Approach*, London: Routledge.

Aglietta, M. (1976) *A Theory of Capitalist Regulation, the US Experience*, London: New Left Books.

Anderson, K. (2025) *The Late Marx's Revolutionary Roads: Colonialism, Gender, and Indigenous Communism*, London: Verso.

Armstrong, P., A. Glyn and J. Harrison (1978) "In Defence of Value: a Reply to Ian Steedman", *Capital and Class*, vol 2, no 2, pp. 1–31.

Arnon, A. (1984) "Marx's Theory of Money: the Formative Years", *History of Political Economy*, vol 16, no 4, pp. 555–75.

Ball, M. (1980) "On Marx's Theory of Agricultural Rent: a Reply to Ben Fine", *Economy and Society*, vol 9, no 3, pp. 304–26.

Ball, M., V. Bentivegna, F. Folin and M. Edwards (eds) (1985) *Land Rent, Housing and Urban Planning: a European Perspective*, London: Croom Helm.

Banaji, J. (1979) "From the Commodity to Capital: Hegel's Dialectic in Marx's 'Capital'", in Elson (ed.) (1979), pp. 14–45.

Bayliss, K. and B. Fine (2021) *A Guide to the Systems of Provision Approach: Who Gets What, How and Why*, Basingstoke: Palgrave.

Bayliss, K., B. Fine and M. Robertson (2017) "Introduction to Special Issue on the Material Cultures of Financialisation", *New Political Economy*, vol 22, no 4, pp. 371–82, reproduced in Bayliss et al. (eds) (2018), pp. 1–16.

Bayliss, K., B. Fine and M. Robertson (eds) (2018) *Material Cultures of Financialisation*, London: Routledge, reproduced from special issue for *New Political Economy*, vol 22, no 4, 2017.

Bayliss, K., B. Fine, M. Robertson and A. Saad-Filho (2019) *Neoliberalism, Financialisation and Welfare: the Political Economy of Social Provision in the UK*, Cheltenham: Edward Elgar, in preparation, but never finished but see Fine (2024).

Bell, D. (ed.) (2007) *Victorian Visions of Global Order: Empire and International Relations in Nineteenth-Century Political Thought*, Cambridge: Cambridge University Press.

Bellofiore, R. (1989) "A Monetary Labor Theory of Value", *Review of Radical Political Economics*, vol 21, no 1–2, pp. 1–26.

Benton, T. (2019) "The Ecological Marx?", in Davis et al. (eds) (2019), pp. 87–103.

Bhaduri, A. (1977) "On the Formation of Usurious Interest Rates in Backward Agriculture," *Cambridge Journal of Economics*, vol 1, no 4, pp. 341–352.

Bradley, L. and M. Howard (eds) (1982) *Classical and Marxian Political Economy*, London: MacMillan.

Braverman, H. (1974) *Labor and Monopoly Capital*, New York: Monthly Review Press.

Brennan, D., D. Kristjanson-Gural, C. Mulder and E. Olsen (eds) (2017) *Routledge Handbook of Marxian Economics*, London: Routledge.

Broome, J. (1978) "The Allegedly Invariable Value of Sraffa's Standard Commodity", Department of Economics, Birkbeck Discussion Paper, no 64.

Caravale, G. (ed.) (1991) *Marx and Modern Economic Analysis, Volume II: The Future of Capitalism and the History of Thought*, Aldershot: Edward Elgar.

Carchedi, G. (1984) "The Logic of Price as Values", *Economy and Society*, vol 13, no 4, pp. 431–55, reproduced in Fine (ed.) (1986), pp. 215–40.

Catephores, G. (1980) "The Historical Transformation Problem – a Reply", *Economy and Society* vol 9, no 3, pp. 332–36.

Chang, K.-S., B. Fine and L. Weiss (eds) (2012) *Developmental Politics in Transition: the Neoliberal Era and Beyond*, London: Palgrave.

Chiodi, G. and M. Messori (1984) "Marx's Analysis of the Relationship Between the Rate of Interest and the Rate of Profit: Comment", *Cambridge Journal of Economics*, vol 8, no 1, pp. 81–84.

Christophers, B. (2015) "The Limits to Financialization", *Dialogues in Human Geography*, vol 5, no 2, pp. 183–200.

Christophers, B. (2017) "Seeing Financialization? Stylized Facts and the Economy Multiple", *Geoforum*, vol 85, October, pp. 259–68.

Christophers, B. (2018) *The New Enclosure: the Appropriation of Public Land in Neoliberal Britain*, London: Verso.

Christophers, B. and B. Fine (2020) "The Value of Financialization and the Financialization of Value", in Mader et al. (eds) (2020), pp. 19–30.

Colletti, L. (1973) *Marxism and Hegel*, London: New Left Books.

Davis, M., H. Bains, B. de la Motte and M. Jump (eds) (2019) *Marx200 – the Significance of Marxism in the 21st Century*, Glasgow: Praxis Press.

de Brunhoff, S. (1976) *Marx on Money*, New York: Urizen Books.

de Vroey, M. (1982) "On the Obsolescence of the Marxian Theory of Value: a Critical Review", *Capital and Class*, no 17, pp. 34–59.

de Vroey, M. (1985) "La Theorie Marxiste de la Valeur, Version Travail Abstrait: un Bilan Critique", in Dostaler and Lagueux (eds) (1985), pp. 31–57.

Dobb, M. (1940) *Political Economy and Capitalism*, London: Routledge and Kegan Paul.

dos Santos, P. (2007) "On Alfredo Saad-Filho's 'The Value of Marx' and Ben Fine's and Alfredo Saad-Filho's 'Marx's "Capital"'", *Historical Materialism*, vol 15, no 2, pp. 218–32.

dos Santos, P. (2009) "On the Content of Banking in Contemporary Capitalism", Research on Money and Finance, Discussion Paper no 3, Department of Economics, School of Oriental and African Studies, www.soas.ac.uk/rmf/papers/47509.pdf, *Historical Materialism*, vol 17, no 2, pp. 180–213.

Dostaler, G. and M. Lagueux (eds) (1985) *Un Echiquier Centenaire: Théorie de la Valeur et Formation des Prix*, Paris: La Découverte.

Duménil, G. (1980) *De la Valeur aux Prix de Production*, Paris: Economica.

Duménil, G. (1983–84) "Beyond the Transformation Riddle: a Labor Theory of Value", *Science and Society*, vol 33, no 4, pp. 427–40.

Duménil, G. (1984) "The So-Called 'Transformation Problem' Revisited: a Brief Comment", *Journal of Economic Theory*, vol 33, no 2, pp. 340–348.

Duménil, G. and D. Lévy (1991) "Szumski's Validation of the Labour Theory of Value: a Comment", *Cambridge Journal of Economics*, vol 15, no 3, pp. 359–64.

Duménil, G. and D. Lévy (1993) *The Economics of the Profit Rate: Competition, Crises and Historical Tendencies in Capitalism*, Aldershot: Edward Elgar.

Duménil, G. and D. Lévy (2000) "The Conservation of Value: a Rejoinder to Alan Freeman", *Review of Radical Political Economics* vol 32, no 1, pp. 119–46.

Dymski, G. (2015) "How to Engage with the Global Crisis: the Shape of Jazz to Come", International Initiative for Promoting Political Economy. 29 December 2017, http://iippe.org/wp/wp-content/uploads/2015/10/Dymski-IIPPE-keynote-as-presented.pdf.

Eatwell, J. (1982) "Competition", in Bradley and Howard (eds) (1982), pp. 203–228.

Ehrbar, H. (1989) "Mathematics and the Labor Theory of Value", *Review of Radical Political Economics*, vol 21, no 3, pp. 7–12.

Elson, D. (1979) "The Value Theory of Labour", in Elson (ed.) (1979), pp. 115–80.

Elson, D. (ed.) (1979) *Value: The Representation of Labour in Capitalism*, London: CSE Books.

Engels, F. (1971) "Supplement, to *Capital*, Volume 3", Moscow: Progress Publishers.

Epstein, G. (2005) "Introduction: Financialization and the World Economy", in Epstein (ed.) (2005), pp. 3–16.

Epstein, G. (ed.) (2005) *Financialization and the World Economy*, Cheltenham: Edward Elgar.

Ernst, J. (1982) "Simultaneous Valuation Extirpated: a Contribution to the Critique of the Neo-Ricardian Concept of Value", *Review of Radical Political Economics*, vol 14, no 2, pp. 85–94.

Faccarello, G. (1982) "Sraffa versus Ricardo: the Historical Irrelevance of the 'Corn-Profit' Model", *Economy and Society*, vol 11, no 2, pp. 122–37.

Faccarello, G. and H. Kurz (2018) "Marx at 200: Introductory Remarks", *European Journal of the History of Economic Thought*, vol 25, no 5, pp. 665–78.

Fasenfest, D. (ed.) (2022) *Marx Matters*, Leiden: Brill.

Fine, B. (1973) "A Note on Productive and Unproductive Labour", *Bulletin of the Conference of Socialist Economists*, vol 2, no 3, issue 6, pp. 99–103.

Fine, B. (1975a) *Marx's 'Capital'*, London: Macmillan, first edition; see Fine and Saad-Filho (2026[1975]).

Fine, B. (1975b) “The Circulation of Capital, Ideology and Crisis”, *Bulletin of the Conference of Socialist Economists*, vol 4, no 3, issue 12, pp. 82–96.

Fine, B. (1975c) “From Marx to Morishima” *Bulletin of the Conference of Socialist Economists*, vol 4, no 3, issue 12, pp. BR1–BR6, reproduced in Mohun (ed.) (1994), pp. 91–95.

Fine, B. (1979) “On Marx’s Theory of Agricultural Rent”, *Economy and Society*, vol 9, no 3, pp. 241–278, reproduced in Fine (ed.) (1986), pp. 114–87.

Fine, B. (1980a) “On Marx’s Theory of Agricultural Rent: a Rejoinder”, *Economy and Society*, vol 10, no 3, pp. 327–31.

Fine, B. (1980b) “On the Historical Transformation Problem”, *Economy and Society*, vol 9, no 3, pp. 337–39. See Chapter 3.

Fine, B. (1980c) *Economic Theory and Ideology*, London: Edward Arnold.

Fine, B. (1982) *Theories of the Capitalist Economy*, London: Edward Arnold.

Fine, B. (1983a) “On the Economics of Ricardo and Sraffa”, *Economy and Society*, vol 12, no 2, pp. 271–75. See Chapter 3.

Fine, B. (1983b) “A Dissenting Note on the Transformation Problem”, *Economy and Society*, vol 12, no 4, pp. 520–25, reproduced in Fine (ed.) (1986), pp. 209–14.

Fine, B. (1985–86) “Banking Capital and the Theory of Interest”, *Science and Society*, vol XLIX, no 4, pp. 387–413. See Chapter 11.

Fine, B. (1988) “From Capital in Production to Capital in Exchange”, *Science and Society*, vol 52, no 3, pp. 326–37. See Chapter 12.

Fine, B. (1989) *Marx’s ‘Capital’*, London: MacMillan, third edition, see Fine and Saad-Filho (2026[1975]).

Fine, B. (1990a) “On the Composition of Capital: a Comment on Groll and Orzech”, *History of Political Economy*, vol 22, no 1, pp. 149–65. See Chapter 8.

Fine, B. (1990b) *The Coal Question: Political Economy and Industrial Change from the Nineteenth Century to the Present Day*, London: Routledge, Routledge Revival, 2013.

Fine, B. (1991) “On the Falling Rate of Profit”, in Caravale (ed.) (1991), pp. 110–28.

Fine, B. (1992) *Women’s Employment and the Capitalist Family*, London: Routledge, reprinted as Routledge Revival, hardback, 2011, and paperback, 2012.

Fine, B. (1994) “Coal, Diamonds and Oil: Towards a Comparative Theory of Mining”, *Review of Political Economy*, vol 6, no 3, pp. 279–302.

Fine, B. (1997a) “The Continuing Imperative of Value Theory: a Personal Account”, *Utopia*, no 28, pp. 9–27, in Greek. See Chapter 2.

Fine, B. (1997b) “The New Revolution in Economics”, *Capital and Class*, no 61, pp. 143–48.

Fine, B. (1998a) *Labour Market Theory: A Constructive Reassessment*, London: Routledge, reprinted 2013.

Fine, B. (1998b) *The Political Economy of Diet, Health and Food Policy*, London: Routledge.

Fine, B. (2001a) *Social Capital versus Social Theory: Political Economy and Social Science at the Turn of the Millennium*, London: Routledge.

Fine, B. (2001b) "The Continuing Imperative of Value Theory", *Capital and Class*, no 75, pp. 41–52, translated into Turkish, *Fiscaoeconomia*, 2019, vol 3, Special Issue (1), pp. 70–94. See Chapter 2.

Fine, B. (2002) *The World of Consumption: The Cultural and Material Revisited*, London: Routledge.

Fine, B. (2003) "Value Theory and the Study of Contemporary Capitalism: a Continuing Commitment", in Westra and Zuege (eds) (2003), pp. 3–22.

Fine, B. (2006a) "Debating Critical Realism in Economics", *Capital and Class*, no 89, pp. 121–29.

Fine, B. (2006b) "Debating the 'New' Imperialism", *Historical Materialism*, vol 14, no 4, pp. 133–56.

Fine, B. (2007a) "Rethinking Critical Realism: Labour Markets or Capitalism?", *Capital and Class*, no 91, pp. 125–29.

Fine, B. (2007b) "Financialisation, Poverty, and Marxist Political Economy", Poverty and Capital Conference, 2–4 July 2007, University of Manchester, https://eprints.soas.ac.uk/5685/1/brooks.pdf.

Fine, B. (2008) "Debating Lebowitz: Is Class Conflict the Moral and Historical Element in the Value of Labour Power", *Historical Materialism*, vol 16, no 3, pp. 105–114.

Fine, B. (2009a) "Looking at the Crisis through Marx", *International Socialist Review*, Issue 64, March–April, pp. 40–47.

Fine, B. (2009b) "Financialisation, the Value of Labour Power, the Degree of Separation, and Exploitation by Banking", SOAS Research Students, Summer Seminar Series, April 30th.

Fine, B. (2010) "Locating Financialisation", *Historical Materialism*, vol 18, no 2, pp. 97–116.

Fine, B. (2012a) "Revisiting Rosa Luxemburg's Political Economy", *Critique*, vol 40, no 3, pp. 423–30.

Fine, B. (2012b) "Financialisation and Social Policy", in Utting et al. (eds) (2012), pp. 103–22.

Fine, B. (2012c) "Neoliberalism in Retrospect? – It's Financialisation, Stupid", in Chang et al. (eds) (2012), pp. 51–69.

Fine, B. (2012d) "Foreword", in Pilling (ed.) (2012), pp. xix–xxiii.

Fine, B. (2013) "Consumption Matters", *Ephemera*, vol 13, no 2, pp. 217–48, http://www.ephemerajournal.org/contribution/consumption-matters.

Fine, B. (2014a) "Financialisation from a Marxist Perspective", *International Journal of Political Economy*, vol 42, no 4, pp. 47–66.

Fine, B. (2014b) "The Continuing Enigmas of Social Policy", prepared for the UNRISD project on Towards Universal Social Security in Emerging Economies, UNRISD Working Paper 2014–10, http://www.unrisd.org/Fine.

Fine, B. (2016) "The Endemic and Systemic Malaise of Mainstream Economics", FESSUD Working Paper Series, no 190, http://fessud.eu/wp-content/uploads/2015/03/FESSUD_WP190_The-EndemicSystemic-Malaise-of-Mainstream-Economics.pdf.

Fine, B. (2017a) "The Material and Culture of Financialisation", *New Political Economy*, vol 22, no 4, pp. 371–82.

Fine, B. (2017b) "A Note towards an Approach towards Social Reproduction", International Initiative for Promoting Political Economy. 29 December 2017. http://iippe.org/wp/wp-content/uploads/2017/01/sroverviewben.pdf.

Fine, B. (2017c) "The Continuing Enigmas of Social Policy", in Ye (ed.) (2017), pp. 29–60.

Fine, B. (2017d) "Neither Equilibrium as Such nor as Abstraction: Debating Fred Moseley's Transformation", *International Journal of Political Economy*, vol 46, no 1, pp. 22–28. See Chapter 10.

Fine, B. (2019a) "Marx and Value: The Enigma Code for Contemporary Capitalism", in Davis et al. (eds) (2019), pp. 7–11.

Fine, B. (2019b) "Marx's Rent Theory Revisited? Landed Property, Nature and Value", *Economy and Society*, vol 48, no 3, pp. 450–61. See Chapter 13.

Fine, B. (2022) "From Marxist Political Economy to Financialisation or Is It the Other Way about?", in Fasenfest (ed.) (2022), pp. 43–66.

Fine, B. (2023) "Mathematical Economics as Aid or Obstacle to Heterodox Economists? A Personal Experience", Special Issue for Duncan Foley and Anwar Shaikh, *New School Economic Review*, vol 12, December, pp. 21–29.

Fine, B. (2024) *The Financialisation of Social Reproduction in the Age of Neoliberalism: from Theory to Case Studies: Critical Reconstructions of Political Economy*, Volume 4, with Kate Bayliss, Mary Robertson and Alfredo Saad-Filho, Leiden: Brill, and Chicago: Haymarket.

Fine, B. (ed.) (1986) *The Value Dimension: Marx versus Ricardo and Sraffa*, London: Routledge & Kegan Paul, Routledge Revival, 2013.

Fine, B., G. Gimm and H. Jeon (2010) "Value is as Value Does: Twixt Knowledge and the World Economy", *Capital and Class*, Special Issue, no 100, pp. 69–83. See Chapter 4.

Fine, B. and D. Hall (2012) "Terrains of Neoliberalism: Constraints and Opportunities for Alternative Models of Service Delivery", in McDonald and Ruiters (eds) (2012), pp. 45–70.

Fine, B. and L. Harris (1975a) "The British Economy since March 1974", *Bulletin of the Conference of Socialist Economists*, vol 4, no 3, issue 12, pp. 43–62.

Fine, B. and L. Harris (1975b) "Marxism, the State and the Economics of the Conjuncture", Department of Economics, Birkbeck College Working Paper, no 39, June.

Fine, B. and L. Harris (1976a) "The British Economy from May 1975–January 1976", *Bulletin of the Conference of Socialist Economists*, vol 5, no 2, issue 14, pp. 1–24.

Fine, B. and L. Harris (1976b) "Controversial Issues in Marxist Economics", in R. Miliband and J. Saville (eds) *Socialist Register*, vol 13, pp. 141–178.

Fine, B. and L. Harris (1977) "Surveying the Foundations", in R. Miliband and J. Saville (eds) *Socialist Register*, vol 14, pp. 106–120.

Fine, B. and L. Harris (1979) *Rereading 'Capital'*, London: Macmillan.

Fine, B. and L. Harris (with K. O'Donnell and M. Prevezer) (1985) *The Peculiarities of the British Economy*, London: Lawrence and Wishart.

Fine, B., M. Heasman and J. Wright (1996) *Consumption in the Age of Affluence: the World of Food*, London: Routledge.

Fine, B., C. Lapavitsas and A. Saad-Filho (2004) "Transforming the Transformation Problem: Why the 'New Solution' Is a Wrong Turning", *Review of Radical Political Economics*, vol 36, no 1, pp. 3–19. See Chapter 9.

Fine, B., C. Lapavitsas and D. Milonakis (1999) "Addressing the World Economy: Two Steps Back", *Capital and Class*, no 67, Spring, pp. 47–90.

Fine, B. and E. Leopold (1993) *The World of Consumption*, London: Routledge.

Fine, B. and P. Mendes Loureiro (2021) "From Social Choice to Inequality-Decomposition: in the Spirit of Arrow and Atkinson by Way of Sen and Shorrocks", *International Review of Applied Economics*, vol 35, no 1, pp. 765–91.

Fine, B., A. Petropoulos and H. Sato (2005) "Beyond Brenner's Investment Overhang Hypothesis: the Case of the Steel Industry", *New Political Economy*, vol 10, no 1, pp. 43–64.

Fine, B. and Z. Rustomjee (1996) *South Africa's Political Economy: from Minerals-Energy Complex to Industrialisation*, London: Hurst.

Fine, B. and A. Saad-Filho (2008) "Production vs. Realisation in Marx's Theory of Value: a Reply to Kincaid", *Historical Materialism*, vol 16, no 4, pp. 167–80. See Chapter 6.

Fine, B. and A. Saad-Filho (2009) "Twixt Ricardo and Rubin: Debating Kincaid Once More", *Historical Materialism*, vol 17, no 3, pp. 192–207. See Chapter 7.

Fine, B. and A. Saad-Filho (2016) "Thirteen Things You Need to Know about Neoliberalism", *Critical Sociology*, vol 43, no 4–5, pp. 685–706.

Fine, B. and A. Saad-Filho (2018) "Marx 200: the Abiding Relevance of the Labour Theory of Value", *Review of Political Economy*, vol 30, no 3, pp. 339–54, reproduced in Chinese, *Political Economy Quarterly*, vol 2, no 4, 2019, pp. 50–69. See Chapter 5.

Fine, B. and A. Saad-Filho (2026[1975]) *Marx's 'Capital'*, London: Pluto, seventh edition; see Fine (1975a).

Fine, B., A. Saad-Filho and M. Boffo (eds) (2012) *The Elgar Companion to Marxist Economics*, Cheltenham: Edward Elgar.

Foley, D. (1982) "The Value of Money, the Value of Labour Power and the Marxian Transformation Problem", *Review of Radical Political Economics*, vol 14, no 2, pp. 37–47.

Foley, D. (1983) "On Marx's Theory of Money", *Social Concept*, vol 1, no 1, pp. 5–19.

Foley, D. (1986) *Understanding Capital: Marx's Economic Theory*, Cambridge, Mass.: Harvard University Press.

Foley, D. (2000) "Recent Developments in the Labor Theory of Value", *Review of Radical Political Economics*, vol 32, no 1, pp. 1–39.

Fratini, S. (2018) "Is Marx's Absolute Rent due to a Monopoly Price?", *European Journal of the History of Economic Thought*, vol 25, no 5, pp. 961–85.

Freeman, A. and G. Carchedi (eds) (1996) *Marx and Non-Equilibrium Economics*, Aldershot: Edward Elgar.

Gleicher, D. (1989) "Labor Specialization and the Transformation Problem", *Review of Radical Political Economics*, vol 21, no 1–2, pp. 75–95.

Glyn, A. (2007) *Capitalism Unleashed: Finance, Globalization, and Welfare*, Oxford: Clarendon Press.

Gough, I. and J. Harrison (1975) "Unproductive Labour and Housework Again," *Bulletin of the Conference of Socialist Economists*, vol 4, no 1, pp. 1–7.

Groll, S. and Z. Orzech (1987) "Technical Progress and Values in Marx's Theory of the Decline in the Rate of Profit: an Exegetical Approach", *History of Political Economy*, vol 19, no 4, pp. 591–613.

Groll, S. and Z. Orzech (1990) "Capital-labor Relations: Consistency or Complication? A Reply to Ben Fine", *History of Political Economy*, vol 22, no 1, pp. 155–65.

Hardt, M. and A. Negri (2004) *Multitude: War and Democracy in the Age of Empire*, New York: Penguin.

Harris, L. (1976) "On Interest, Credit and Capital", *Economy and Society*, vol 5, no 2, pp. 145–177.

Harris, L. (1981a) "Marx's Theory of Interest: A Comment", mimeo.

Harris, L. (1981b) *Monetary Theory*, New York: McGraw Hill.

Harvey, D. (1985) *The Urbanization of Capital: Studies in the Theory and History of Capitalist Urbanization*, Oxford: Blackwell.

Hassard, J. and M. Rowlinson (1994) "Economics, Politics and Labour Process Theory", *Capital and Class*, no 53, pp. 65–97.

Hassard, J. and M. Rowlinson (2000) "Marxist Political Economy, Revolutionary Politics, and Labor Process Theory", *International Studies of Management and Organisation*, vol 30, no 4, pp. 85–111.

Heinrich, M. (2004) *Kritik der Politischen Ökonomie: Eine Einführung*, 2nd Auflage, Stuttgart: Schmetterling Velag.

Hilferding, R. (1981) *Finance Capital*, London: Routledge & Kegan Paul.

Himmelweit, S. and S. Mohun (1978) "The Anomalies of Capital", *Capital and Class*, vol 2, no 3, issue 6, pp. 67–105.

Hodgson, G. (1977) "Papering over the Cracks", in R. Miliband and J. Saville (eds) *Socialist Register*, vol 14, pp. 88–105.

Hollander, S. (1979) *The Economics of David Ricardo*, London: Heinemann.

Hont, I. (2005) *Jealousy of Trade: International Competition and the Nation-State in Historical Perspective*, Cambridge: Harvard University Press.

Horder, Lord (1938) *Obscurantism*, Conway Memorial Lecture, London: Watts and Co.

Howard, M. and J. King (1989, 1991) *A History of Marxian Economics*, 2 Vols. Princeton: Princeton University Press.

Itoh, M. and C. Lapavitsas (1999) *Political Economy of Money and Finance*. London: Macmillan.

Jeon, H. (2008) "Korean Debate on the Value of Software and Knowledge Labour", presented in the 2nd IIPPE international research workshop, http://www.iippe.org/wiki/Second_IIPPE_International_Research_Workshop.

Jeon, H. (2009) "Knowledge Work and Debate on the Value of Information Goods", *Marxism 21*, vol 6, no 1, pp. 230–72, in Korean.

Kang, N., S. Kang, D. Rieu, S. Park, K. Lee, C. Lee and M. Cha (2007) *Debate on the Value of Information Commodities*, Osan: Hanshin University Press, in Korean.

Kim, S. (1982) *Theories of Economic Crisis: a Critical Appraisal of Some Japanese and European Formulations*, Ph.D. thesis, University of London.

Kincaid, J. (2007), "Production versus Realisation: a Critique of Fine and Saad-Filho on Value Theory", *Historical Materialism*, vol 15, no 4, pp. 137–64.

Kincaid, J. (2008) "Production versus Capital in Motion: a Reply to Fine and Saad-Filho", *Historical Materialism*, vol 16, no 4, pp. 205–27.

Kincaid, J. (2009) "The Logical Construction of Value Theory: More on Fine and Saad-Filho", *Historical Materialism*, vol 17, no 3, pp. 208–20.

Knafo, S. (2007) "Political Marxism and Value Theory: Bridging the Gap between Theory and History", *Historical Materialism*, vol 15, no 2, pp. 75–104.

Laibman, D. (1982) "Technical Change, the Real Wage and the Rate of Exploitation", *Review of Radical Political Economics*, vol 14, no 2, pp. 95–105.

Lapavitsas, C. (1986) *Value, Money and the Credit System: a Structural Analysis of the Forms of Money and their Relation to Production and Exchange*, PhD thesis, Birkbeck College, University of London.

Lapavitsas, C. (1996) "The Classical Adjustment Mechanism of International Balances: Marx's Critique", *Contributions to Political Economy*, vol 15, pp. 63–79.

Lapavitsas, C. (2000) "Money and the Analysis of Capitalism: the Significance of Commodity Money", *Review of Radical Political Economics*, vol 32, no 4, pp. 631–56.

Lapavitsas, C. (2009) "Financialised Capitalism: Crisis and Financial Expropriation", Research on Money and Finance, Discussion Paper no 1, Department of Economics, School of Oriental and African Studies, www.soas.ac.uk/rmf/papers/47508.pdf, *Historical Materialism*, vol 17, no 2, pp. 114–48.

Lavoie, D. (1986) "Marx, the Quantity Theory, and the Theory of Value", *History of Political Economy*, vol 18, no 1, pp. 155–70.

Lebowitz, M. (1992) *Beyond 'Capital': Marx's Political Economy of the Working Class*. London: Macmillan.

Lebowitz, M. (2003) *Beyond 'Capital': Marx's Political Economy of the Working Class*, Basingstoke: Palgrave Macmillan, second edition.

Lebowitz, M. (2006) "The Politics of Assumption, the Assumption of Politics", *Historical Materialism*, vol 14, no 2, pp. 29–47.

Lebowitz, M. (2010) "Trapped inside the Box? Five Questions for Ben Fine", *Historical Materialism*, vol 18, no 1, pp. 131–49.

Lee, C. (1993) "Marx's Labour Theory of Value Revisited", *Cambridge Journal of Economics*, vol 17 no 4, pp. 463–78.

Lipietz, A. (1982) "The So-Called 'Transformation Problem' Revisited", *Journal of Economic Theory*, vol 26, no 1, pp. 59–88.

Lipietz, A. (1983) *Le Monde Enchanté: De la Valeur à l'Envol Inflationniste*, Paris: Maspéro.

Lipietz, A. (1984) "The So-Called 'Transformation Problem' Revisited: a Brief Reply to Brief Comments", *Journal of Economic Theory*, vol 33, no 2, pp. 352–55.

Mader, P., D. Mertens and N. van der Zwan (eds) (2020) *International Handbook of Financialization*, London: Routledge.

Malm, A. (2013) *Fossil Capital: the Rise of Steam Power and the Roots of Global Warming*, London: Verso.

Marx, K. (1972a) *Capital*, Volume II, London: Lawrence and Wishart.

Marx, K. (1972b) *Capital*, Volume III (London: Lawrence and Wishart).

Marx, K. (1973/1993[1857–58]) *Grundrisse*, London: Pelican.

Marx, K. (1981) *Capital*, Volume III, Harmondsworth: Penguin.

Marx, K. (1987a) *Theories of Surplus Value*, Part 3, London: Lawrence and Wishart.

Marx, K. (1987b[1859]) *A Contribution to the Critique of Political Economy*, Collected Works, vol 29, pp. 257–417, London: Lawrence & Wishart.

Marx, K. (1990[1867]) *Capital*, Volume I, Harmondsworth: Penguin.

Marx, K. (1991[1894]) *Capital*, Volume III, Harmondsworth: Penguin.

McDonald, D. and G. Ruiters (eds) (2012) *Alternatives to Privatization: Exploring Non-Commercial Service Delivery Options in the Global South*, London: Routledge.

Meek, R. (1956) *Studies in the Labour Theory of Value*, New York: Monthly Review Press.

Meiksins, P. (1994) "Labor and Monopoly Capital for the 1990s: a Review and Critique of the Labor Process Debate", *Monthly Review*, vol 46, no 6, pp. 45–59.

Michell, J. and J. Toporowski (2014) "Critical Observations on Financialization and the Financial Process", *International Journal of Political Economy*, vol 42, no 4, pp. 67–82.

Milonakis, D. and B. Fine (2009) *From Political Economy to Economics: Method, the Social and the Historical in the Evolution of Economic Theory*, London: Routledge.

Mintz, S. (1985) *Sweetness and Power: the Place of Sugar in Modern History*, London: Penguin.

Mohun, S. (1994) "A Re(in)statement of the Labour Theory of Value", *Cambridge Journal of Economics*, vol 18, no 4, pp. 391–412.

Mohun, S. (ed.) (1994) *Debates in Value Theory*, London: MacMillan.

Morishima, M. (1973[2009]) *Marx's Economics: a Dual Theory of Value and Growth*, Cambridge: Cambridge University Press.

Morishima, M. and G. Catephores (1975) "Is There an 'Historical Transformation Problem'?", *Economic Journal*, vol 85, Issue 338, pp. 309–328.

Moseley, F. (2000) "The 'New Solution' to the Transformation Problem: a Sympathetic Critique", *Review of Radical Political Economics*, vol 32, no 2, pp. 282–316.

Moseley, F. (2015) *Money and Totality*, Leiden: Brill.

Moseley, F. (2016) *Money and Totality: Marx's Logical Method in 'Capital' and the End of the 'Transformation Problem'*, Leiden: Brill.

Moseley, F. (2017) "Money and Totality: a Macro-Monetary Interpretation of Marx's Logic in 'Capital' and the End of the 'Transformation Problem'", *International Journal of Political Economy*, vol 46, no 1, pp. 2–21.

Moseley, F. (ed.) (1993) *Marx's Method in 'Capital': a Re-examination*, Atlantic Highlands, N.J.: Humanities Press.

Moulier-Boutang, Y. (2006) "Antagonism under Cognitive Capitalism: Class Composition, Class Consciousness and Beyond", presented in Conference on Immaterial Labour, Multitudes and New Social Subjects: Class Composition in Cognitive Capitalism, King's College, Cambridge.

Naples, M. (1989) "A Radical Economic Revision of the Transformation Problem", *Review of Radical Political Economics*, vol 21, no 1–2, pp. 137–58.

National Housing Federation (2017) "Public Expenditure on Housing: the Shift from Capital Spend to Housing Allowances: a European trend?", http://s3-eu-west-1.amazonaws.com/pub.housing.org.uk/public_spending_housing_europe_uk_briefing.pdf.

Negri, A. (2008) *Reflections on Empire*, Cambridge: Polity Press.

Negri, A. and Vercellone, C. (2007) "Il Rapporto Capitale/Lavoro Nel Capitalismo Cognitivo", *Posse*, http://www.posseweb.net/spip.php?article17.

Oakley, A. (1983) *The Making of Marx's Critical Theory: a Bibliographical Analysis*, London: Routledge & Kegan Paul.

Oakley, A. (1984, 1985) *Marx's Critique of Political Economy: Intellectual Sources and Evolution*, Vols 1 and 2, London: Routledge and Kegan Paul.

Okishio, N. (1961) "Technical Change and the Rate of Proft", *Kobe University Economic Review*, vol 7, pp. 85–99.

Panico, C. (1980) "Marx's Analysis of the Relationship between the Rate of Interest and the Rate of Profit", *Cambridge Journal of Economics*, vol 4, no 4, pp. 363–78.

Panico, C. (1983) "Interest and Profit: a Study in Marx's Writings, I–III", Research Paper Series, nos. 26–8, Faculty of Economics and Politics, Cambridge.

Panico, C. (1984) *Interest and Profit in the Theories of Value and Distribution*, PhD thesis, University of Cambridge, and London: MacMillan; and New York: St. Martin's Press, 1987.

Panico, C. (1985) "Market Forces and the Relation Between the Rates on Interest and Profits", *Contributions to Political Economy*, vol 4, no 1, pp. 37–60.

Panico, C. (1988) "Marx on the Banking Sector and the Interest Rate: Some Notes for a Discussion", *Science & Society*, vol 52, no 3, pp. 310–25.

Patinkin, D. (1966) *Money, Interest and Prices: An Integration of Monetary and Value Theory*, 2nd edition. New York: Harper and Row.

Paulré, B. (2004) "Introduction au Capitalisme Cognitif", Le Journée d'Étude Organisée par le GRES et MATISSE-ISYS CNRS-Université Paris 1, Paris, le 25 novembre, http://seminaire.samizdat.net/spip.php?article61.

Pilling, D. (ed.) (2012) *Marxist Political Economy, Essays in Retrieval: Selected Works of Geoff Pilling*, London: Routledge.

Pilling, G. (1972) "The Law of Value in Ricardo and Marx", *Economy and Society*, vol 1, no 3, pp. 281–307, reproduced in Fine (ed.) (1986), pp. 18–44.

Pilling, G. (1980) *Marx's 'Capital': Philosophy and Political Economy*, London: Routledge and Kegan Paul.

Pomeranz, K. and S. Topik (2005) *The World that Trade Created: Society, Culture, and the World Economy, 1400 to the Present*, Armonk: M. E. Sharpe, second edition.

Potts N. (ed.) (2015) *Is Marx's Theory of Profit Right? The Simultaneist-Temporalist Debate*, Lexington Books, Lanham, MD.

Radin, M. (1996) *Contested Commodities*, Cambridge, MA: Harvard University Press.

Reati, A. (1986) "The Deviation of Prices from Labour Values: an Extension to the Non-Competitive Case", *Cambridge Journal of Economics*, vol 10, no 1, pp. 35–42.

Reuten, G. and M. Williams (1989) *Value-Form and the State: the Tendencies of Accumulation and the Determination of Economic Policy in Capitalist Society*, London: Routledge.

Ricardo, D. (1951a[1816]) "Proposals for an Economical and Secure Currency", in *The Works and Correspondence of David Ricardo*, Volume 4, Cambridge: Cambridge University Press.

Ricardo, D. (1951a) *Principles of Political Economy and Taxation, the Works and Correspondence of David Ricardo*, Volume 1, Cambridge: Cambridge University Press.

Ricardo, D. (1951b) *The Works and Correspondence of David Ricardo*, vol 4, Cambridge: Cambridge University Press.

Robertson, M. (2014) *The Financialization of British Housing – a Systems of Provision Approach*, Unpublished doctoral dissertation, School of Oriental and African Studies, University of London.

Robertson, M. (2016) "The System of Provision for Housing in Selected Case Study Countries", FESSUD Working Paper Series, no 193, http://fessud.eu/wp-content/uploads/2015/03/FESSUD_WP193_The-System-of-Provision-for-Housing-in-Selected-Case-Study-Countries.pdf.

Rosdolsky, R. (1977) *The Making of Marx's 'Capital'*, London: Pluto.

Rowthorn, B. (1980) *Capitalism, Conflict and Inflation*, London: Lawrence and Wishart.

Rubin, I. (1975[1928]) *Essays on Marx's Theory of Value*, Montréal: Black Rose Books.

Rubin, I. (1978[1927]) "Abstract Labour and Value in Marx's System", *Capital and Class*, no 5, pp. 107–40.

Saad-Filho, A. (1993) "Money, Labour and 'Labour-Money': a Review of Marx's Critique of John Gray's Monetary Analysis", *History of Political Economy*, vol 25, no 1, pp. 65–84.

Saad-Filho, A. (1996) "The Value of Money, the Value of Labour Power, and the Net Product: an Appraisal of the 'New Approach' to the Transformation Problem", in Freeman and Carchedi (eds) (1996), pp. 116–35.

Saad-Filho, A. (2002) *The Value of Marx: Political Economy for Contemporary Capitalism*, London: Routledge.

Saad-Filho, A. (2017) "Neoliberalism", in Brennan et al. (eds) (2017), pp. 245–54.

Saito, K. (2017) *Karl Marx's Ecosocialism: Capital, Nature, and the Unfinished Critique of Political Economy*, New York: Monthly Review Press.

Samuelson, P. (1966) "A Summing Up", *Quarterly Journal of Economics*, vol 80, no 4, pp. 568–83.

Samuelson, P. (1971) "Understanding the Marxian Notion of Exploitation, a Summary of the So-Called Transformation Problem Between Marxian Values and Competitive Prices", *Journal of Economic Literature*, vol 9, no 2, pp. 399–431.

Shaikh, A. (2016) *Capitalism: Competition, Conflict, Crises*, Oxford: Oxford University Press.

Shamsavari, A. (1991) *Dialectic and Social Theory: the Logic of 'Capital'*, Braunton: Merlin Books.

Solow, B. (1987) "Capitalism and Slavery in the Exceedingly Long Run", in Solow and Engerman (eds) (1987), pp. 51–78.

Solow, B. and S. Engerman (eds) (1987) *British Capitalism and Caribbean Slavery: the Legacy of Eric Williams*, Cambridge: Cambridge University Press.

Spencer, D. (2000) "Braverman and the Contribution of Labour Process Analysis to the Critique of Capitalist Production – Twenty-Five years on", *Work, Employment and Society*, vol 14, no 2, pp. 223–44.

Sraffa, P. (1926) "The Law of Returns under Competitive Conditions", *Economic Journal*, vol 36, no 144, pp. 535–50.

Sraffa, P. (1951) "Introduction", to Ricardo (1951a), pp. xiii–lxii.

Sraffa, P. (1960) *Production of Commodities by Means of Commodities*, London: Cambridge University Press.

Stedman Jones, G. (2007) "Radicalism and the Extra-European World: the Case of Karl Marx", in Bell (ed.) (2007), pp. 186–214.

Steedman, I. (1977) *Marx after Sraffa*, London: New Left Books.

Steedman, I. (ed.) (1981) *The Value Controversy*, London: Verso.

Sweezy, P. (1968) *The Theory of Capitalist Development*, New York: Monthly Review Press.

Szumski, J. (1989) "The Transformation Problem Solved?", *Cambridge Journal of Economics*, vol 13, no 3, pp. 431–52.

Szumski, J. (1991) "On Duménil and Lévy's Denial of the Existence of the So-Called Transformation Problem: a Reply", *Cambridge Journal of Economics*, vol 15, no 3, pp. 365–71.

Takenaga, S. (2018) "Marx on Rent: New Insights from the New MEGA", *European Journal of the History of Economic Thought*, vol 25, no 5, pp. 926–60.

Trentmann, F. (2009) "Crossing Divides: Consumption and Globalization in History", *Journal of Consumer Culture*, vol 9, no 2, pp. 187–220.

Utting, P., S. Razavi and R. Buchholz (eds) (2012) *Global Crisis and Transformative Social Change*, London: Palgrave.

Vercellone, C. (2004) "Sens et Enjeux de la Transition vers le Capitalisme Cognitif: Une Mise en Perspective Historique", Paper presented at the seminar, "Transformations du Travail et Crise de l'Économie Politique", Université de Paris 1 Panthéon-Sorbonne, 12 October, http://www.geocities.com/immateriallabour/vercellone-capitalisme-cognitif.html.

Vercellone, C. (2007) "From Formal Subsumption to General Intellect: Elements for a Marxist Reading of the Thesis of Cognitive Capitalism", *Historical Materialism*, vol 15, no 1, pp. 13–36.

Vercellone, C. (2008a) "Finance, Rente et Travail dans le Capitalisme Cognitif", *Multitudes*, no 32, http://multitudes.samizdat.net.

Vercellone, C. (2008b) "The New Articulation of Wages, Rent and Profit in Cognitive Capitalism", Queen Mary University School of Business and Management, London, http://hal.archives-ouvertes.fr/docs/00/26/55/84/PDF/The_new_articulation_of_wagesHall1.pdf.

Wardell, M. (1999) "Labor Processes: Moving beyond Braverman and the Deskilling Debate" in Wardell et al. (eds) (1999), pp. 1–16.

Wardell, M., T. Steiger and P. Meiksins (eds) (1999) *Rethinking the Labor Process*, Albany: State University of New York Press.

Weeks, J. (1980) *Value, Capital and Social Relations*, manuscript, possibly draft for Weeks (1981).

Weeks, J. (1981) *Capital and Exploitation*, London: Edward Arnold.

Wells, D. (1992) "Consumerism and the Value of Labour Power", *Review of Radical Political Economics*, vol 24, no 2, pp. 26–33.

Westra, R. and A. Zuege (eds) (2003) *Value and the World Economy Today*, London: Macmillan.

Williams, E. (1944) *Capitalism and Slavery*, Chapel Hill: University of North Carolina Press.

Worth, O. (2010) "Introduction: *Capital & Class* at 100", *Capital and Class*, vol 34, no 1, pp. 3–6.

Yaffe, D. (1973) "The Marxian Theory of Crisis, Capital and the State," *Economy and Society*, vol 2, no 2, pp. 186–232.

Ye, I. (ed.) (2017) *Towards Universal Health Care in Emerging Economies: Opportunities and Challenges*, London: Palgrave.

Zelizer, V. (1994) *Pricing the Invaluable Child: the Changing Social Value of Children*, Ithaca: Princeton University Press.

# Index

www.ingramcontent.com/pod-product-compliance
Ingram Content Group UK Ltd.
Pitfield, Milton Keynes, MK11 3LW, UK
UKHW020258051026
15470UKWH00020B/1311

9 789004 766259